THE ROAD THAT CH... ...ORIDA

and

THE NATION

Alligator Alley

LATE 20TH CENTURY CONSERVATION in FLORIDA
from
1969 TO 2005

By L. Jack Moller

Barringer Publishing, Naples, Florida
www.barringerpublishing.com

Design and layout by Linda S. Duider

ISBN 978-1-954396-56-2

Library of Congress Cataloging-in-Publication Data
ALLIGATOR ALLEY:
The Road That Changed Florida and the Nation

Printed in U.S.A.

Table of Contents

Zebra butterfly going to roost.

Letters, Maps and Other Documents

∞

Sunset at panther pond, south of camp red bug. this is a sawgrass-willow pond surrounded by a pine ridge and cabbage-oak island where we would often see panthers.

Storm coming—deep lake unit, big cypress national preserve.

The author takes you through the turbulent years of the twentieth century as experienced by him and many others who worked as hunter/conservationist/environmentalist to save the undeveloped parts of Florida for generations to come. The book illustrates how politics, hunting, fishing and outdoor recreational activities are connected to a single road project in Florida. The significance of this road project was thoroughly understood and thus became the reason millions of acres of land are protected from development and are made available for all who love to enjoy the outdoors.

L. J. Moller standing in a place that no
one will ever see again.

Acknowledgements

∞

This book was written because of the deep appreciation I have for my family who put up with me all too often being away from home as I explored the Big Cypress and Everglades ecosystems and attended the all too frequent meetings concerning the conservation of Florida's and the nation's natural resources. We worked to do our part to make sure some of Florida's natural resources can remain for future generations to appreciate as my dad and I did. I met many good friends who also enjoyed the outdoors. To all these people, I am greatly indebted for their support, leadership, guidance, and friendship as we worked together to protect not only the natural resources but also the ability of future generations to enjoy and appreciate the world of the hunter, fisher, camper, and outdoors person in Florida's swamps.

I would not have attempted this work without the support and encouragement of my wife, Donna, who waded through all the rough drafts, and the encouragement of our daughter, Dr. Kathryn Wright.

To my wife, daughter, parents, friends—

Thank you and happy hunting, fishing, and camping to all.

L. Jack Moller

Acronyms

∞

FWC—Florida Fish, Wildlife and Conservation Commission; previously GFC, Florida Game and Fish Commission

SFWMD—South Florida Water Management District

ACoE—Army Corps of Engineers

NPS—National Park Service

DOI—Department of Interior

BCNP—Big Cypress National Preserve also BICY

ENP—Everglades National Park

CERP—Comprehensive Everglades Restoration Program

EEL—Environmentally Endangered Lands and Recreation Lands Act

P2000—Preservation 2000 Lands Act

CARL—Conservation and Recreation Lands Act

FF—Florida Forever Lands Act

BOT—Board of Trustee, the Governor and Cabinet of Florida

FWF—Florida Wildlife Federation

NWF—National Wildlife Federation

DEP—Department of Environmental Protection of Florida

SCI—Safari Club International

NRA—National Rifle Association

ARC—Acquisition and Restoration Council

USFWS—United States Fish and Wildlife Service

ORV/OHV/ATC/ATV—Off Road Vehicle, Off Highway Vehicle, All Terrain Cycle, All Terrain Vehicle, swamp buggy, airboat

EIS—Environmental Impact State

WMA—Wildlife Management Area, managed by the Florida Fish, Wildlife and Conservation Commission

WCA—Water Conservation Area

FDOT/DOT—Florida Department of Transportation

ATLAS—Across Trophic Land Scapes

NPCA—National Parks and Conservation Association

FHWA—Federal Highway Administration

LAMAC—Land Acquisition , Management Advisory Council

DOJ—U.S. Department of Justice

LOTAC—Lake Okeechobee Technical Advisory Council

STA—Storm Water Treatment Area

DSL—Division of State Lands, Florida

Keys—The local name for all the islands in Monroe County, FL, that string out toward Cuba.

Sunrise in cypress trees, barely visible in the top of the cypress trees is a pine island south of camp red bug.

Prologue

∞

The author lived during a time of action to protect vast areas of Florida from development and to improve the water management problems caused by the actions taken since statehood to drain the everglades and other parts of Florida. He was influenced by many people who had the same desire to ensure there were vast areas of Florida that were not drained and developed. Some of these people are Tom Shirley, Ralph Johnson, Freddy Fisikelly, Wes Sarves, Dr Pete Rosenthal, Dr. Larry Harris, Dr. Art Marshall, Dr. Paul Parks, Dr. George Dalrymple, Johnny Jones, Cal Stone, Dave Balman, and Franny Taylor. There were many others who worked tirelessly to bring about actions to restore the everglades, to protect habitat and the Gladesmen culture. Through the efforts of these people and the organizations they belonged to, many thousands of acres of Florida are now in public ownership and the comprehensive everglades restoration (CERP) is being worked on.

Cigar orchid.

Chapter One

◆ ● ◆

The Big Cypress is a mysterious and wonderful place. Many think the area is nothing but cypress and wetlands; however, there are many thousands of acres of upland. These uplands are pine, cabbage palm-tree, palmetto, and oak islands. There are many names that local 'swampers' give to these uplands. Some like to call all uplands 'hammocks' or islands, others call them 'hummocks.' There are true islands that are usually in the deeper water areas and are dominated by hardwoods, the majestic oak, or tropical hardwoods. But then, there are places that are ridges and generally support pines, palmettos, cabbage, and oak trees. It is on these ridges and hammocks that the deer, turkey, quail, and hog are most plentiful.

Exploring a cypress pond

But then there is the Cypress, which makes the Big Cypress what it is. It is 'Big' not because of the size of the cypress trees but because of the large expanse of cypress trees. Louisiana is second to Florida for the acreage of cypress trees. There are different types of cypress. For many years, experts have debated the differences in these trees. Some see them as different species or subspecies. There are cypress trees that grow in the wide-open flats that rarely achieve any size. It is as if they all get to be just high enough to snatch your hat off as you ride a horse or swamp buggy through them. There are also trees that grew to tremendous size, both in height and girth. In my opinion, the difference in the two types of trees is the location of their germination. The hat-rack trees, hat rack cypress, all live in the marl prairie habitats with low water, poor soils, and cap rock that is only a few inches below the surface. That's right, the soil is not deep here, and the trees have a hard time getting their roots into the ground and only poor nutrition is obtained from the ground. These roots have a difficult time following the water as it recedes in the annual drought. This hydrological cycle creates the ebb and flow of life in the Everglades as well as the Big Cypress.

There were huge cypress trees that brought the lumbermen into the Big Cypress in the early 1930s. Logging lasted through the 1950s. These huge trees grew in the sloughs and ponds. These shallow depressions in the rock strata have deeper soil, which is not a muck base soil but a sand base and contain water for longer periods of time. These cypress can get their roots to follow the water table on its annual rise and fall. When coupled with the richer soils, very large trees can result.

People ask why a hunter cares so much about the geology, soil, water, and vegetation types in the Cypress. Well, it is simple; these are the factors, along with fire, that allow wildlife to be plentiful. Change any of this system and the wildlife, which has developed over the eons, will leave or die. Those who understand the water and plant cycles can be more successful hunters. I cannot tell you how many people who come from other parts of the U.S.A. as good hunters are unable to even see a deer, hog, or turkey in the Cypress, see wildlife in the snow from a hillside or traveling from a feeding area to a bedding area. You have to remember that these animals do not have to travel far to get everything they need. They only have to stand up and move to the edge of the high ground to get their water or find a low spot in the uplands to obtain a drink. Further, they have plenty of year-round, thick vegetation to hide in. Therefore, it is not necessary for them to expose themselves to observation by either photographer or hunter.

Dense vegetation makes it almost impossible to walk through much less to walk in a manner that would allow you to sneak (slip) up on a deer or hog. The same density prevents you from seeing animals as they flee. It is nearly impossible for a person to see any wildlife in the Cypress by walking. Because of the dense vegetation and the wet soil, walking in these conditions is not conducive to stalking animals. The movement of your foot almost always creates a loud slurping sound.

Yet, evidence of abundant wildlife is everywhere. Muddy conditions cause most of them to leave tracks that can be seen by any casual observer. It

A big bear track, 3-inch 12-gauge shotgun shell

is most frustrating for many to come out of a thicket and not see or hear a thing but then find fresh tracks in the mud.

Many people do not realize that black bears live in South Florida. Black bears, though not legally hunted since 1969, are plentiful and always exciting to see or their presence known. It is a common sight to see their tracks in the mud. It is a common thought that because of our high human population bears cannot survive in the Cypress. Moreover, people are surprised to learn that we have very large bears. The boar bear that left the print would have tipped the scales at better than six hundred pounds. When seen from a tree stand around thirty yards, he looked like a Volkswagen sedan with four legs, and seemed to have had no fear or worry in the world. The boar bear is the king of the Cypress and saunters about wherever they want to go. Bears have a remarkable way of feeding. They will eat anything they can find and that includes meat. But, like black bears everywhere, they primarily feed on plants. And so, we are right back to dependence on the plant cycle that is connected to the water cycle that is connected to geology. If one is to be a successful bear hunter—photographer or gun—then basic ecological knowledge helps.

The very fact that such a large animal lives in the Cypress is extremely exciting. Many people have never seen a bear of any kind. Those who do should consider themselves lucky. Those who hunted with me saw several each year. However, in most cases we were not fortunate enough to be able to get a photograph. We could not get any photos because bears are usually seen in the poor light of dense hammocks or from a distance through the cypress trees.

While we do not hunt bears anymore, we find them very exciting to just see and to know they are around. What we really hunt is deer, turkey, and wild hog. The deer are not particularly big in the cypress. In fact, hunters from up north think our deer are all young because of their smaller size. In comparison, deer in the northern United States are very small— eighty to one hundred-ten pounds.

I like to tell my northern deer hunting friends that we have to be better hunters in the Cypress because we have smaller targets to find/hit. When one considers that we have thick vegetation year-round, no snow to accentuate the deer's brown body, no major differences in elevation, and wet conditions to slog through, we have the most elusive of deer in the United States. Additionally, there are no farm fields, food plots, or feeders. It is often said that if you can harvest a white-tail deer in the cypress, you can get one anywhere.

Two does in a grass flat by a pine-palmetto patch.

As can be seen in the picture, one of the does is not easy to see. As soon as they take one or two jumps, they are out of sight. In fact, one is more easily seen as she is in the northern edges of the Cypress. While the second doe much closer to the palmettos is almost impossible to see.

To the north of the Big Cypress is Fisheating Creek. This is a creek that runs into Lake Okeechobee from the northwest. The creek drains water to the lake from the Lake Wales Ridge. This ridge runs north and south and is west of the lake. For many years, most of the creek belonged to the Lyke's family. They owned a tremendous amount of land in this part of the Florida. Some say their holdings were around 350,000 acres. Their family homesteaded this area around the time of statehood and held on for nearly one hundred and fifty years. They raised cattle, timber, citrus, and leased their land to hunters. These hunt leases were prime leases in Florida, and some would go for as much as $60.00 an acre in the 1990s with a minimum lease size of 1,000 acres. This is a lot of money to spend for the opportunity to hunt deer, quail, dove, hog, turkey, and have a cabin to enjoy. But then, the pressures of society and work on those who could afford such a lease would make the luxury of getting out of town in an hour or two more than worth the cost. Even in this area of improved pasture and higher ground, understanding the water cycle plays an important role in being a successful hunter.

Big live oak tree on the Lyke's Ranch at Fisheating Creek.

*In 1947, there was 60,000,000 board feet of cypress lumber
removed from the Big Cypress.*

Chapter Two

◆ ◆ ◆

My First Trips to the Everglades
and Big Cypress

When I was in sixth grade, my church youth group, the Royal Ambassadors for Christ (RAS), went on a camping trip. We left the city hall of Opa-locka, Florida, in homemade swamp buggies and headed for the Everglades. We did not go to the Big Cypress as that was too far away. These buggies belonged to friends of my father who were our RA leaders. I knew my mother was terrified that I would be snake or gator bit or even worse, fall into quicksand and never return. Well, we left about 5 p.m. and headed up what is now 32nd Avenue crossing the current property of St. Thomas University and then on to the Everglades. We followed a canal, Snake Creek (C9), by riding on the levee road that was created from the spoil dug up by the Army Corps of Engineers (ACoE) when digging the canal. I did not know it then, but this was the beginning of my love for the outdoors and the Everglades system.

It seemed like forever before we reached the end of the levee where we found a huge dragline digging twenty-four hours a day, seven days a week. We also realized we could not go any farther to the west because of this work. Turning the swamp buggies around was much more difficult than we expected. This is because buggies have a very large turning radius, no breaks, and there was only a small space to maneuver in. Everyone but the driver got off and with much yelling and flashlights shining on the canal's edge we soon were going back to the east.

Turning north, we traveled for a good while along a levee that is now Flamingo Road. This road is now a four-lane divided highway in southwest

Broward County, Florida. Along the way, I started to fall asleep and actually managed to roll off the slow-moving buggy into the swamp. We managed to reach a suitable place to camp on the north side of Hollywood Boulevard, Broward County, Florida, which is now CB Smith Park today. The rest of the trip was uneventful; we fished in rock pits, shot guns at targets, and rode swamp buggies all over western Pembroke Pines. We left town on Thursday night and returned on Saturday so as not to miss church. I was extremely tired and figured I could get my parents to pick me up faster if I made Mother think I was snake bit. I knew she was sure I would be. Well, when I called from the leader's house, I told Mom I was snake-bit and in no time she and dad were there. They had to have been speeding the six or so miles from our house to where I was. Anyway, they got there in a hurry and for that lie I picked up rocks and pulled weeds for a month. It would have been much better to have not told Mother that little lie because I could not leave the yard while on punishment, except for school. You know, during

my punishment time, the weather was great and the woods around the house were calling every day, but I did not give in and did my time! From that day on, I was in the swamps at every possible opportunity. I did not realize it at the time but the canals we were riding

Cypress, marl, and palmetto is a typical habitat type in the Big Cypress.

next to during that first visit were for the purpose of draining the swamps and to create ground on which to build houses.

The next year, I was invited to go on a deer hunt in the Everglades with my dad's friends. Dad had several jobs and was working nights while attending the University of Miami and Mom was teaching elementary school. We did not have much money, but we had a good home and lots of friends. That deer season, I was lucky enough to go hunting several times. This meant that I was able to ride the buggies as they lumbered slowly through the tall sawgrass, soft mud, and shallow water. We would hunt to the east of U.S. 27 as it was being drained by the Army Corps of Engineers (ACoE) for future homes.

I was in junior high when I went on my second deer hunt. This trip was to Brown's Farm in Palm Beach County. The men had moved their buggies from Andy Town to the Broward-Palm Beach County line, which is no longer there because of the I-75 and U.S. 27 intersection and had parked them at the South Florida Water Management District (SFWMD) pumping station. We drove the buggies the rest of the way on U.S. 27 to a narrow wooden bridge. U.S. 27 did not have four lanes at this time and was only a narrow, high-crowned dangerous road. It was called Bloody-27. The men had to stop traffic while they maneuvered the buggies so they would line up straight with the bridge before getting off the highway because the outside of the fat airplane tires would hang over the outside of the bridge. Once

This was the type of swamp buggy my dad's friends used in 1961.

they were on the other side, they had to make a many point turn by easing forward and backward because they had to head ninety-degrees off the narrow wooden bridge onto the levee. We hunted in an old, abandoned farming area called Brown's Farm. This was a huge piece of land laced with small ditches that were lined with barbed-wire fences on each side. The muck was deep and soft so it was necessary to drive on the tall, thick sawgrass and other bushes in order to jump deer. It was not possible to walk in these glades or see anything other than the tall sawgrass a few inches in front of your face. We had a great time, and the men took a nice buck. My next hunting trip that year was in the same area. This time, not only did they get a good buck, but we also saw a panther running down the levee toward Palm Beach.

While in senior high, I was fortunate enough to work on different construction projects and a neighbor of my future wife, Donna K. King, worked for the Army Corps of Engineers. He was working on two projects; one was the levee on the north side of old U.S. 41 where the new road is currently located. He was building the S-12 structures. This levee was built to hold back water and stop it from draining into Everglades National Park. Our neighbor explained that one day we would see water backed up like a lake all the way to Palm Beach County.

The other project was a levee in South Dade. This saltwater/freshwater levee left what is now called Black Point and ran way out into Biscayne Bay. When I explained to my dad what we were doing and how this levee went way out into the Bay toward these islands off in the distance, and further that the levee was being built to roadbed specifications, Dad enlightened me as to what was really going on. He said many years ago a group of wealthy folks had purchased these islands and wanted a south bay causeway built to them so they could develop the islands as Miami Beach had been. We were not really building a saltwater/freshwater levee but a roadbed to these islands. These islands were later protected when they became Biscayne National Park. But in those days, we would free dive for hours after work, getting lobsters and spearing fish.

This desire to be in the Everglades and Big Cypress led me to purchase land. While I was in high school, I purchased five acres from Webb Realty. The terms were $15 down and $15 a month and no interest. I figured since

Me with a week's gear while back packing in loop road unit, 1964

I could use the family car now and then, why purchase a car? Since I was still underage, Dad co-signed with me and I earned the money by doing odd jobs. I had my land in the middle of the swamps—land that I could build a camp (cabin) on. While I never built one on that land, I did build one on the 1.25 acres I purchased on Baxter's Islands, Collier County, Florida.

I thought I would be going into an area that had not seen by modern man. Boy, was I surprised. As I walked about stands of cypress and even into the thickest hammocks, islands, and swamps, I could not find a place that modern man had not already been. As a young man, I did not realize the Big Cypress had been explored and exploited for many decades before I arrived in the 1960s. During my senior year, 1965, while in high school, several friends, Larry Hawthorn, Ronnie Myers, Johnny Crowe, and I would take off to the Big Cypress because it was much easier to walk in and many times more interesting than the vast expanse of grass and water called the Everglades. Many folks do not realize there is a significant difference and hence they call all the lands of South Florida Everglades. Each habitat has its own beauty and mysteries.

Like many others before us, we started to explore the Loop Road area and Monument Road. The Loop Road area, now known as the Loop Road Unit of the Big Cypress National Preserve, is located off U.S. 41 and north of Loop Road. When he was a

One of our rough camps in what is now the loop unit of the Big Cypress National Preserve.

young man, my dad had used this area and he told me of several interesting places to go. We proceeded to look for these places and we found them.

Thinking that we had located places that no one had been to in a very long time, we proceeded to develop a small, rough camp area. We carried in nails and material to build a chickee with no roof. Our plan was to carry a plastic tarp in and out each trip. This would help assure that we would not arrive at camp and find someone else there. If there was no roof—no need to stay there. We dug a small hole in the ground on the edge of the island to allow water to seep in so we could dip water for our needs. We had a fine camp, but we soon learned we would not be alone when hunting season came. When hunting season opened up, the mile we had walked through thigh-deep water, marl, muck and pinnacle rock was not enough to assure we were alone. There were others who had known of our camp area many years before us, and they showed up to do what we were doing—hunting deer and hogs—only they were better prepared with dogs and buggies. Both allowed them to locate and follow the game while we were basically stuck to the few hammocks around our camp location.

Considering this situation, we decided to abandon this camp and look for a new site in a more secluded location. This led us deeper into the Loop unit and we found signs of man there as well. We found evidence of the logging that had gone on in the 1940s. These men had cut cypress for the war industry and then the housing boom that followed. In 1947, the year of my birth, the Big Cypress was giving up sixty million board feet of cypress lumber a year.

We finally settled several miles to the west of our first place, which had been close to Trail Center. Trail Center was a restaurant and gas station on the Dade Collier line. Today this is an NPS ranger abode or something like that. We were about two miles west of there and a mile south of U.S. 41 on two big oak hammocks.

Our new location was reached by an hour's hard walk through more water, sawgrass, cypress, and the dangerous pinnacle rock to the southwest from where we jumped off U.S. 41. We found a big island with old Indian farms on it, with several fingers of sawgrass sloughs coming into it and a smaller island to the north. The first season, we camped on the southern end of the big island. We soon learned that this was where we wanted to hunt, so we moved to the smaller but lower island to the north. Here we built another small lean-to camp. I would sleep in my jungle hammock and Larry on the ground. Over the season, we carried in some pots and pans that we left for our use. We had a good season and, as was the normal case, heard plenty of game and saw some running but we did not shoot any big game. It seemed we were never to shoot anything and would starve on "track soup." (Track soup is what we called seeing game tracks all day and taking no game.)

It was at this campsite that I would have my first close encounter with serious accidents. The first would come one cold, windy night. I was in my hammock and could not get warm, so I decided to light my catalytic hand heater. This was a major mistake, as I did not realize the flames would jump up and nearly catch the roof of my jungle hammock on fire. I had to quickly dump the hand warmer out of the hammock and then to extinguish the grass fire. So much for new ideas; I NEVER used one again.

On another trip, four of us went in before hunting season. In those days, there was neither archery nor black powder seasons and everyone carried modern guns in the woods. We would shoot vermin and pests as we came upon them, even if this was with a high-powered deer rifle. It started raining so we got under a low, tarp lean-to. Soon the water was so deep we had to put a plastic tarp on the ground and raise the edges several inches to build a dry spot to sit in. As the rain let up, Larry got up to stretch his legs. He instinctively stepped over the bore line of a friend's .243. It was good thing, at about the same time, the owner of the gun released the safety and the gun discharged. The bullet hit the ground right between Larry's legs. If he had not stepped over the bore line, he would have lost his leg. Apparently, the gun had been worked on and the trigger was much too unstable to be counted on. NEVER get in front of a gun barrel!

Another time, I went in by myself. While cutting wood with a hand hatchet, I hit a four-inch limb as it leaned against another log. This would allow me to cut the limb faster. The tool did its job well and the top part of the limb flipped up and hit me right on the tip of my shoulder. The shoulder and arm went numb at once. For several hours, I sat there with pain and nausea eating at me as tried to figure how I would walk out with my pack and gun. Finally, around noon, the pain let up and the feeling came back in my arm.

The last and most serious incident that occurred was also the last time I used this camp location. I had again gone in by myself—not good. This was a particularly snaky looking day. It had been cool for a few days and it was now warm. Conditions like this cause hungry snakes to be out and about. So, I loaded my .22 H&R, which was on the pack frame belt, with a round under the hammer. After walking a good distance in the knee-deep water and pinnacle rock, I reached my campsite and removed the pack. In my tiredness, I forgot to place the safety loop over the hammer of the pistol and the gun flipped out. The gun's hammer struck a rock and discharged. The .22 grazed my right wrist. There seemed to be no real damage as the bullet had only cut the skin. There was little blood but the thought of what could have happened sent my nerves to race. I spent several hours in the hammock before hiking out and drove directly to the hospital. Finally, nearly seven hours later, a doctor looked at my injury. All ended well—I was lucky and NEVER did that again!

We checked out the Stair-Step area and soon found that being able to cover lots of country was essential to being able to hunt. We also found that when the water was down in the spring, we could walk quite easily. However, most of the year and particularly during hunting season there would be water on the ground that became extremely soft and difficult to walk on. It was like walking in mashed potatoes. In fact, years later, this is how one of the National Audubon researchers, Dr. Deuver, explained the ground conditions. We enjoyed the wide-open vistas of the area and the excitement of exploring one island after another. Again, we found that modern man had been everywhere we went. All these nice buggy and airboat trails lead to someone's camp or cabin. There were many nice structures in the Stair-Steps and some even had airports associated with them. Years later, I would learn that even Al Capon had a speakeasy on Loop Road and had built airboat trails from Florida Bay through the mangroves and cypress strands on to his place. It was said this was so he could smuggle in his booze and other contraband items. Merle Vann's place on Loop Road still has the stairs from Capon's establishment. Little did I know that the Off Road Vehicle (ORVs) uses of Capon and others would be the center of many interesting and difficult years ahead.

By now, Donna King and I were engaged, and she put up with a great deal. On some trips, she would willingly go with me. Today, I realize she went along to be with me. This was not because she liked to walk in the mud, sand, and rocks, with mosquitoes and

Donna and me on Monument Road.

snakes. But she went and we had a great time as we walked along those big old buggy trails. One of our favorite walkabouts was Monument Road. This road left Tamiami Trail, U.S. 41, at Monument Lake and went north. In those days, I did not know where it went and longed to hike the length of it. Little did I know at this time that one branch of Monument Road went to Immokalee and the other went to Clewiston. Anyway, we would spend some Saturdays hiking this sandy road because it was not covered with grass or mud, and we could read the many animal tracks as we strolled along.

Monument Lake, which is really a rock-pit, got its name because there was a monument placed by it to recognize a meeting with Seminole Indians as a truce was discussed. The Seminoles are one nation that has never been conquered by the U.S. Army, but they did come to a truce agreement.

Larry and I continued to explore on foot. We would walk south of Loop Road looking for animal tracks. What we found was mostly where others had been. We would walk north of U.S. 41 and continue to find where others had been. Of course, on every trip we saw plenty of deer and hog tracks. But we just could not find a place we could call "ours." We found many good-looking places, but they already had folks there. We found some very rough camps like the ones we had been building and better ones like "Fool's Paradise."

The area around Fool's Paradise was an interesting place. We had been walking in a very large cypress swamp at the northern end of Robert's Lake Strand for hours when off in the distance we could see the outline of green trees on the horizon. When walking in cypress strands you navigate by looking off in the distance and reading the tree line you can see in the thinning tops

Phillip King and me at fool's paradise inside of loop road unit.

of the cypress trees. This is fairly easy in the winter when the cypress is dormant but it is much more difficult in the summer months when every plant is much greener and thicker.

We headed toward this line of green oak trees. We could tell the difference between oak trees and pine trees; what we could not tell was how big or little the hammock or island was. As we approached the island, we could see some signs of others being there. This was not unusual, so we continued. We found a nice, oak hammock that was about ten acres in size with several human trails in it. We soon learned why there were well-used trails; there was a cabin on the north end. The owners had walked into the area carrying in all the material by hand. They had done a lot of work. We looked around and walked their trail out to the road so as to know where not to go in the future. In these days, before the NPS, the land was open for people to use. Sure, someone owned it, but these absentee owners had not posted or fenced their land and did not even know where it was, people used the land and often built camps or cabins on a place they liked.

Many times, when we found a place that we wanted to be able to return to, we walked as straight as possible on a compass reading. On the way, Larry would walk ahead while I used a small sliding steel pocket ruler to sight on his upper torso. I would get the distance in fractions of an inch and a compass reading. Then I walked up to him, and he would start off again. We recorded these readings and compass headings in a small book and later, while we took a break, used triangulation to figure out the direction and length of each leg. This information allowed us to return without having to mark a trail or to stumble around looking for it again. Of course, today a GPS does this much better and faster.

The hunting season of 1966 found us heading to Loop Road. We had located a good place north of the road. This area was on what is called the Plank Road. Many years earlier, during the logging days, this buggy trail was planked with slab lumber cut by the lumbermen. Lumbermen driving log trucks would carry out logs and return with slabs. The slabs would be laid down to provide a smoother ride over the rough, highly irregular rock structures or to prevent the trucks from getting stuck in the soft mud or axles breaking. Again, what we did not realize was there would be many other people there too. We had carefully measured the road by making several trips from a known location and reading the car odometer so we would know how to find our starting point to get into the woods when it was dark. We left home around four in the morning and headed for our spot. What we found was a road with people camping on both sides from the time you entered the eastern side almost all the way to its western end. There were people camping right where we wanted to park and depart from. We could not stop, so we drove on figuring out the mileage and how to get to our hunting place by walking across the swamps. The only place we found to park with no one camping was in the middle of Roberts Lake Strand. In the dark of night, we jumped off the road into the thigh deep water and made our way back to the east-northeast trying to figure out the location of the island where we wanted to hunt. To make a long story short, we never got to where we wanted to hunt and never found dry ground. Tired to the bone by early afternoon, we headed south to Loop Road. When arriving at the road, we had to figure out if we should walk to the west or to the east. After some discussion, we walked west. It was a long time before we arrived at our car. We were tired, but we had a good day. Again, we took no game.

In the early 1960s, my dad's brother, Joe Moller, lived with us. He and dad had opened an auto body repair business, which failed. They both lost everything except the house we lived in. Joe was a pilot and went to work for a helicopter service that was contracted to fly the first rough routing of Alligator Alley (S.R. 84/I-75.) He told us they landed at Andy Town, now

Larry and me after camping a week south of S.R. 84

gone to make way for the I-75/U.S. 27 interchange and flew west stopping to set out survey stakes until they reached the eastern part of Naples. He told us about real big pine and oak islands in Collier County, but he was not really sure of exactly where they were. This was all we needed to know, and the report encouraged us to move our exploration to the northern end of the Big Cypress.

We continued to backpack but moved up to the newly opened Alligator Alley. Here we found a different type of terrain. We found more marl, deeper sloughs, and much bigger pine islands and hammocks. We liked this area much better. However, we were never alone.

We were looking for that great hunting place. We did find lots of neat places that already had someone using them. We found many camps, some better than others and some not so good. In the next few years, we continued to explore and learn the Big Cypress. When we were off the Alley, we could move about easier with fewer people in the woods than there were on U.S. 41. We also found a lot more game, but, as usual, we did not shoot any big game.

We saw deer running away and heard them jumping in the water but never fired a shot at a deer or hog. We were young and tough, had good knees, and were full of energy. We could walk with heavy packs all day and carried the very minimum amount of food as we lived off what we could get. Sometimes this was a snipe or other bird. Sometimes it was a squirrel, frog or pot of crawfish.

In 1968, the second or third year we hunted south of S.R.84, the Florida Game and Fish Commission of Florida (GFC) held a two-day doe hunt. This was not public land, and they had no way to control who participated or to know how many does were shot. The GFC (now the Florida Fish, Wildlife and Conservation Commission of Florida—FWC) had received a report from a well-known deer expert that said there were too many deer in the Big Cypress, and they were going to harm the habitat, if the size of the herd was not reduced. A special deer hunt was held in Collier County that brought people from all over the state to the Big Cypress. From that season on, there were many more people in the Big Cypress and the deer herd had been seriously reduced.

My favorite camping gear was a jungle hammock that I made from a surplus military hammock. I took the top off the military jungle hammock and sewed it onto a heavy white canvas hammock. This worked well for me. I also carried a light double aluminum pot for boiling water and cooking in. All we carried was dried food—like rice, fruit, and already cooked boiled eggs and potatoes. Any meat we ate was what we shot.

I continued to go to the Cypress by myself. Even though this is not considered a good idea, I could not always find someone to go with me, which was frequently the case in my early years of hiking and backpacking. When I was older with a cabin and a buggy, the tough wet country continued to make it difficult to find people to go to the swamps for more than a brief visit. In both cases, I really enjoyed the solitude and experiences when I was alone in the swamps.

During one backpack hunting trip in my early years of exploring south of I-75, I had walked about three hours south and set up camp on a cabbage hammock located on a large marl prairie between two big cypress strands. I did not know it at the time, but I was in Mullet Slough. I had planned to sit on the island and watch the edge of the cypress for deer feeding along its edge. I turned in early that evening to get away from the mosquitoes and to have a good night's rest in a cold-camp (a cold-camp is one with no fire) so I would be ready for a full day of hunting the next day. During the night, I woke up and thought I had dreamed about a bear coming into camp. The bear had sniffed me in the hammock and finally slapped it making it spin like a top. I turned on the flashlight, looked around and saw nothing. In the morning after I drank my cold instant coffee, I looked around the edge of the small island and to my surprise I found fresh, large bear tracks. There had indeed been a bear visit at the camp that night. I was not too concerned as I always slept with a .357 magnum in the hammock with me. But then it would not be a pleasant experience to have to deal with a bear attack while sleeping in a jungle hammock. Thus, the next day I packed up my camp and left the woods considering my dream as a warning to not stay around any longer.

Chapter Three

◆ ◆ ◆

The Road that Changed Florida

These were good days. When we stayed longer than a day, one of our parents would take us to the swamps. This meant a trip of seventy-five miles each way. But by doing this, we did not have to worry about our car being stolen. However, in those days, this was not really a problem and many left their cars, trucks, and trailers on the sides of roads all over South Florida. Some even left their swamp buggies at the trailheads all hunting season.

Larry Hawthorne on alligator alley in 1967.

When we were dropped off by our parents, we had a set time and date for them to pick us up. We always arrived early to make sure they did not have to wait on us. Above you see Larry standing on *The Road that Changed Florida and The Nation,* Alligator Alley (S.R. 84 or Alley or I-75), while we waited for our ride. If it was a cool day, we could actually lie on the road to stay warm as there was so little traffic.

One day, my dad asked me what I would do if we ever shot a deer way back in the swamps while backpack camping. I said we would camp there until we ate enough of the deer to walk out or he would have to send my Uncle Joe with a helicopter.

Soon after Larry and I went to the Alley to hike in the Cypress, my family started fishing along the road. It was a good place to fish and we had plenty of room to pull off the road.

Our family camping on S.R. 84, 1a968.

We also had plenty of space to spread out. We could walk the banks for miles, without others being in the way, much as my dad and his hunting friend had done when the Tamiami Trail was first built. The fish were extremely hungry and aggressive. I think this was because they had not been heavily fished. Anything we threw in the water was hit and hit hard by a largemouth bass.

Fishing remained like this for a number of years. Then the bass started to get smart and would be more cautious before hitting a lure. They would often pick up a plastic worm and carry it around in their lips before eating the bait. This required fisherman to have a real feel for their fishing line. For many years, there were times when we would catch over one-hundred bass a day while walking along the bank. Most of the time we would use artificial bait. We used anything from plastic worms to top water lures. One of the best lures was the four-inch, shallow-running Rappala.

This fishing led to our family camping on the Alley. This seventy-five-mile-long road connecting the East Coast with the West Coast of Florida had become a real outdoor lovers' paradise. There were positive newspaper articles about how families could camp and enjoy the outdoors on the Alley. There were people camping and fishing all along the full length of the road. I did not know it at that time, but we could do this because of the actions of the Florida Wildlife Federation. John J. Jones, the president of Florida Wildlife Federation (FWF), had agreed not to fight the road if sportsmen were allowed to use it; there was no FDOT fence and sportsmen could also leave the right-of-way every other section to hunt, camp, and fish in the Everglades and Cypress.

At night, traffic on the road would die down enough to allow us a good night's sleep. Everyone had a great long park to enjoy. We did not know it then, but this would soon change as many had great plans for eastern Collier County and western Broward County.

Our camping and fishing trips soon led to the next phase of our becoming swampers. I learned why my dad had asked me about bringing out our game. He had it in his mind to purchase a swamp buggy. It was not a big one but one that would get us into the backcountry and out. He purchased our Onan buggy from Mr. Smith who had a cabin in the Stair-Step unit. As I said, it was small and could take four people with some gear back into the swamps at a speed that was a little faster rate than walking.

With the purchase of this buggy, I started looking at other swamp buggies to learn how they were made and why. I took a good number of pictures so that I would be able to reference them later as I planned to build my own.

Now that we had a buggy, Dad, brother Ed, and

Dad and Eddy in sawgrass country where Silver Lakes community is today.

I would ride in the area that is now Weston, Chapel Trails, and Silver Lakes housing developments. Today, there are 500,000 people living where we used our swamp buggy and hunted. When my dad was a young man, these places were Everglades, but they had become dried out sawgrass areas with a few large islands. The area was full of deer as almost all the vegetation in this type of habitat is good deer food. The limiting factor for the size of a deer herd is the amount of high ground when the water is high. Drained sawgrass country has no herd limiting factors thus there were lots of deer. The Onan buggy worked well in this terrain, but it was slow and much too low to see over the eight to ten-foot-tall sawgrass. The deer we saw were running through the tall sawgrass and would get away. Not only were there deer in this part of western Broward County, there were panthers, too. Every now and then we would see one. But most of the time, we only saw their tracks in the mud or hear them scream at night.

My first swamp buggy was a sight for sore eyes. Not being rich (I am still not), I used what I could get for next to nothing. I used a surplus U.S. Mail cart, turned it upside down, put the drive axle in the front, and drove a three-speed truck transmission with belts from a single-cylinder Wisconsin engine. The transmission turned the pinion via a chain drive connection. There was no steering wheel, just a joystick that steered with a push-pull. It would not go fast but two people could get in the woods a fair distance and back out. We used it for a number of years, and I even managed to run over my wife, Donna's, leg without hurting her.

Donna and Sue on our first swamp buggy.

But finally, it died and went to the buggy graveyard—the Alley Auto Parts Junk Yard.

By now, I had paid off the loan for the five acres I purchased while in high school. This land was a long way up Monument Road on its west fork and about half-way between U.S. 41 and the Alley. I had never seen it, but I wanted to build a cabin on it. There were many thousands of others who had purchased land just as I had. Some folks purchased land for the same reason but most wanted to drain the swamps and build roads and regular houses.

Now and then, we could borrow my dad's Onan buggy and go camping. Larry and I would wander around the Cypress, south of the Alley. We were looking for a good place to hunt and camp. We came across many camps and cabins. Some of them were really big and well-built while others were like what we had been building—tar-paper covered areas to sleep and eat under.

Larry cooking the turkey he shot.

On one trip, Larry shot a nice gobbler. His well-placed 30-06 round did little damage to the edible meat and so we had roast turkey for a few days. We never really found our perfect hunting place but did find the big pine islands my uncle told me about. Baxter Island was one of these and it would soon become a motivating reason for my life to take another change.

We enjoyed the Cypress much more than the Everglades. We could walk in the Cypress and when it was dry, we could really hike a great deal with little problem because we knew how to read the vegetation. There were thick swamps that took a great deal of care to get through or one had to learn how to go around them. However, the thick palmettos and swamps would eventually give way to open prairie country. This was flat marl soil with some water on it and in the spring these areas would be covered with flowers. However, even though these marl areas had no real thick vegetation, they were not easy to walk in when wet. We had a saying, "One step forward and slide back one-half step." This walking was really hard on the legs.

As we moved around camping either via buggy or hiking, we greatly appreciated full moon nights. The moon would emit enough light that we would actually see to move about with a certain degree of safety. But to sit by the campfire or lie in a hammock and watch the moonrise over the massive pine trees was worth all the effort. These trees had either not been cut by the loggers in the 1940s and '50s or they had grown from seedlings since then. Whatever the case, they were great to look at.

During the day, the heat and humidity would become absolutely oppressive. The air would become so still we could hardly breathe. But off in the distance, we could hear the rumble of the storm coming and see the huge cumulus clouds building to awesome heights. We would then begin to feel the breeze growing stronger and know the storm was coming our way. At least, we hoped it would come so that the wind and rain would cool off the entire area including us.

But like all good things, such as the Alley, good times would pass, and it would become difficult to get into the woods from the Alley. These storms would only last a short time and then move out as fast as they came. The results would be greater oppressive heat with higher humidity. The tall, white clouds would reflect the sun so that we now received twice the amount of heat coming from the sun. It was not a time to walk or work in the Cypress after a storm passed.

Larry moved off to college and on, so I was left with no one to accompany me into the woods. Marriage would soon change that as Donna would go with me on some trips and these were exciting times because it always seemed like something was going to happen at any moment. One time, we tried to go down an old logging tram with our best car—a Corvair. It did not go too far and soon sat down on the rear engine. This was just one more dumb thing that I did.

Chapter Four

◆ ◆ ◆

Growing Political Action

We met a new couple in our apartment building—Mike Sweeny. Mike soon had me going to his brother's cabin south of the Alley. John, Mike's brother, had purchased forty acres and was building a nice cabin in the swamps. We would load everything on the truck, drive to Turner River Road, off-load the supplies onto a barge made of oil drums, pull the barge across the canal and then, while wading in swamp water, load the big Dodge power wagon swamp buggy. This buggy still sits in front of where John's cabin once stood. It is one of many cabins the NPS burned. The buggy burned in the 1971 fire and the NPS burned John's cabin in the 1980s.

The buggy can be seen along the new NPS ORV trail from gate #2. Once we were loaded, the fun would start. At a pace about like a slow walk, we would head to his cabin. The distance was not much as the crow flies but by the way the swamps said we had to go; it was about three miles. These miles were all slow going, as we had to go through Deep Lake Strand on the east side of Turner River Road. The strand had many fingers of cypress and open areas between these deep-water courses. Luckily. we would arrive at camp in two hours after leaving the barge. That is if we did not get stuck or break down.

This was 1969, and the land boom was at its highest point in modern times. People were selling swampland and folks would purchase it sight unseen. I knew I wanted to build a cabin of my own so when I saw a survey truck on the Alley, I stopped to talk with them. After some discussion, they loosened up and told me where there were some good locations to purchase property. They also told me that others were in the swamps doing the same

Jockey Club east of Turner River Road.

thing. Donna and I talked it over and I went back to the area to find a good chunk of land, which we purchased. We began to build our cabin, Camp Red Bug—a project that became a lifelong effort, a family joy, and point of contention. But all being said, it was more joy than grief.

In 1970, while we worked on our cabin and explored the Big Cypress, most of our productive hunting came from areas to the east—places like Brown's Farm, Ray Rottenberger, and Holely Lands. Some game was taken from the Miami River, the Mud Canal, and the area north of S.R. 84. We spent many an hour on our homemade freestanding ladder stands. When we wanted meat, we would go to one of these places. There was a lot of game in these semi-drained Everglades, but the country was not as pretty as the Cypress.

These drained Everglades-type habitats would be in my life again and again over the years. Some would require litigation to save them and others would be lost to the ever-pressing problem of where to store dirty water in a system that had become overused by 1975.

By 1970, we had our property cleared as much as we wanted, and a cabin begun. I had spent a lot of time planning the building and by having good plans, I was able to purchase scrap lumber, or get some material off construction jobs as they were cleaned up. At the same time, my dad and brother sold their little Onan buggy, and were building a new, big, 4x4 buggy out of an International Harvester truck. However, before they could finish it, I had to get building materials in, and the structure started. You see, the Big Cypress had become a national issue and many were pushing to make it a National Park.

Calvin Stone (Cal) told me there was not enough support to make it a National Park. However, Cal did not want the area to be either a National Park or developed so he was able to assemble a meeting at his camp, Calusa Ranch. This meeting would create a new "breed of cat" in the NPS portfolio. These state and national leaders spent a week at Cal's. Deals were made as to how it would be managed and by what agency. There were nearby private airports owned by members of the Everglades Conservation and Sportsmen Club. Cal was president of that club and president of the FWF, while John J. Jones was the paid Executive Director. From these little airports folks flew around Big Cypress and then rode swamp buggies to see what land they were going to convince the State of Florida and Congress to purchase.

According to Cal, everyone came away with a firm commitment to make this happen and to put 570,000 acres under the control of the NPS as Preserve. There were two problems: no money to do this and there was no legal avenue to take people's land. Thus, to save the water from being drained off by the creation of the new Dade-Collier Jet port and the development that would follow, these men conspired to take the land that belonged to many others. They also had decided to make sure the hunters and cabin owners who were in the swamps at that time could remain. The plan was to require the I-75 Environmental Impact Statement (EIS) to stipulate that I-75 would be fenced with no service roads, no interchanges except for the Indian Reservation. Additionally, the EIS would go on to state that by doing this the land in the Big Cypress would become land-locked and the value depressed. Once this land was worthless, agencies could purchase the land cheaply. Thus, a complex law was created—the Big Cypress National Preserve Act of 1974. As you can see by the date, it was not a quick or easy law to pass since the action that began in 1969 by Joe Browder was not completed until 1974.

Additionally, Assistant Secretary Nat Reed was telling (see letter and testimony in appendix) people, including landowners, what they wanted to hear. He said the land would be purchased at market value. This sounded good for those who had just paid $1,000 an acre for swamp or uplands in the Big Cypress. Little did we realize that Nat meant the land would be purchased at its tax-appraised value. Once the Big Cypress Act was signed into law, all drainage and roadwork outlawed, and the NPS given condemnation rights on all the land, the property had very little value. People lost a lot of money, had their dreams destroyed and, in some cases, lost their retirement investment plans. This did not matter as long as I-75 could be built on S.R. 84 so wealthier and very influential people could be satisfied. These influential people owned companies like Deltona Corporation, Mackle Brothers Corporation, and Gulf American Land Company. These and other major landowners wanted I-75 to follow the route to Naples and across Florida to Miami so their property would become more valuable. Their collective thoughts were that of attracting new people into Southwest Florida and building new towns.

About this same time, one of my students who hunted with his dad and knew I hunted asked me to attend a meeting of the Dade County Halftrack Conservation Club. I did and my eyes and mind were opened to a big world of who was doing what to protect our lands and hunting. I was introduced to Cal, and he assured me that our cabins would remain and we would be able to use our swamp buggies and hunt if we could only get Florida and the U.S. Congress to protect the Big Cypress. I left feeling very confident all was in good order. Why not? Here was the President of the Florida Wildlife Federation, President of the Everglades Conservation Sportsmen's Club, an officer in the Everglades Coordinating Council, and a big executive type for Florida Power and Light with the same interest as me.

If anyone would know what was happening and what was going to happen, it should have been Cal.

Every year the Dade County Halftrack Conservation Club sponsors a conservation display at the Miami Dade County Youth Fair. We had a really big display, with live animals, vehicles, photographs and plants. When the fair first started, Freddy Fisikelli had us doing nighttime security and car problem help for the full fourteen days. As the fair matured, they decided that we had to give them a percentage of the coins pitched into our conservation kettle. We decided that we were no longer needed at the

Country Cadillac built by Ed Moller on display at the Dade County Youth Fair

fair and stopped going. This was a mistake because it was a place where many thousands of people would see what the Everglades and Cypress were like. It was also a place where we could promote saving these places from development impacts. But like all good things it, too, went by the wayside.

So, I continued to work on our little cabin. I obtained most of the lumber secondhand and drew up the plans. Once the material was on hand, I cut each piece, and color-coded and numbered it as per the plans. We then started taking material to the land. This was a job in itself as I did not have a swamp buggy and had to carry much of it in. The closest route was a three-quarter mile hike straight through a cypress swamp. We did this most of the time by either carrying the material or floating it. Before most of the material was in, Dad and brother finished their big 4x4 buggy. We then took the rest of the material in and stored it off the ground under the sub-floor. My neighbor, Rick, my youngest brother in-law, and I put the entire place up with the roof on and the windows and doors in during one full day's work. The only thing that did not go on was the wall sheeting. This went on the next week. Then I took another twenty years to get it to a point that was 99% finished. I had material and furnishings given to me. I was invited to salvage buildings and got good buys on throwaway lumber at the Immokalee sawmill. In the end, I had a kitchen paneled in mahogany cove molding and the rest of the house with one-inch pecky cypress I made from rough lumber obtained at the Immokalee sawmill. The house had a drop ceiling and R19 insulation throughout the walls and ceiling. It was a cool place in the heat of the summer.

In the '70s, not only was I hunting and exploring the Cypress, but I was also fishing with my neighbor, Rick, and longtime friend, Denny. We would go to sea on Friday night and fish all weekend. Then, we sold the fish on the mainland on Sunday or Monday. Rick had all his commercial fishing permits and licenses, and we would make good

Rick docking his boat at Papa Joes.

money fishing as well as having a great time. Rick could catch fish at a rate of ten to one of mine. He knew where the fish would be at what time of the year.

On one very productive trip, we anchored on the upstream edge of a reef off Alligator light. We could see fish on the depth finder, so we stayed there for hours and chummed. Finally, they started to bite around midnight. Using fifteen-pound line, no weights, and glass minnows we had caught in the cast net earlier that day, we were catching fish as fast as we could.

Using two poles, we would cast straight out the side of the boat, set the rod in the rod holder, go the stern rod to set the hook, bring in the yellow tail, move the other rod down, break the line off so the fish fell in the big ice box, tie on a new hook. We would then start the process over. We fished until nearly dawn and were exhausted from pulling in fish.

We did have one real surprise. Rick yelled for me to get the pliers and help him. He had not caught a yellow tail but a big mangrove snapper. By the light of the moon, he had not looked closely and did not notice what fish was on his hook. He placed his thumb in the fish's mouth. This was a mistake. If you have ever seen a mangrove snapper, you will know why. Its big teeth had gone clean through Rick's thumbnail and Rick was holding on to the fish for dear life. I got the pliers and freed Rick. From then on, we both made sure to look closer and to break the line on the line-break attached to the icebox.

There was a very brief time fish traps could be used. Rick built two and used them. We only used them for one or two trips and then stopped. They could clean out the ocean. We worked to make them illegal and they still are today.

If we did not go to the Keys or Marco to fish on weekends, we often spent late hours shrimping in Miami. For many years, there were not too many boats even on the hottest shrimp runs. Rick and I used a small, fourteen-foot jon boat. We started pulling a big net. One night, while working the net in the Miami Port ship channel, a huge sea tug almost sank us. We came really close to going down as the tug was making huge waves and we had a full sock of shrimp. I think that night we sold six hundred pounds to a restaurant in Hialeah.

Another brainstorm sort of worked. Rick decided to build a long trout-line for dolphins. We reasoned if we got in a bunch of school dolphin and got them to the boat, we could throw this trout-line out behind the slow-moving boat and catch a bunch of the dolphin. They would bite the

A big bull dolphin off Miami.

bait and shake the line and the others would get hooked as well. The idea worked. Rick reported to me it worked so well the first and only time it was used, a huge, reef, bull shark took the second fish from the boat and left with all of them in tow. The shark had cut the trout-line and left only one fish. No more ideas like that!

Rick had to close his part-time commercial fish venture as the laws changed and fisherman had to prove they made a certain percentage of their total income from fishing. There was no way we could do that. He was out of business and I was out of work.

I would also fish with Dennis Wilson—Denny. With Denny, I usually went dolphin fishing or diving. We caught enough to eat for months and kept the fish good to eat by freezing it in water. If we did not dolphin fish we would free-dive to spear fish and gather lobsters by hand.

Diving in the surge channels of Florida Bay was an exciting and sometimes dangerous activity. Denny was a good diver and fed his family and friends with what he took. We would dive in the surge channels when there was a slack falling tide. This provided the clearest water, if there had been no storms for a few days and no current. We would dive until we found groupers, snapper, or other good eating fishing. The first such fish speared would be strung on the spear and left on the bottom. The sounds and smell would bring more fish to the area. Then we could really fill the coolers with good-size handpicked fish. But this practice would also bring in big sharks and barracudas.

On one such trip, I had a good size grouper on the bottom and was working to get another when out of the corner of my eye I saw a large greenish, gray-green shark circling me with that hungry look. He was coming closer on each circle, had a large belly and a real ugly smile. I got Denny's attention, picked up my fish, and we got out of the water. After a few minutes, we figured the shark had gone. So back in we went. I speared another fish, and the shark was right there saying in his own way that it was his fish. We were vacating the water in a hurry. Denny was swimming to the boat on his stomach and I on my back next to Denny's flippers. This way we could look in all directions for the big reef bull shark that wanted our fish. I looked to the boat to make sure I would not drive Denny into the boat and then looked behind me. Looking back again, I saw the big bull shark with his mouth open coming for my legs or his fish. Well, he got the fish on the spear, and I was out of the water like a big penguin. That was my last time diving, not because of the bull shark but because diving made my bad knee hurt for days afterwards.

I realize it is hard to believe but the building of I-75 and the deals cut to build this road affected the Keys and marine fishing nearly as much as it did the uplands and freshwater habitats. How the Keys were saved will be brought out later in the book.

Chapter Five

◆ ◆ ◆

The DOI/NPS Arrive

On weekends, when we were not fishing, we would head to the camp Red Bug and we always had a load of building material. There was always something to be done. At about this same time, big parts of the east coast had communities that were changing. Some were developing high rates of crime and heavy drug use problems.

Some people living in these parts of the East Coast saw the Cypress (Big Cypress area) as a place to live and commute to town to work. Living in the Cypress, they could do what they wanted and not be worried about crime. A real estate company, Pines & Palms Inc., built a rock road, Cypress

Ed and Donna with the family at camp target range.

Lane, into the area east of Baxter Island. The company gave Wildcat Excavation Company ten acres on S.R. 84 and forty acres one and a half miles south of the Alley to build Cypress Land and several other roads. With all these roads, many people saw the Baxter Island area as a place to live in the woods. One of these was a New York penal employee who owned seven one-and-a-half-acre lots south of me. He paid the road builder to build a road to his property from Cypress Lane. This road onto Baxter Island was not popular with those who had places on Baxter Island; some of the men had a talk with the excavator who then decided he had plenty of other work to do before finishing the New Yorker's road. By the time the New Yorker was ready to move his trailer onto his land, someone had stolen his sixty-foot trailer and the Big Cypress National Preserve law had passed locking up 880 square miles of land in a Federal Law. He could not build anything. In those days, it was legal to build a hunting cabin on your land and the building and zoning departments did little to nothing to verify what you were doing. I know this because I took them to see my little cabin and they said it was built better than places next to the Collier Courthouse and not to worry about anything. All they wanted to do was talk about hunting.

One time, the zoning department did attempt to take some action on a more recently built structure. It was said they flew to the area via helicopter and sat down in the man's front yard. Reportedly, to their surprise, he started shooting at the helicopter or at least over it. The pilot took off leaving the inspectors on the ground. The inspectors ran all the way back to the Alley from Baxter Island. I never heard what happened or if they ever returned.

Baxter Island got its name because an eco-tour guide named Baxter would take northern tourists to it in the springtime. He used a modified Maxwell touring car as a swamp buggy and would leave from Ft Myers in the late 1940s. He would then drive to Immokalee and further south on the buggy trail that went to Baxter Island. He had a campsite near my place. This campsite was called 'Whiskey Bottle Camp,' at least until the artist, Russ Smiley, purchased it. The reason for this name is there was car-size pile of whiskey bottles there. I learned this from Joe Brown of Immokalee at one of Russ's famous artist parties he held in the swamps. These were awesome parties with lots of interesting folks attending. Russ sold his place to Raleigh Burney and Raleigh and his wife moved from Hialeah, Florida, to Baxter Island.

Joe Brown also explained to me how Mullet Slough was named. When I first went through Mullet Slough, I could see the remains of a wooden, thirty-gallon barrel. This barrel, what was left of it, and the steel bands were in a cypress tree on the north side of the buggy trail. Joe Brown told me that on one of Baxter's eco-tour trips to the Big Cypress, his Maxwell Touring car-swamp buggy broke down on the high oak island on the north side of the slough at a crossing we called Cleat Rock Hammock. Baxter and his sidekick/assistant, walked back to Immokalee to get a replacement part. They did not find the part there and had to go all the way to Ft. Myers. They obtained the part and by the time they returned to where they left their northern tourists these good people had eaten all the salted mullet and hung the barrel in the tree. Thus, the slough became known as Mullet Slough. Some think it is so named because mullet would swim up Turner River and then swim to this deep slough. This is just not so.

The following pre-legislative history of the Big Cypress National Preserve was told to me by Cal Stone, John J. Jones, and Joe Browder.

While Senator Lawton Chiles is considered the legislative father of the Big Cypress National Preserve, in my opinion, Joe Browder is the creator of the Preserve. Joe had been working hard to save the area because of its importance to the natural water flow to the western Everglades National Park. He was not getting anywhere at making it a park. Cal Stone had several sections of land he owned and another ten sections he leased in what is now the middle of the Big Cypress National Preserve. According to Cal, he did not want the area to become houses such as already in Miami and the new airport would certainly cause this. Cal told me he met Joe and they talked about how to save the Cypress. Cal was the President of the Florida Wildlife Federation (FWF) and had many contacts in South Florida and Tallahassee. Further, many of his wood's neighbors had a lot of influence with important people in decision-making positions. Cal was a good friend of Governor Ruben Askew. One time while visiting Cal at his house, he showed me a fine .270 Winchester bolt-action rifle Governor Askew had given him.

From his meeting with Joe Browder, Cal arranged another meeting but this one would be at his camp where Joe and many others were flown in to meet and confer. The group included federal bureaucrats from the DOI/NPS, people from Tallahassee, environmental leaders of the day, and elected officials from both the state and Washington DC. They spent a week working on the concepts and making agreements on what should happen, who should manage the area, and what the area would be for. They also figured out what political actions had to be done to get the task completed and who knew whom.

The list of who knew whom was most impressive:

Cal knew Congressman Claude Pepper. Congressman Pepper was not known for his environmental positions, but he was really for the common-man and sportsmen. Cal was an officer in the local IBEW, and he knew that Congressman Pepper was a Union man. Cal told Pepper the taking of these private lands would be good for the common man. The average man could go to the Cypress to enjoy hunting and not have to go out west and spend a lot of money. Congressman Pepper bought in and supported it.

John Chandler who owned a camp, 'Boar's Den' (now owned by Carl Greer), next to Cal's camp, knew Congressman Dante Fascel really well. John talked to Dante and he was on board.

Many local city mayors and county elected officials hunted in the Big Cypress. These people knew all the right people who could make things happen. They also knew that I-75 was coming and very influential people wanted this road built to open up their lands for development.

Johnny C. Jones, Executive Director of the Florida Wildlife Federation (FWF), knew Tom Kimball, President of the National Wildlife Federation (NWF). Johnny talked with Tom and got his support for the most massive land purchase by the NPS in a very long time. After all, if the FWF with a 40,000-hunter membership was for it, how could Tom be against it. Johnny went to Governor Askew whom he also knew and between Cal and Johnny the governor was on board. They then went to work on the Board of Trustees for Florida, the Cabinet. Each member eventually signed on. Now, all this was a real change in position because just a few years before when ENP expanded to the west and took in the Ten Thousand Islands, the FWF had taken a position that opposed this action.

The FWF president at that time stated there was no need to protect any more mosquito-ridden swamps in South Florida.

The shocker came when Johnny went to DC and spoke to Senator Bible's interior subcommittee. Johnny was told that those in DC were tired of Florida always coming to DC with their hand out for money and doing nothing for themselves. Johnny asked the senator what it would take for the senator to support the Big Cypress National Preserve. He was told that Florida would have to put up $40,000,000. Johnny agreed to this and returned to Florida. On his return to Florida, he contacted Governor Askew with the news.

A year earlier, 1972, Johnny and others were able to get the Environmental Endangered and Recreation Lands (EEL) bill signed into law and funded. However, the forty million dollars required by the U.S. Congress to fund the Big Cypress came after the Board of Trustees (BOT agreed with National Audubon's ten item resolution threat to file litigation and I-75 was built.) This agreement was signed on April 14, 1973, and signing it stopped Audubon from filing a suit against the state. This suit would prevent the building of I-75 from Tampa to Miami, see appendix, and one of the resolution's conditions was for the state to spend forty million dollars to purchase the state's portion of the Big Cypress National Preserve. Johnny worked with state Senator Bob Graham and Representative Richard A. Pettigrew to get $40 million from EEL. Most of this money was used to purchase the Bear Island Unit and other portions of the original Preserve. EEL also provided money to purchase much of Ray Rottenberger's, Three Lakes Wildlife Management Area and other areas in Florida. Even though in 1964 there was already a small bill, commonly called the "bathing suit tax" for conservation and recreation lands, EEL was the real beginning of the movement in Florida to purchase property for environmental and natural resource outdoor recreation. Several bills followed EEL: Conservation and Recreation Lands Act (CARL), Preservation-2000 (P2000), and the Florida Forever Act. In 1968, money that was generated by the bathing suit tax was replaced by a documentary stamp tax (DOC stamp). This DOC stamp tax was placed on all real estate and mortgage transactions and used to fund all future land acquisition acts. By 2004, the DOC stamp tax was generating $2,000,000,000 a year.

JOHN C. & MARIANA B. JONES
4080 North Haverhill Road
West Palm Beach, Florida 33417-8116
June 21, 2001

Mr. L. Jack Moller
610 N.W. 93rd Avenue
Pembroke Pines, Florida 33024

Dear Jack,

I have read your history of the Big Cypress acquisition and want to congratulate you on the time and effort you have taken to document the events of the past thirty years. I would like to add some of my recollections, especially what happened in the early 1970's. You are welcome to use any of these remarks that you feel will be helpful.

The Big Cypress acquisition was not a particularly popular concept among many of the residents of South Florida. Many people were still smarting from the loss of fishing and hunting opportunities that occurred when the Everglades National Park was created in the late 1940's. Many had moved their hunting camps from what is now the ENP to the Big Cypress and now they feared they would be forced out of the Big Cypress. Many of these landowners had built their camps with the intention to eventually retire to the area to live full time. The landowners were equally concerned they would lose their right to use their swamp buggies for transportation and as a way to traverse the area to hunt. There was a consensus of opinion, which of course proved to be true over time, that there was oil under the Big Cypress, and the federal government was attempting a "land grab" to get free access to the oil.

At the same time, the jetport was under consideration in Big Cypress and there were other massive agricultural developments being planned. Interstate 75 had been designated across the Big Cypress. I could see that time was of the essence, and if immediate steps were not taken, the Big Cypress would be lost to development. I believed that the Big Cypress was important for its recreational opportunities, but I also learned that the watershed was vital to Everglades National Park and the fishery in Florida Bay.

Joe Browder and Nat Reed were in Washington, and there was a bill before Congress to purchase the Big Cypress. In addition to the opposition in Florida, there was many in Congress who were less than happy about forking over $160 million to buy Big Cypress. It had only been a little over twenty years since the federal government had purchased Everglades National Park, and now Florida was back knocking at the door for more money.

The Florida Wildlife Federation was moving on several fronts to protect the Big Cypress. We were trying to get the state to declare the Big Cypress an "area of critical state concern" to limit development. We were opposing the I-75 route across Alligator Alley, at least until the Big Cypress could be purchased. We were opposing the construction of the jetport in the Big Cypress.

I was also personally working to calm the fears of the landowners. I tried to assure them I would do all within my power to protect their rights to hunt, fish and recreate, and I especially worked to get the use of swamp buggies protected. I worked with Joe Browder in Washington and with Nat Reed who was then the Assistant Secretary of the Interior to give the landowners who desired it, a lifetime tenancy. I suggested to Nat Reed that to allay the fears of those who were crying "federal land grab" that the government permit the owners to retain their mineral and oil rights.

I went to Washington, I think in the spring of 1973, to testify before the Senate Interior Sub Committee on Lands. Senator Allan Bible, from Nevada was the chairman of the committee. Cal Stone was the president of the FWF and was a landowner in the Big Cypress. He was a member of the large Everglades Sportsman's Club on the Tamiami Trail. The club was a political force, and the membership was divided over the Big Cypress acquisition. I had persuaded Cal to support the acquisition, and he accompanied me on the trip to Washington. While we were there we visited Senator Lawton Chiles, Nat Reed and Joe Browder. The executive director of the National Wildlife Federation, Thomas L. Kimball also accompanied Cal and myself. We got commitments from Chiles, Reed and Browder to allow the owners to retain the oil and mineral rights, and to give them a lifetime tenancy. We also got a commitment that traditional uses would be permitted. Those uses included hunting, fishing, camping, frogging, *and the use of traditional swamp buggies.* The Big Cypress was never intended to be a park or wilderness area, but a buffer to Everglades National Park.

When we went before Senator Bible's committee, I felt hostility. After the hearing, I said to Tom Kimball, "Senator Bible is against us for some reason." I asked Tom if he knew him, and if he could get us into see him. Tom knew him quite well, and got us an appointment that afternoon.

When we got into Sen. Bible's office, I asked him, "What is it you don't like about the bill?" He scowled at me, "You people in Florida just got the Everglades National Park bought with federal money, and now you're back up here wanting more. Florida hasn't put any money on the table." I asked him, "How much money do you want from Florida?" He answered, "Forty percent," which amounted to $40 million. "If I can get Florida to put up the forty million, will you let the bill out of committee?" I asked. Sen. Bible agreed.

The Florida Legislature was in session, so I went to back to Tallahassee. I went straight to Governor Reubin Askew's office. I told him that we're not going to get the Big Cypress approved by Congress unless we put up $40 million. We had just approved the Environmentally Endangered Lands Bonding Program in November 1972, so we had $240 million available, but the enabling legislation had not yet become effective, so we needed to pass a bill to get the money appropriated. Gov. Askew sent me to Senator Bob Graham's office, where his staff chairman, Al Galbraith, Ernie Litz and I wrote a measure that would appropriate the $40 million. In the House, Rep. Richard Pettigrew also had a bill that would put up $40 million, if the federal government agreed to the purchase of the entire Big Cypress. Graham's bill bought the first $40 million, regardless of what the feds did. Graham's bill passed the Senate and when it was sent to the House, Rep. Pettigrew adopted Graham's version of the bill.

When the measure was passed into law, we notified Sen. Bible of Florida's commitment to the purchase of Big Cypress. He still refused to let the bill out of his committee.

Senator Henry "Scoop" Jackson, of Washington State, was chairman of the full Interior Committee. Tom Kimball went to Jackson and told him what Bible had said. Senator Jackson pulled the bill out of Bible's committee, and signed on as a sponsor. He and Senator Chiles held hearings in Miami, and Jackson brought the bill to the floor of the Senate where it was approved.

Joe Browder, Nat Reed, and Lawton Chiles deserve the credit for getting the Big Cypress protected. Joe Browder once wrote that without the support of the hunters and fishermen, the acquisition would have never become a reality.

On November 22, 1974, Assistant Secretary for Fish and Wildlife and Parks, Nat Reed, wrote me:

"The recent enactment of the Big Cypress National Preserve is a major step forward in the annals of American conservation. The protection of this priceless resource will do much to assure future generations of Americans that we have acted wisely as custodians of our unique national heritage. Your tireless support of this legislation—and especially your faith and activity when its prospects seemed bleak—were instrumental in achieving this great victory for the environment. Please accept my belated thanks for your vital efforts in preserving Big Cypress."

As you know, I retired from conservation work in 1986. One of my greatest regrets is that I did not follow the Big Cypress issue through to its conclusion. I believe if I had remained active in the public debate that continued, I might have been able to keep alive the issue of traditional uses. I am still convinced that the traditional swamp buggies, which were built lightweight, with limited horsepower and wide tires, should be allowed. The Big Cypress is a watershed that provides water to the Park. It is not, and never was intended to be an extension of Everglades National Park. It was to be a buffer and recreational uses were to be maximized. Senator Chiles was particularly adamant about keeping the Big Cypress open to hunting, fishing and camping. I am outraged that the bureaucrats are attempting to subvert the intent of the original law to fit their own intents and purposes.

If this huge area is closed to public use, I wonder who is going to be the watchdog to see any abuses or degradation that occurs? As the Japanese say, "If there is no eye to behold the beauty, What is the good?"

Keep up the good work.

With best personal regards, I am,

Sincerely,

John C. Jones

At the same time EEL was being developed, the legislators also created a bill that under certain conditions would allow the State of Florida to take control of local zoning and development matters. A bill was created titled the Area of Critical State Concern. It was applied to the Big Cypress Basin, Green Swamp, and Florida Keys. In 2004, the regulations and oversight brought by this action were still in effect; it created contention between landowners who opposed it and conservationists who supported it.

Johnny also told Tom Kimball that he did not think Senator Bible was going to support the Cypress bill even if he did get the money as requested. Tom said he knew the chairman of the committee well enough to talk with him. The Chair, Senator S. Jackson, said he would not even allow the subcommittee to act on the bill and took it right to the full committee. This Big Cypress bill would also be Senator Jackson's green action for his Presidential race. When the state had the money to satisfy Senator Bible and others with the same concern the bill looked ready to move in DC.

The time line is simple: 1) Powerful and influential people want I-75 to go from Tampa to Miami Lakes and across Florida on S.R. 84.; 2) The state learns that the Congress wants a bunch of money for the state to apply to the purchase of the Big Cypress; 3) The state passes EEL; 4) The state signs and agrees to National Audubon demands to allow the state to build an illegal road; 5) The state applies a new law to the Big Cypress basin— Area of Critical State Concern and spends $40 million to satisfy Congress. While all this sounds good the political work had only just begun.

There were people that no one even heard of working to save the Cypress. Many of those who were interested owned camps in the Cypress. One was Mr. Ellis, Lawton Chiles' cousin. Mr. Ellis had a long history in south Florida as he once was the bridge tender on the old Marco Bridge and his brother operated the walking dragline used to build U.S. 41. He was a big supporter of the idea to save the Cypress and was able to talk with Senator Chiles at will.

Mr. Ellis, 2000, at his camp deep in the Big Cypress National Preserve

In fact, because of the desire to build I-75 from Tampa to Naples to Hialeah-Miami Lakes, there would be more deals to come. There was a committee that included Art Marshal that reviewed a few routes for I-75. These routes included one along the mangrove line, one several miles south of U.S. 41, one halfway between U.S. 41 and Alligator Alley (S.R. 84), and two more to the north. The committee recommended the one from Ft. Myers to U.S. 27 and then south along Highway 27 to Miami. However, this would not open up land development opportunities to Naples. Besides, the congressman from southwest Florida had promised his voters they would have an Interstate Road and not a toll road like the Florida Turnpike on the East Coast of Florida.

The situation becomes much more interesting. According to Cal Stone, he learned that his two partners in their Big Cypress land venture had been to see Governor Askew. These partners had convinced the Governor to run I-75 down the middle of the area between U.S. 41 and S.R. 84. This route would open their property. Cal told me that he went back to the Governor and convinced him this was a bad idea, and it would be better to run I-75 on S.R. 84. After all, the State already owned a 600-foot right-of-way that the landowners along the road had donated to the State for ingress and egress for perpetuity. All the State had to do was purchase this perpetuity agreement and a great deal of money would be saved.

Cal told me, after talking to Governor Askew, he contacted his partners for a business dinner. He told them he knew what they had done and was invoking the part of their partnership that allowed any partner to buy out the others or the others had to buy out the one who was seeking the purchase. Cal said he would offer them $50 an acre that was a little more than they had paid. They told him that he did not have the funds. What they did not know was that Cal had talked with another camp owner near his place, L. Nipper. Mr. Nipper was a big banker from up north and had this cabin in the Cypress to hide out in when he needed a rest. It seemed that the Cypress was a place to escape the pressures of the world. I know Camp Red Bug was that kind of place for myself and others. Cal said he called their hand when he pulled out a signed blank check from Mr. Nipper. The bluff worked and the partners bought out Cal's interest in the majority of the property and left him with his camp property. Then he told them that Governor Askew was going to run I-75 on the Alley.

While this was going on there was a falling-out between Johnny and Cal. I attended the Dade Halftrack Conservation Club meeting when a vote to support one man or the other was taken. There were over 400 members present and a great deal of talk and debate about who they should vote to support—Cal or Johnny. The point that sent the vote to Johnny, in my opinion, was a report that Cal had ten sections of land in the middle of the cypress, and had it posted so no one could hunt it. No one knew if this was true or not, but those who hunted in that part of the Big Cypress were respected members of the club and because they said so, it was so.

Years later, Cal told me that he had ten sections of land leased and it was posted but that the signs meant nothing. They were there because the bank he leased the land from required it. He also said that he could not allow any structures on this land and if one was built, he had to remove it and it had to be removed either by the builder doing so or by the match. He told me he had to allow folks to hunt it because in order to get hogs from the Fish and Game Commission (GFC); now the Fish, Wildlife and Conservation Commission (FWC), he had to allow them to consider it a Wildlife Management Area (WMA). No one knew there was a WMA in the middle of the Big Cypress except Cal and a few in the FWC. This political battle had weakened the Florida Wildlife Federation (FWF) and our ability to work on the finalized Big Cypress National Preserve act. This was a problem that has haunted us to this day.

While the FWF was having political battles, Florida Audubon discovered that this road was not legal. They figured out the wrong agency did the Environmental Impact Statement (EIS). They used this card to their advantage. They drafted ten resolutions that the Board of Trustees would have to agree to if they did not want Audubon to file suit. The Board agreed (see attached appendix documents) and the Big Cypress had a State sponsor, forty million dollars, no impacts on six mile cypress strand in Lee County, no access from I-75, no frontage roads, only access at either end and for the Indians' Snake Road, improvement of the visual corridor, taking four sections of land around S.R. 29, taking the Fakahatchee Strand, no interchange at S.R. 29, cutting off Turner River Road by I-75 and more. All this was agreed to the day before the Board of Trustee (BOT) meeting.

Not only did I-75 change the future of southwest Florida and southeast Florida by providing a rapid transportation conduit to bring in people and development, but it also set in motion the mechanisms to take thousands of acres of land, approximately 1,500,000 acres. Further, it established in the mind of Floridians that purchasing land for the environment and recreation was a good thing and even better if it was usually from willing sellers.

We did not receive the information in this NWF letter and how the road was illegal until the 1980s. The letter was found in Johnny's files after he retired.

Getting ready to few the new EXXON oil work.

Everyone wanted the Big Cypress National Preserve. The Greater Miami Chamber supported it because it would be good for business. Hunters and fishermen would spend money when they came to south Florida to pursue their activity. According to Joe Browder, the Collier Enterprise people wanted it because the land they had outside of the Preserve would become more valuable. Supply and demand principles apply to land when there are sufficient actions to keep property from being sold. Further, they could keep their oil and gas rights. By then everyone knew there was oil under the Big Cypress. After all, the Sunnyland oil field and Bear Island oil field were producing good quantities of oil. The Cypress falls in a dome alignment from Tampa to Miami International Airport. In the end, most were happy hunters, fisherman, businessmen, major landowners, and non-hunting environmental groups. The bill was set to go.

On January 23, 1971, the daughter of Richard Nixon, Julie, walked in Robert's Lake Strand. This one act finalized DC politics to make it happen. Joe Browder had a knack of being able to get issues tied into national politics and this time it worked. The final bill that passed Congress had January 23, 1971, as the exemption date for certain improved properties to qualify for non-purchase. The bill was signed by President G. Ford (President Nixon had resigned). The date President Nixon's daughter walked in the Big Cypress was inserted in the bill even though the act did not pass until 1974. This action cost a good number of people their improved property because they had not "begun" their improvements by January 23, 1971.

During all this activity of the early '70s, Governor Askew had appointed an Everglades Recreation Committee that Wes Sarvis chaired. Wes was chairman of the Everglades Coordinating Council and an officer in the FWF. Everyone interested in the issue was on this committee except the National Park Service (NPS). The NPS was not there because in those days they only owned Everglades National Park. Today, the Department of Interior (DOI) and NPS own or have control of seventy-five percent of all public land in south Florida. Both tribes of Indians were on it, county governments, the South Florida Water Management District (SFWMD), and various types of sportsmen groups. It was here that I first heard of and saw the SFWMD present photos of how they were killing the tree islands in the Everglades with high water. They had slides showing dead rings of trees around each island that were the result of artificially holding the water high. This issue would impact Florida and the nation forever.

It was amazing that even the most ardent and hunter-unfriendly environmental groups testified before Congress in favor of the Big Cypress National Preserve; it was a 'new breed of cat' in the National Park Service's property types. They all said what we, sportsmen, wanted to hear. Why even the Assistant Secretary of Interior sounded friendly to us. It was what we did not hear, see, or understand that would get us many years later. Statements in the House and Senate Reports like "restore the Big Cypress to its wilderness character" and "carefully manage ORVs." No one in 1970-74 could imagine what these few words could mean twenty-seven years later. We also did not understand how the newly-passed Endangered Species Act (ESA) would be used against the hunters of the nation nor did we understand how the Wilderness Act or Clean Water Act (WCA) would be used against sportsman.

Chapter Six

◆ ◆ ◆

The NPS Strategy Starts

Around 1973, the oil companies decided they wanted to explore again for oil in the Big Cypress. In those days, there were some regulations about how to remove oil in Florida but not many, if any, on how to explore for oil. This oil work that was going on near my little cabin caused me to wake up and take notice. Not that I am against oil being removed but the method of exploring for it was bad on the land. Some of the landowners on Baxter Island would not let the oil companies cross their property. The oil company had to go around these folks. There were real concerns about the dynamite blasting as the seismic work might destroy water wells. The company was able to do their work and drilled wells all around my place.

Oil well in Bear Island, 1989.

To the southeast, they drilled one about five miles away. To the southwest one about two miles off, to the north on about a mile and to the northeast one about two miles away. It certainly seems to me there is oil under my acre and a quarter of the land which I owned twelve percent of the mineral rights for. I also own twenty-five percent under my five acres further into the interior. I own these rights because when the NPS took my land I kept the oil and gas rights as allowed by the Big Cypress National Preserve Act.

During these early years of oil development, my name was used twice to give the FWF standing in litigation to make sure the oil companies did their work properly. We had reports about how the Raccoon Point oil work was not being done right, the road was too high, the work not friendly to the Big Cypress. In the first case, my name remained on the plaintiff's list. This case settled out of court and allowed FWF board members to visit the work location and provided one FWC officer and his equipment to work in the Raccoon Point area and the first Florida panther recover funds. In the second case, the judge did not allow my name to remain on the list of plaintiffs because my property was too far from the work location. During one trip to Washington DC to support the Everglades's restoration and the Big Cypress, I had lunch with Senator Paula Hawkins. During this lunch meeting, she told us that there were more than a million barrels of oil coming from Raccoon Point a year and that it was the only well field east of the Mississippi that was free flowing. I do not know if this true or not but that is what the senator told us.

Raccoon Point oil field, 1980.

Along came the Big Cypress Advisory Oil Committee and they decided that once the oil company built an oil road, the public could not use it. This made good sense because with such a road people could flood into the interior of the Big Cypress. However, the catch was that in many places such a rule would lock the public out of the entire area. These oil roads had to be built on existing ORV trails, as much as possible. This too made good sense. But by doing this, they effectively closed off much of the land to access for the public. There had to be some give and it was worked out that there could be some use for short distances and crossing established.

This was the first time the Florida panther came into play. During a public workshop addressing oil, there was an exempt landowner in the Raccoon Point area. He pointed out that there were panthers in that area, and they were an Endangered Species. Further, he said that these roads would allow too many people into that part of the cypress. Later in the hallway, a local club leader soundly thrashed him. She really got all over the gentleman and explained how his statement would run him out of the woods. How right she was!

Panther track, 1983

Florida panther

This almost came true. The USFWS made a section 7 ruling that either the public had to be denied use of the eleven-mile road, with crossings established or all hunting east of the road form U.S. 41 to S.R. 84 east to the Everglades (L28) had to be stopped. Naturally, all the sportsmen supported taking the public off these roads. But the eleven-mile road is mostly on open prairie country and such a regulation would not be a problem. Such a ruling would shut down most of the area if applied in the same manner across Big Cypress.

This was the second time the USFWS used their section 7 power. The first time was when they took the deer and hog dogs out of the Cypress.

They ruled that either the dogs had to come out because they would disturb the panther or hunting would have to be closed. The USFWS said that because of inbreeding all the Florida panthers had a heart murmur. During the FWC meeting where this new hunting regulation was to be approved, we put about 200 hunters in the meeting hall. No one liked removal of the deer-hog dogs and I believe the FWC was ready to call the hands of the USFWS. However, it was not worth the risk as all knew if hunting was ever closed, for whatever reason in the Cypress, the NPS would not reopen it. Reluctantly, we agreed to stop the dog hunting. The USFWS did allow dogs to remain for bird hunting.

It was not long before the oil companies started removing some of their rock oil roads from the Big Cypress National Preserve near my camp. I watched them as they did this and realized they were removing way too much material. Essentially, they were removing all the topsoil. I figured that these old, buggy trails would not revegetate and thus we would be blamed for the problem. I told Johnny Jones about what I saw, and he arranged for me to take an ACoE inspector to see the work. I did this. This inspector wrote a report about the problem and agreed with me there was too much dirt being removed. Years later, I investigated what was done with these findings. I learned that the file had been purged from the ACoE and the inspector transferred to Alaska. Nothing was ever done about the topsoil being removed, yet years later the NPS and their environmental supporters would blame these impacts on the hunters who used ORVs to access the Big Cypress in the traditional manner.

Things were really starting to heat up as the Big Cypress National Preserve had its first manager, Mr. E. Mortinson, who was moved out and a new superintendent was assigned. Everyone thought things would change for the better. They thought the reason the Big Cypress was being managed more toward a National Park and not a National Preserve was because if the unit only had a manager it came under Everglades National Park. This idea of ours seemed to be true for a good while. The DOI/NPS decided we were right, and the Big Cypress should not be under Everglades National Park but be its own stand-alone unit. When this was done, they moved in the first superintendent—Fred Fagergren. It was not long before oil came into play again.

Freddy Fisikelli and I went to Tallahassee to address the Board of Trustees about the eleven-mile road. The NPS wanted the road off their property and run north to S.R. 84. We succeeded in stopping this from happening as their road was already in and fully under the jurisdiction of the NPS. By taking a new road north, it would not be controllable and would open the interior to unacceptable levels of human use and then the ESA panther would come into play causing us to stop hunting there. The handwriting was on the wall and from then on, we would

Scorpion Head Camp belonged to Merle Van. On a clear day, you could see the Florida Bay from the 2nd Story.

come under attack by the NPS leadership. After all, we had spoken out against what they wanted and won; they wanted us off their land. We had taken the best stand for the cypress and not supported the superintendent. From that day on, he tried to make the Preserve a park. According to Freddy at the superintendent's departure party, Superintendent Fagergren made the statement that had done his best to make the Preserve a park.

It was obvious he had done this. After all, he had won a long, drawn out court case to save the 'trespass camps'—Like Camp Scorpion Head in the Stair-Step twenty miles south of Loop Road. Remember earlier, I explained people would find a good place to hunt and build a camp or cabin. When Big Cypress legislation was being worked on, everyone involved, including elected and appointed decision-makers, kept saying hunters could continue going to camp. This was what we wanted to hear because we in the south do not say we are going to our cabin or lodge as one in DC would say. When we say 'going to camp,' we mean going to our cabin. When they say going to camp, they mean going to a tent camp. This was the start of many such plays on words that we would run into.

By now, I was becoming more involved in politics. This involvement was via donations, working for candidates, or working with those who were running campaigns. This activity became all too normal and evident after the word was out that I-75 would be built on Alligator Alley, S.R. 84. All those who owned land along the right of way would have to sell their ingress and egress rights. Never mind the land donation agreement that allowed access forever, the State would purchase this by condemnation if need be, NO willing sellers here. Remember, the Constitution gives us the right to own property and the government the right to take property via purchase.

Someone in our Baxter Island project hired a good lawyer to investigate legal options to protect his access rights. The attorney's opinion was simple and in a nutshell: They write the laws, they enforce the laws, and you cannot beat them in court so play politics. I knew then that I had

John Sweeny & me on our Honda 90s.

to become more informed and more involved in the politics of conservation and hunting. That is, if I wanted a chance to keep our little cabin and maybe have access via public access.

After the trespass camps lost their court case, I attended one of many political fund-raisers, this one just happened to be for Senator Chiles. He told me that the NPS did not have to take the 'trespass camps' and could have left them if they wanted by creating a lease agreement. This is all too evident as now that the NPS owns most of Biscayne Bay as a National Park, they have received enough public and political pressure to keep the trespass houses in the bay known as Stilt's Vile and then lease them.

In about this same time frame, there was a new ORV on the scene. It was the Honda three-wheeler or ATCs. We bought five of them and proceeded to learn how to ride them. These little 90cc motorcycles with fat balloon tires were awesome. They would change the way people used the outdoors forever. As big as I was, I could go anyplace I wanted, and faster than a buggy. Further, I could now carry almost everything I needed to camp except a load of ice for cooling game. But never mind as this was the early 1970s and we were still not shooting much big game. Up to 1979 or 1980, we might have taken one or two bucks and no hogs. There were deer but they were located where we could not get to them or build a tree stand. During this same time frame, the FWC made all hogs south of S.R. 84 game animals as they were prime food for the panther. This happened the week after John Sweeny released some hogs on his forty acres east of Turner River Road. These hogs were no longer his because they were neither branded nor had no registered ear notch.

The 1980s found us having many family weekends at Camp Red Bug. A new owner had taken over Camp Comfort. Wayne Hoffmann was in the process of purchasing it from the first owner, Hendry Torres. Camp Comfort was my northern neighbor who shared a common property line. Our daughter, Kathryn, was in middle school and she had decided to learn how to play the French horn. Wayne being a neighbor was most fortunate, as he was a top-notch, middle school band director. On top of that his dad, Harry Hoffmann, was a retired band director. Harry was a founding member of the Everglades National Park Historical Society and he had been a bugler in the U.S. Army. On weekends when all were at camp, Wayne or his dad would blow their French horn with the come-on-over call. Little Kathryn would get her horn and go take a horn lesson

Kathryn & Wayne Hoffmann practicing the French horn.

in the woods. We often laughed out loud thinking about what someone might have thought if they were in the woods and heard these French horns playing.

It was interesting to talk with employees of the NPS who worked on the bill and learn from them on their side about what was being created and what happened when it was sent to them to be implemented. Dr. Pete Rosenthal was one of these folks. He explained to me how as a new biologist working for ENP, he and others like him were told to brainstorm and figure out what had to be done to get rid of the hunters and buggy owners. We should have known there were problems on the horizon when the Assistant Secretary sent Cal Stone and Johnny Jones a letter, see appendix, begging them to hold the course and not stop fighting to create the Big Cypress National Preserve. We did not see this letter until nearly thirty years later.

Family and friends at Camp Red Bug.

During these years, we continued to hunt hard, improve the cabin and our buggies. We knew we would have great wildlife habitat if only the poachers could be removed. In the 1970s, I was told neither the NPS nor the FWC were going to enforce too many rules or regulations because there were so many mad people. It was best to live with the current conditions, do minimal enforcement, and wait for the social conditions to change. When these social issues changed so would the wildlife conditions. There was a lot of truth to this because when we first started Camp Red Bug, we could mow the grass fire breaks, take a Coca-Cola break, return to finish mowing, and find fresh deer or turkey tracks in the newly mowed fire break. We would have big family parties at Camp Red Bug. We might have eight to twelve people for three or four days. Yet, deer and turkey were all around the Red Bug.

In the early '80s, we hunted in East Henson Strand to the west of camp. We did take a few bucks out of this strand over several years, but we really had to work hard. We had to walk them up and move them in front of ground standers. One of the better bucks was this deer taken by Denny.

On this hunt we had five people in the crew. I sent Denny and Ronnie to known locations as standers. Now this is all going on in a cypress swamp with water no lower than knee high unless you stepped up on an island or log. Everything was located under the canopy of the huge cypress trees. Once the standers were in place, the three of us would very slowly walk, quietly, and one at a time toward the standers. I had pointed to some very large pine trees way off in the distance for Joe Paysint to head toward. All he had to do was keep his eye on them and keep them to his face and me to his right. Rick would flank me on my right. We slowly moved as quietly as possible one at a time toward the standers. After about three hours of this leapfrog moving, we heard the loud boom that only a 12-gauge can make in such heavy overstory. There were several shots and then lots of yelling. The buck was down, and we had to get him out. That was an even harder chore as we were more than two miles from the buggy and more than four miles from camp.

However, we could not start working our way out because we had lost Joe. Somehow he had lost sight of the big pines I had pointed to on the horizon and went someplace else. After some time, we were able to find Joe and start working on going back to Camp Red Bug.

Not only did we have to get him and ourselves to the buggy but also the buggy back to camp. The small, 1947 Jeep, Red Buggee-1, with 10.5x24 tractor tires was loaded well over its carrying capacity. We also had to go through the East Crossing. This is a trail that goes through a very big cypress strand and the water is about four or five feet deep for more than four-hundred yards. There is no way to ride the ridge or edge as the huge cypress trees keep you in the trail. It is a trail that was used during the Third Seminole Indian War.

Red Buggee 1 in phase one of development.

When I first went into that country, I saw a brass plaque stating this was a battle site between Chief Bowlegs and some military general. I was too young to know I should have written down the information and do not remember more than this.

As expected, the plaque is long gone. I was always of the opinion that some souvenir collector took the plaque. However, years later while talking with some Indian friends, I learned that it was probably an Indian who removed it. This is because I was told there are two factions in the tribe. One thinks it is honorable to recognize their war with the U.S.A. and the other thinks it is not honorable. Thus, recognition of such events do not remain in place long.

We hunted where the Seminoles had lived and hunted. We were walking the same swamps and islands that Chief Billy Bowleggs, Charlie Fowl, Charlie Billy had walked. We knew we had a great habitat for wildlife and it was not long before we started seeing a tremendous number of animals.

As mentioned earlier, the 1970s found many people heading to the Cypress. The reasons were many: bad or changing neighborhoods in the cities of the east coast, no work, cheap land, and ability to get good money from the NPS for little investment in a structure as they condemned land to make the Big Cypress National Preserve. I also think the years of reduced rainfall helped. After the floods of the late 1960s and the early 1970s, we had a real low rain cycle. This meant the cypress was dry and easy to get around in. Many folks could bring in their house trailers or building material and set up a house. Anyway, at one time, Everglades City Schools sent a school bus to Baxter Island to pick up twenty-two schoolchildren. Children who lived north of S.R. 84 went to Immokalee and those living south went to Everglades City.

During the days of public hearings on I-75 routing, people would pack high school gyms. By and large, the public present spoke against the routing and did not want I-75 on the Alley. Or they wanted to have access roads along I-75. Little did we know that whatever we said made no difference because the Florida Board of Trustees had already agreed to the Audubon's ten resolutions. We did not realize that these hearings were a farce and held only to comply with the public hearing law. We did not realize what big, influential, powerful, landowners would benefit from the building of I-75 on Alligator Alley. It was interesting to hear the passionate speeches of landowners in the Baxter Island area. Some went so far as to threaten to blow up the equipment if they started this project. However, these folks were the first to take their NPS buyout money and leave the swamps.

Not only were threats being made by citizens over I-75 but the Big Cypress National Preserve brought out the bad side of some. One case really stands out. An individual had posted wanted dead or alive posters of Nat Reed, Bob Graham, and Joe Browder, with a dollar amount included. Joe Browder told me that Gater Bill had a talk with this bad actor and the posters came down. Gater Bill was a real outdoorsman who lived by taking frogs from the Stair-Step area and some say a gator skin now and then. As soon as the NPS gained control of the Big Cypress, they proceeded to address Gater Bill's profession and it was not long before they ran him out of the Big Cypress National Preserve.

Shortly after the public hearings on I-75 were held and it was obvious that we were going to lose our access to the public lands along the roadway, the officers of the Dade County Halftrack Club talked to the FDOT person who was running the project. This FDOT person told us that there was no!*!*! way you we were going to get off the road to shoot the deer. He was really set against us being able to enjoy these public lands. The FDOT man didn't know it but a local city mayor was on the phone listening as he too wanted off the road to shoot these deer. In a few years, this FDOT man was no longer with FDOT, and a new and more balanced person took over this road project—Tom Berry. After many meetings, debates and the building of I-75, Tom eventually became the Secretary of FDOT and remained a friend all the time.

The increased population on Baxter Island worked very well for me as I paid one of the resident young men, I think he was in sixth grade at the time, to mow my camp grass. On the weekends, he would often go hunting or exploring with us. When it was not hunting season, we would still hunt. Only, we could not carry a gun anymore as it was NPS land and a Florida WMA. But we hunted with cameras and our eyes looking for places to hunt come hunting season.

My yardman also made a good watchman for my camp. Anything that went on was observed and I was informed. One weekend, when I arrived at camp Michael, the young man who mowed my lawn came over. He said the NPS had been to my place and rolled a wheel on a stick all the way from Cypress Road. I knew what they were up to. They were measuring from a known spot to see if I was on my property or theirs. If I was on their property, they could condemn my place as a trespass camp. This was also after I had my "exemption" papers from the NPS. When I went home, I called the NPS land office and asked them what they wanted. They played really dumb until I told them the date, time and what they had done. Then they became talkative. I told them to stay off my land unless I invited them and they did.

Another time, I arrived at camp and found my woods trailer gone. I left a small single axle buggy trailer there so I could take my buggy to other parts of the Preserve easily. My yardman told me that L.B. Hart had borrowed my trailer. Sure enough, I looked around a bit and found a note Mr. Hart had left, saying he had an emergency and needed my trailer and would return it in a few days. No harm done. I knew where it was. Besides, I hunted on land he was running his wild swamp cattle on. He had fenced off a bunch of land east of Turner River Road. When the fence went up, I went straight away to his cow camp at the Orange Grove and asked if he would mind if we hunted on the land. He said no, go ahead. Years later, I learned from Raleigh Burney that L.B. did not own the land but merely fenced it off. According to Raleigh he would fence off property by using a double "U-nail" locking the barbed-wire to the tree with a nail slid into the two "U-nails." He would connect the fence to a canal so the cattle would have water if none was in the swamps. When he was done, he would pull the locking nails, leaving the "U-nails" so he could return in a few years. It seemed to work in this frontier area.

Many places had special names that associated them with some particular person or activity. On the northern end of Turner River Road, south of I-75, there is a culvert bridge. This was the location of the NPS gate number #2, in 2002. At this location, a Yankee purchased a good bit of land and cleared all the big cypress off it. He then built a few ditches with no dikes and installed a big screw pump. When the rains came in the summer, he turned on his pump and as fast as he pumped water out it ran back into his groves. He packed up and went back north. Thus, the

*Green Camp
burned and left
by the NPS.*

*Some of the NPS trash on
Baxter Island, 1992.*

*More NPS trash on
Baxter Island.*

NPS heavy equipment used to clean Baxter Island parked at Camp Red Bug.

name Orange Groves was placed on this location. There were many similar activities going on all over the Big Cypress in the 1960s and 1970s.

In a few years, the NPS had purchased most of the improved property. Some of these folks could have remained in the Big Cypress National Preserve; me and about seventy others did. However, a lot of people did not want to live under the thumb of the NPS or they had not seen the amount of money the NPS was paying for such property. Whatever the reason, my yardman left with his family along with the others who lived on Baxter Island. All over the Big Cypress, people were leaving the area. They sold all their property and walked off and left it as directed by the NPS.

Years later, Superintendent Donahue, not wanting the rest of the world to know how the NPS had not properly managed the Preserve, blamed all his **NPS-trash** on the people who had trespassed on his land. When the truth was that the NPS had purchased the property for good money, told the people to leave their belongings, and turned it into trash. Some had removed items when they left but they had to return them before they could close the sale to the NPS. Then for many years the NPS did nothing about cleaning up their trash. These pictures of the NPS trash removed from the Baxter Island area are but a little of what they had to remove from around Camp Red Bug. Frequently, they would burn a person's house and leave it as trash as if to say to those who went into the woods do not think about setting up camp here. When I left the area in 2002, they had not cleaned up Green Camp and its burned remains are still there today.

During the NPS Baxter Island cleanup operations, I allowed the NPS maintenance foreman to stay at Camp Red Bug and to park his equipment in sight of the house. The foreman had access to the front porch and bathroom. This allowed the NPS employees to avoid commuting to work, their equipment to be safe, and more time placed on cleaning the woods of the NPS trash instead of spending time commuting.

The NPS did own a large amount of trash all over the preserve; this is because there had been a lot of people living in the Big Cypress. They were encouraged to sell their belongings to the NPS and leave it. At one time, the NPS sold what they could to other folks who bought what was left for salvage. Some merely moved the stuff to another part of the Preserve and then the NPS bought it again. And, again it was left in the swamps.

It was really a shame to see Florida go from a rural/frontier state to an urban/suburban state. In 2003, Florida was growing by 800 new people a DAY. This is a town the size of Tampa in one year. Open spaces like the old Big Cypress were all gone. Life had sure changed in Florida by 2003.

In 2004, oil continued to play a big role in the conversion of Southwest Florida from rural to urban. The Colliers owned most of the mineral rights under the Big Cypress National Preserve and the Florida Panther National Wildlife Refuge. A few years earlier, they had tried to make people think they were going to implement a massive oil drilling campaign and flooded the NPS with applications. They had not done any seismic work in the Preserve since we took them to court many years ago. Yet, they were applying for these massive drilling schemes. It was clear to me and others who understood the big picture that they really did not want to drill in the Big Cypress as it was too expensive and risky; besides, they had not done their exploration work yet. President Bush included $40 million in his national budget as the first of three payments for these mineral rights.

Many of the environmental groups in the Everglades Coalition heard the Collier presentation and started pushing to buy out their mineral interest in these two units of public land. This is exactly what the Collier's wanted, money for not working and no risk. Those who understood the full matter opposed it. The Colliers were known as big Republican supporters and did not get what they wanted under the Democratic controlled state and Federal administrations. So, they sat back and waited. Then when the Republicans came into control, the company once again started talking about all the drilling and the road building, they were going to do. The long and short of it is, if they got the buyout, everyone in the Everglades Coalition thought this would be great and the Republican's had an environmental plus. This plus did not make any difference as the membership of the Coalition did not support either Governor Bush or President Bush.

What the Coalition membership and particularly the big national environmental organization leadership did not consider was that the Colliers were not selling all their mineral rights only those which were most likely to not have production value. Further, the Collier's wanted money so they could develop huge new towns around Immokalee. Also, the minor mineral owners would not be bought out. The Coalition membership had not considered the likelihood that the federal government would make exploration for oil easier on all federally owned lands soon. Well, it was not long after this mineral buy out was set that the Collier's presented their massive new town projects around Immokalee. We already knew these were in the works because folks who were doing the survey work on the ground were letting us know what was going on—so much for good environmental decision-making. I am sure the real issue with these Coalition members was that they knew the purchase of the mineral rights, even part of them, would move the Big Cypress National Preserve that much closer to a National Park which is what they desired (see the NPCA letter in the appendix).

This oil buy out issue is a good example of how politics and the environment are intertwined. The groups in the Everglades Coalition never supported either President Bush or Governor Bush no matter what they did to help the environment. Even with this buy out, they continued to bash these leaders. Further, the buyout issue became more interesting because the Democratic Senators, led by none other than Senator Bob Graham, refused to approve the funds of the buyout. The other interesting lesson here is that the agreement to allow oil removal from under the Big Cypress National Preserve was necessary to make the legislation come about. Yet, the very people who agreed to this oil issue were the ones now breaking this agreement. The same situation was also occurring in the Big Thicket National Preserve; the NPCA and other like-minded groups wanted to take the mineral rights from this NPS unit as well. So much for honoring the commitments made by earlier leaders.

Chapter Seven

◆ ◆ ◆

We Had Lots of Good Times and Great Hunts

The Camp Red Bug crew enjoying the camp and cypress.

We had lots of memorable hunts. They were all good but some will stand out forever. One such hunt took place on December of 1987. Raleigh Burney, who was 78 years old, and I were the only two hunters at Camp Red Bug that weekend. We sat around the campfire on Friday night talking about where to hunt the next day. Burney was a great one to listen to and learn from. He had grown up on S.R. 29. His family leased hammocks in the Fakahatchee Strand from the Colliers, to farm and grow citrus. That weekend, we had a strong cold front upon us and that meant we would have a strong north wind the next day or two.

It was always an exciting evening sitting by the campfire whenever Burney, Joe Brown and/or Neal Brown would start talking about what it was like in southwest Florida before the roads were paved. The techniques of preserving food, although I am sure were not unique to the area, were extremely interesting. For example, Burney would tell how he would go out with one or two shells to get game, which meant whatever he saw. If he took a deer or hog, his folks would strip out the meat and partially cook it. Then, they would jar it or put it in a lard can. The lard can would be made by layering lard and partially cooked meat until the can was full and capped off with lard. The cans and jars would then be stored under the house that was built up off the ground. This was the coolest place they had.

Another thing that was interesting was how they moved their citrus to the Del Monte Citrus packing plant in Copeland. The family citrus farms were on hammocks in the Fakahatchee Strand and leased from the Colliers. They and the others who did the same would place the picked fruit in a cypress plank sluice and send the fruit by water to the plant.

Burney and his last deer.

One day while we were hunting on an old farm field in the Big Cypress, Burney explained to us how vegetables were grown on these marl flats. The farmers would wait for winter to come and the ground to dry up. While it was still muddy but not good dry and hard, they would stake out where their furrows would be plowed. A mule with a breaking plow was guided to these stakes thereby keeping the furrows straight. The mule could not walk in the marl as it was still muddy, so a mud board was tied to its hooves. It would take some time, but the mule would get used to walking by swinging its hoofs in an arc instead of the normal gait. Once the furrows were made, people would come along with a hole-making hoe. Then planters would come along and place a tomato start in these holes and a shovel of manure was placed on each plant. The last step in the process was to guide the mule down the other side of the furrow throwing dirt on the plant and manure. Vegetable farming was active in Bear Island Unit until 1974 when the NPS took control of the land.

Burney's older brother worked one of the bulldozers cutting lines for the logging company as they made roads and laid railroad tracks in the Cypress. He also provided food for these work crews by hunting deer and hogs in the Cypress. One day, Burney said his older brother would like to come to camp for the weekend. His brother asked us to take him to Mincy's place so he could camp out there for the weekend. We tried to get the elderly gentlemen to stay at Camp Red Bug and in a house, but he would have no part of it. So, we took him to Mincy's. A few months later he died. I suppose he knew this was coming and wanted one more camping trip in the solitude of the Big Cypress with his little pup tent.

As to our memorable hunt in December 1987, we knew the acorns were gone as it had rained enough to make those on the ground rotten. We also knew that the cabbage berries were starting to drop, and the willows were beginning to send out their tender new shoots. This made things simple. We would hunt were these plants existed in abundance. The only problem was how—we would either find a place where there were willow shoots and climb a likely pick off spot with our climbing tree stands or we could do a small drive with only one stander.

We decided to use the second strategy. That meant we needed the vegetation to have a certain configuration; the driver would walk with the wind to get the greatest effect of moving through the thick vegetation. I parked the buggy several hundred yards from Dick's Stand. Then Burney and I walked the rest of the way in the knee-deep water and mud to his tree at the gap by Dick's Stand and I walked the half-mile or so on toward East Crossing. Once there, I used my climbing stand to climb my favorite cabbage tree in Chevron Island Camp. I was tucked inside the island and could see the outer edges of a small section of the strand as well as a good bit of real estate along the interface between the hammock and the deep cypress swamp. Burney was at a gap between three islands. He could see two cypress strand edges, the edge of a willow pond and some open cypress country. Around ten o'clock as designed, I got down from my stand and started to walk as slowly and as quietly as possible toward Burney. I had walked in the thick understory of the hammock for about fifteen minutes when I heard two rifle shots. I was sure that they had come from Burney since no one else should be in the area. But in the thicket, with the wind blowing behind me, it was difficult to tell where the shot sounds had come from.

I finished the drive to find that Burney was not in his stand. I thought he must have gotten cold and had gone back to the buggy. Then, I looked to the southwest and saw him sitting on the ground. At the age of 78, he was tired and overworked from the early morning hike in the mud and water and from climbing the tree. But he was even more excited than exhausted from the fine shot he made on a great buck. Burney hunted for about five more years with us before old age made him stay home. We always figured this hunt added a good number of years to his life.

Another top hunt took place in the Bear Island Unit. Denny, Debbie, my brother, Ed, and Burney sat around the kitchen table planning the hunt for the next day—Saturday. The wind was blowing hard from the north, and it was really cold. We would go to what we called Hog Island. We would drive up slowly from the south, park the buggy in a gap between two islands, and then Denny and Debbie would walk to the east. They would take a stand along the eastern side of the island with Debbie on an isthmus with sawgrass ponds on either side. Brother would sit on the buggy; at that time, we could still legally shoot off a stopped non-powered buggy. I would

walk north on the west side of the six-hundred-acre island and push with the wind back toward the south. Burney would take his ATC and park on the northeast corner of the island to back stand.

Ed, Debbie, and me with our game taken in Bear Island.

It was so cold that day that stepping in the water really hurt. The wind was howling, and it was not a good day to deer hunt, but we bundled up and headed to the Bear Island Unit and Hog Island. This was nearly twenty miles from Camp Red Bug. It required us to leave around three a.m. and to not get lost, stuck or waste time. All had to go like clockwork.

We arrived on time, just before dawn. I gave Denny and Debbie twenty minutes to get around to where they were supposed to go. Then I started working north on the west side as quietly as possible. Getting to the north end of the island system was no problem and I was glad to be walking and not sitting. I started my push with a real loud hoop and continued to bark like a dog and beat bushes. After doing this for about fifteen minutes, I heard one little pop to the southeast. It could have been Denny, Debbie, or someone else far off. I did not know. Then I heard Denny yelling about the big buck Debbie had shot with one round from her Ruger 44 mag. I yelled for Denny to get back in his stand and to stay put while I finished the drive.

In a few more steps, I heard four shots from Ed's direction. I yelled and could not hear him answer. I was not sure what had happened or who had shot. As it turned out, he could not hear me as the wind was blowing all the sound away from him. He had killed one of the biggest boar hogs

The federal archeologist after a long buggy ride.

we had ever seen. The hog had come out of the thicket where I was pushing and walked right to the buggy. Ed fired his 12-gauge magnum with 00-buck shot. The first three rounds only made the hog shake his head. Then, after the third round, he turned broadside, and the fourth round hit him broadside at about ten yards. Ed said he was about to use his 06 when the hog fell over.

We were heading back to Camp Red Bug by nine a.m. and passed several people just getting into the woods. All of them gave us a stare of amazement since on the little Red Buggee there was me at 275, Denny and Debbie at around 350 together, Ed at 350, a 200-pound boar hog, and a 100-pound eight-point. We had to tie our coolers and stands on the front bumper and more gear on the back bumper. It was slow going, but we got out.

During the springtime, I would work for federal archeologists. Superintendent Fagergren, before we crossed him on the eleven-mile road issue, had connected me with these federal employees. Until that time, I had never met such dedicated, knowledgeable, hard-working federal employees. Of course, I had not met many, other than a few NPS folks. We would work on the weekends and school holidays.

I had a contract to guide them for one hundred dollars a day and a copy of their findings. They had to provide their sleeping accommodation and food. I did not want to provide the food just in case one of them became sick. I also did not want to list that I provided board on the contract. I was already becoming very distrustful of the NPS leadership and their ultimate goals. I feared that if I listed board, they would say my cabin was now commercial property and as such it violated my exemption status (see letter in the appendix). It would not

Federal archeologist and the author on the Ox Cart Trail.

matter that the superintendent had connected us. This might have been why he sent these federal employees to me. He wanted to get the goods on me and get rid of me. That sounds like a bit of paranoia, but years later we will see this very action unfolding in other arenas.

I did not have to worry about the cabin and property, so we had a great time driving all over the Preserve. We would meet on Friday night and travel to specific locations they called "hot spots" that were selected by experts looking at aerial photos etc. These hard-working folks would walk in places I would not even consider going to even if there was a fourteen-point buck. They were getting chewed out by their boss for not getting to all the "hot spots." I finally got them to bring down this boss. It seems that the boss had never been in the Big Cypress, and by looking at the local topographic maps, he figured one could get on one of those swamp buggies and run everywhere fast! He had seen the Naples swamp buggy races on television and thought that was how you could travel in the real world. We got him on the buggy and went to the first spot for that weekend. Five hours later we arrived and he was glad to get off the buggy as it was beating him up pretty bad.

We found lots of interesting things. Some of them were of more modern times like the handmade crock jug. Then there were items that were much older like the clay pot leg. Not only did we find an abundance of pottery chards, but we

Federal archeologist with handmade fired crock jug found in the cypress.

also found tons of old animal bones. We found burial mounds. We found living areas where the Indians had lived long enough at that one location to build a ten-acre extension on the island. We worked on this one big oak ridge and soon saw a flat area. The archeologists started digging their test pit. These test pits would be a 10x10-cm hole aligned north and south by the compass and 10-cm deep at each stage. This would continue until they reached what was termed *sterile soil*—soil that had no artifacts in it. At this one location, I had to walk back to the buggy and get a steel chisel so they could chip out lime rock. The lime rock had birds, fish, snake, and turtle bones in it. This rock had been marl soil when the bones were thrown there.

Another location that was small and way back in a big cypress swamp had so much animal bone and waste in it that the soil looked different and felt greasy to the touch. It seems unlikely, but it really did. Considering that the midden dirt was nearly a meter deep, there was a lot of garbage there. Sometimes, these Indian mounds were located where modern man had built a cabin, but most times they were not.

At other locations, we found handmade wooden plank boards. These planks would be about ten or eleven inches wide, more than an inch thick and several feet long. We could tell they were handmade because the broad ax and foot-adz cut marks were still visible.

When we first started, the "hot spots" were not panning out most of the time. The footprints the experts were using to pinpoint these locations were faulty. I pointed out that contrary to what most people thought, the Big Cypress Swamp was not under water all the time. Thus, the basic life need was water and we had to look for permanent water with suitable living areas on dry ground not far away. When we did that, all these "hot spots" proved positive. We could even track where Indian people would travel along slough lines from one low island to another. There were many such travel ways where they might stay a night or two and then move on. If one knows how to read the vegetation, these travel routes are easy to locate and follow. There are specific vegetation indicators created by the Indians to guide them from one major living/ burial area to another.

Federal Archeologist with a clay pot leg.

Then there were areas where the Indians had big farms. It was the practice of the Indians to girdle the oak trees. This would kill them and leave a clear area to plant under. When they did this, they would not have to work so hard to clear land. Also, when the water was up, this soil would be the driest. A quirk of this type of soil is that it holds the moisture better than other soils of the area during the annual low water period or a drought. These conditions allowed the Indians to create a small-plot farm that would produce plenty of food. One of the biggest Indian farms we found had twenty oak trees treated this way. It was also interesting to note that at this location, we found a very old and overgrown buggy trail in the massive hammock. The hammock was wrapped up in a big cypress strand and could not be seen from any direction outside the cypress strand. In this hammock, we found a number-nine frying-pan in the crotch of an oak tree. The tree had grown around the pan to such an extent that we could not remove the pan. We also found an old Jeep generator/regulator. We could barely make out that it was generator/regulator because it was almost completely crushed in the crotch of the oak tree. This indeed was an old and well-used hammock. It was not only used by Seminole Indians, but also by those before them as there were lots of pottery chards in the ground. European man had used it sometime after 1947, since that is the age of the regulator.

We located Indian camps with known history—camps like Charlie Fowl that you can read about in the early explorations of European men as they crossed the state. We found Concho Bill's winter camp. At this location, there were still partially standing chickees. We found places where there were canoe racks and canoe trails dug into the cypress strand soil. One such place was Jack Clay's.

Years later, I would hear retired Fish and Wildlife Commission Lt. Col. Lou Gainey tell of his travels in the Big Cypress area. He told the following case that involved Jack Clay's campsite that had become a hunters' camp in more recent times.

Canoe racks at Jack Clay's camp.

JACK CLAY'S by Lou Gainey (Major) via LJM

Lou relayed this story to me on January 22, 2003, at an African Safari Club dinner/meeting.

When I was a FWC Sergeant, in the late 1950s, a young officer told me he had a report of a doe deer being killed south of Jack Clay's in the Big Cypress. At this time, Alligator Alley (later I-75) was not built, and this was as far into nowhere as nowhere could be. Today, it is about seven miles south of I-75 and a little east of the major rest/recreation area in Collier County, Florida. My sergeant and I loaded up our swamp buggy and went north from U.S. 41 to Jack Clay's. The information was that there was a doe deer buried in the sawgrass pond to the SE of Jack Clay's. There was camp on Jack Clay's that was owned by some judges from Arcadia. Well, we arrived at the camp late in the evening and found no one there as expected. In those days, many would shoot camp meat—doe deer—when they first arrived at camp. My sergeant and I figured this is what the folks who used Jack Clay's last had done. Well, we scratched around in the dried sawgrass pond and found the bones of a recently killed doe deer. By examining the pelvis, we could tell it was doe. We then looked around the campsite and the fire pit. We found a prescription bottle with the judge's brother's name on the bottle. We had no real proof of who shot the doe but once I was in town, I went to see the judge. We chatted a while; then I mentioned the doe deer at Jack Clay's and left the medicine bottle on his desk. The judge knew I knew and that ended the doe killing at Jack Clay's.

Jack Clay's was a Seminole Indian camp south of I-75. It sits on the extreme edge of the sawgrass country in that part of Florida where the cypress and sawgrass intertwine. In this part of the Cypress, there is not a lot of high ground but there is a lot of cypress, marl prairie, and sawgrass. Jack Clay's place is a long oak hammock that is very high on the south end where the buildings once stood. Buggies would go onto the island passing the old canoe racks that the Indians used to rack their canoes and stop in the yard of a nice hunter's cabin. There are glass beads in the sandy soil around the south end of the island. It is said the Indian's used to build canoes here. There is a very deep, waist deep, moat around this part of the island. It is as if the Indians had dug the moat. From the point where the island rises, one can look to the east and as far as can be seen in the cypress, maybe 1000 yards, there is a ditch going east toward the sawgrass and then turning to the southeast. I have never walked the trail further than that, but it continues on as far as you can see. The main buggy trail is to the west of the island. It runs north and south. It goes north to Big Thompson Pine Island, on to I-75, and then on to Clewiston. To the south, it goes on to Preachers, Drakes, Stones, and U.S. 41. While guiding the federal archaeologists, I took them to Jack Clay's where they removed one of the canoe rack posts. It supposedly went to their storage room in Tallahassee, Florida.

Lou also told me how as a new FWC officer he was told to take a few Tallahassee folks from Naples into the Big Cypress and all the way to Clewiston via Devils Garden. He said they traveled by Jeep swamp buggy and camped along the way. Several days out of Naples, he learned the Collier family had offered the state the opportunity to purchase all this land for $50 an acre. All the family wanted to keep were the timber rights. In those days, oil was not yet a known resource in the area.

I now understood years later why I could not find a place in the Cypress that man had not been. There are none!

Chapter Eight

◆ ◆ ◆

More Regulations, Tense Times Continue, and Good Hunts

While I was taking the archaeologists around, the FWC outlawed the use of All Terrain Cycles (ATCs), now called All-Terrain Vehicles (ATVs). These machines are small motorcycle engines with three or four wheels. They took this action at the request of the NPS because this was the most rapidly growing type of Off-Road Vehicle (ORV) in use in the Big Cypress National Preserve. The FWC said they were taking this action to

Federal archaeologist using an ATC when the ATC was banned for hunting and fishing by the FWC.

not allow the use of the ATV/ATC for the purposes of hunting or fishing to protect the panther. We all knew who was behind this move, the NPS. They wanted to reduce the number of new people going on their land. It had become abundantly clear that NPS considered this 'their' land and not the people's land. While one could ride the ATV to go into the interior, they could not use it to hunt or fish. Sportsmen could not carry a gun or fishing pole on an ATV. They wanted to reduce the number of new people going on their land. It had become abundantly clear that NPS consider this 'their' land and not the people's land. While one could ride the ATV to go into the interior but they could not use it to hunt or fish from. Sportsmen could not carry a gun on or fishing pole on an ATV.

When the FWC outlawed the ATC, some sportsmen clubs got together and decided to file suit against the FWC for taking this action. A lawyer who used an ATC had convinced many that he could win and the FWC did not have the authority to take this action. I told them the law was clear and the FWC did have the authority to take the action they took. I further told them that the problem is the Florida panther, the Endangered Species Act, and if the lawyer will take on that issue as a part of the ATC issue, they might win. The Florida panther was the reason for the action and if the lawyer could get the panther removed from Endangered Species list, we could remove the reason for the FWC action. The lawyer did not take on the ESA issue as he said he would and lost the case.

The Federal Archeologists often used ATCs to go along with me as I drove my Red Buggee. I would carry all the gear and extra gas and one archeologist. Then two guys on ATCs would tag along. We set out a course and headed that way. The ATC fellows would range about looking at whatever they had to while we would ride to designated locations to wait on them or set camp. Though this was before GPS was available, the process worked very well as I knew these 750,000 acres. This strategy allowed us to cover a lot of country.

These little, one-cylinder motorcycles are not as fuel-efficient as one would think. On one long trip, they brought an extra five gallons of gas for their two ATCs. I had a twenty-gallon gas tank in the Red Buggee. By the end of the four-day trip, they had used all of their extra gas and had to borrow a gallon for each ATC from my buggy gas tank. I had several gallons left when we got back to camp Red Bug.

The FWC action of taking out the ATC as a transportation tool for hunters and fishing along with the favorable court ruling allowing the FWC to take this action reinforced what most already knew about what the NPS thought of sportsmen. Shortly after this court case, the NPS took control over ORV permitting in the Big Cypress National Preserve saying that this was not hunting, and the law said they were to manage ORVs. Then the NPS allowed hunters and fishermen to use ATCs again. They had used the FWC as a sounding board. It was our opinion that besides letting the FWC take the heat over this matter, the NPS realized that the swamp buggies were the key to making or breaking the organized sportsmen groups and individuals who opposed the NPS plan to make the Preserve a Park. It was pointed out by Dave Balman that the use of an ATC was a one-person issue, but a buggy owner had friends, and many of them, who would help work on or ride the buggy. Thus, buggies were the reason for socialization and how groups of hunters could create their unique community. It was also how and why they would organize to oppose the actions of the NPS. If the NPS could replace the buggy/airboats with ATVs, they could weaken the opposition that was trying to prevent them from making this a park. Someone who had visited Yellowstone said that the ATV industry had donated a lot of money to the NPS so they could work on a pet project out west. The logic was the NPS wanted to keep the ATV industry folks happy, so they changed the regulation the FWC had implemented for them.

It was also about this time that Florida Audubon introduced bill number one in the Florida House and Senate. This bill stated that the polar bear was Florida's state animal. We all knew this was a joke and most likely would not stay this way. Sure enough, no one paid any attention to the bill and then right at the close of the session the bill was amended to state that the polar bear was no longer Florida's animal but that the Florida panther was. Audubon said they had held a statewide poll of elementary children and they had selected the Florida panther to be the state animal. Those of us who were in education never heard of this survey nor had those of us with elementary school children. In our opinion, the legislation was introduced in this manner to avoid opposition from those who understood what such an action would mean to property rights and the ability of sportsmen to continue to use the lands they had fought so hard to protect from developers. It was a slick bit of legislation and it worked.

It was also about this time that the NPS issued their free good-for-life ORV permit. For years, we had purchased an ORV permit from the FWC. This was brought about because in some communities, buggy and airboat owners were being threatened by municipalities with the towing of buggies because they had no state tag or permit. We went to work on passing a law to require buggies and airboats to have a state permit under the FWC control. When the NPS came on the scene, they wanted to have their own count; therefore, they required us to get their onetime free-for-life, good-forever permit. We got the permits and they registered more than 6,000 ORVs (see appendix—Superintendent Fagergren's letter). It was not long before the NPS changed their mind on this free good-for-ever permit thing. They decided they had to charge for these permits. The superintendent told us the director had ordered that all permits should have a charge that would at least cover the cost of production. This issue was not going away. It would come back in future years in a more hideous manner as Superintendent Hibbard's draft ORV plan raised the price of an ORV permit to $150 as another means to get rid of us. That is no lie; his plan actually stated that by raising the price of the permit, there would be fewer people with ORVs.

Small cypress half track.

Once the NPS took over the ORV permits, it was not long before they outlawed the small cypress track. These ORVs were specialized for use in the Stair-Step area. This area has lots of open prairie with soft ground. We tried to explain to the NPS that they were removing the most terrain-friendly ORV, next to an airboat, from the area. But they would not listen to us. Years later and two superintendents later, new NPS staff wanted to know why we did not use track vehicles instead of using the newer style of large rubber-tired buggy. We could only laugh and explain they had caused the move to the bigger buggy by taking out the trespass camps and by removing the small track vehicle.

You see, when there were lots of trespass camps, most folks would go to their camp and walk out to hunt. Then, when these structures were burned by the NPS, these hunters had no place to go. So, they did what I had done in my younger years; they explored and wandered around the cypress looking for good places to camp and hunt. They frequently only used a camping site once. Bigger buggies were needed to carry all this camping gear and more vehicle trails were put on the ground. (see appendix for NPS ORV base line trail map).

This action of doing away with the trespass camps and folks continuing to want to hunt in the Big Cypress caused many to develop a new type of swamp buggy. This buggy was much bigger and it had to be because in addition to their normal load of food, clothing, guns, coolers and people, camping gear for everyone was now required. Thus, the smaller buggy would not work. These new machines (I do not call them swamp buggies but equipment) initiated additional problems with the way people enjoyed the Big Cypress. The NPS had not done their required ORV management plan.

New style of swamp buggy.

They had taken control of the ORVs from the FWC, who had them on trails in Bear Island and would have moved the same way in the rest of the Preserve. Anyway, people drove their new-style swamp-buggy-equipment machines any place they could. Even though this act of driving wherever you wanted was legal, it eventually led to additional litigations and a draconian ORV management plan that was designed more to get rid of people and hunters than to merely manage ORVs. Some folks who should know said that this was the NPS strategy all along—let people run wild and then use that as a reason to stop their use of the Big Cypress.

All this time in the 1970s, we were going to meetings to help make sure the NPS understood what we wanted in the Cypress and what we did not want. Sometimes, this worked but most of the time they went on and did whatever they wanted. As they continued to move toward the park management concept, we continued to press the political side for support.

By now, I had a pretty good buggy, and we were ranging well away from camp Red Bug. Sometimes we would travel a long distance to the southeast or southwest. Other times, we went to Bear Island and as far north as the Hendry County line. We had to

New style of swamp buggy, 2000.

travel so far because there had been too much poaching in the late '70s around Camp Red Bug, and to find game to hunt we had to look real hard and far. It was said enforcement was not going to act when there were so many mad folks so they would just wait until most people were removed.

We had many memorable hunts on Bear Island. Many times, we started in the northeast corner and moved around after the morning hunt was over, ending up in the southwest corner. Many times, we would sit all day in our climbing tree stands. These tree stands were developed in the early 1980s and are the most effective way to hunt deer and hogs in the cypress. Occasionally, after prime hunting time in the morning, the person up wind of everyone else would slowly walk about heading back toward the buggy. This slow drive would move game about and those in the trees could pick it off. This strategy worked really well.

One of the best hunts was designed on the kitchen table the night before. Our group on this hunt included: Rick; his wife, Linda; their son, Michael; Denny; his wife, Debbie; Jimmy Hightower and me. The week before, we had found a place on Bear Island that was about fifteen miles from Camp Red Bug that had a good amount of deer and hog sign. There were two long, pine ridges with big sawgrass ponds between them. The two parallel pine ridges were connected by another pine ridge which was about two-thirds their length from the south end and then another big sawgrass pond north of that. Then, to the north there was a large flat of low grass.

The plan was for Rick to park his buggy on the western edge of the west pine ridge. I would take mine on to the southern side of the same ridge and park it. Denny and Debbie would ease to the east on a buggy trail. I would slip up the grass pond from the south and climb a pine tree in the connecting ridge. Michael would go with Rick and take a stand to the north of his mother who would remain on the buggy. At this time, we could hunt off a buggy that was not under power.

All went well and as I slipped up on my tree, I could hear hogs rooting on the pine island to the east of me. Then, just as I was situated in my stand, I heard two shots from Denny's and Debbie's direction. I was sure it was them, but I sat still as Rick was to walk about that morning. Plus the hogs were moving my way from the other pine ridge.

All morning, I strained to see a hog or some part that I could identify. We could only shoot hogs that were fifteen inches at the shoulder, so I had to be sure of the target. I could not see anything except a little black now and then. I heard plenty of grunting and growling. I heard them rubbing on palmettos. I could see the bushes moving but never could identify the hogs.

About nine a.m., I saw Rick way off to the north on the other side of the sawgrass pond. I waved and waved until he saw me. Finally, I got his attention, and he understood I wanted him to come to me. There I was, sitting fifteen feet up a tree with a herd of hogs

Linda and Michael with her big boar hog.

under me. When Rick got nearer to me, I used sign language to explain all this to Rick and asked him to go get Jimmy, Michael, and Linda. He did that and we positioned them about the area. We put Linda in the prime location. She was standing in the middle of the connector ridge where the hogs had come from. Michael stood to my right overlooking that sawgrass pond and Jimmy stood to my left overlooking that pond. I remained in the tree like an air-traffic controller. Rick went into the thick palmettos.

He had moved in with his machete and shotgun. He was making all kinds of noise. He looked up at me a couple of times like I was crazy and pulling one over him. The third time he looked at me he said that they must have slipped out before we started our push. I said no, they were there about ten feet in front of him. Rick said that is thick. I said that is where they are. So, Rick took one more step, slapped the bushes with his machete, and the world came alive with hogs. They were running everywhere. I could not shoot because the trees were in the way. Jimmy shot one coming his way. Michael missed one. But deadeye Linda, who was now standing on a big pine stump, fired once, and started yelling. This huge boar hog came running right at her. At the last minute, he turned to her left and she blasted him with the 12-gauge. The kick from the gun knocked her off the stump.

Denny and Debbie heard all the commotion and walked over. Sure enough, they had each taken a hog. This gave us four hogs for the morning's work. Pushing hogs is a most exciting way to hunt.

Later that day, we learned that Linda had missed a big buck that had walked by her while she sat on the buggy. We asked how that happened. She said Rick did not load the shotgun when he handed it to her, and she had not checked it until she pulled the trigger and it went click—the buck ran away.

Many times, we would travel in two buggies. Rick, my neighbor, now had his own as his family had grown enough to require this. It was good having two buggies working together just in case mine broke down or became seriously stuck. On the days we had a stiff wind from the north, we would travel into the wind.

Rick and Denny on Rick's buggy.

In those days, we could go anyplace we could get the buggy and we did just that. Anyway, this one day we moved along, tracking a herd of hogs that had moved about the night before. On this one trip, we traveled a long way and pushed many islands. We would drive up to these islands, hammocks, or palmetto clumps, and we would set our standers; some were on the ground, and some were in climbing stands. Then one or two of us would walk in the thicket trying to kick out the hogs or deer. Sometimes, this worked but most of the time we merely got a lot of exercise. This one day we moved along tracking a herd hogs which had moved about the night before. On this one trip we traveled along way and pushed many islands. We would drive up to these islands, hammocks, or palmetto clumps and we would set our standers; some were on the ground and some were in climbing stands. Then one or two of us would walk in the thicket trying to kick out the hogs or deer. Some times this worked but most of the time we merely got a lot of exercise.

On this one very productive hunt, we had traveled across most of eastern Bear Island and had pushed many thickets. Finally, we found a big hammock with hog tracks going in but none coming out. We set about drawing up a strategy to stand the area and then Denny and I would push it.

We got everybody set in position. Linda was back standing (when a drive is done people have differing positions as established by the direction of the drive; front standing is the person in front of the drivers or pushers, side standing is anyone along the sides of the drive, and back standing is the person with a position where the drive started thus behind the drivers) on the buggy. Debbie was front standing on my buggy. Michael was to the south. Rick was to the northwest and Burney was to the northeast. Once everyone was in position, Denny and I would push the hammock.

Denny and I pushed our way into the thick palmettos, under the canopy of oak trees. I was working a thick stand of palmettos that had their roots growing off the ground. Palmettos do this sometimes. I had my 12-gauge, Browning pump at port and was just about to step on the second root when hogs broke out all around me. I had walked into an entire herd. There was one big one that came out and headed away from me and thank goodness he did. I fired and he rolled over, got up and kept going. I fired two more times but the thick vegetation shielded him. I gave chase. He left that hammock and went into a small but thick stand of palmettos. I stopped to shove more shells in the short-barreled Browning pump. It was a good thing I did because he was waiting for me. As I stepped into the thicket, he charged. I had to back up to get the end of the barrel between him and me. At the sound of the gun, he rolled over.

I could hear all kinds of shooting while I was chasing my boar hog. Denny on my left was firing. Debbie in front was firing. Michael was firing. Burney was firing. Rick was shooting both his shotgun and 06, in that order.

As it turned out, Rick's pump had jammed after the first shot, and he had to finish his hog off with the 06. Burney got off one shot as a hog went under the fence. Denny rolled one right off. Debbie had taken one with the 44 Ruger carbine. Michael had one down near him and Linda had fired but missed. We had worked hard all morning and traveled twenty or so miles from Camp Red Bug, but it paid off. We took six hogs out of Bear Island by noon. We then had a lot of work to do as we needed to get the hogs on ice fast.

By now, black powder and archery were a part of the hunting season. I have never been a great archer, but I like it because it is very challenging. Archery season is also the closest season when Cypress deer are in rut. One of my favorite friends to take archery hunting was Stuart Carver. He would stay in a stand all day even if it was storming and lightning as it frequently does in the cypress, during the September archery season.

Some of the hogs taken on the big shoot out.

One day, as we rode back to camp, we saw a deer feeding in the palmettos. This was a few hundred yards from camp. I stopped the buggy. Stu got out his bow and slipped up to thirty yards before the buck looked at him. As soon as the buck put his head down, Stu drew and let the arrow go. He had shot the buck through a big palmetto leaf. While we sat on the buggy drinking a Coke, I asked him why he did that and how did he know he would hit the buck. Stu explained the leaf was flat to him and the arrow would not be deflected, and the buck's chest was right behind the leaf, so he took the only shot he had. In a few minutes, we split up to look for the buck. Stu tracked him from where he was shot. I flanked along the edge of the palmetto island and along a cypress pond. I figured the buck would head to the nearest water. Sure enough, in a few dozen yards, I found the four-point.

Bucks in the Cypress come into rut around August 15. This may sound unusual until you think of the environmental driving forces behind all South Florida. It does not snow as in northern latitudes. There is lots of water. If the doe is bred at the wrong time, the fawn falls in the water or it has too little

The author carrying out a 10 pt after a successful evening black powder hunt.

dry ground to survive. Not only must it survive the water itself but also the major predators of the area—alligators, panthers, bears and bobcats. If the fawn and doe are restricted to smaller, dry ground areas they become easier prey. If the fawn is dropped when it is dry in January to March, then there are many more acres of dry ground and fewer bugs.

All this makes good sense and was learned by the FWC while doing deer studies in the early 1980s when they took does all year long for a few years. We expressed great concern over this action because at that time the NPS had stated they wanted to reduce hunting by 50% because there were not enough deer for the endangered Florida panther. By doing the recruitment math for fifteen does taken over several years, we figured the FWC was removing thousands of deer during a ten-year period of time. We all knew that if you wanted to impact deer herd size, you take out the doe deer. This was clearly evident in how the FWC had managed the Everglades deer herd.

Black powder fast became my absolute favorite type of hunting. The guns are powerful and usually dependable but one never really knows if it would fire or not. This was because of the humidity, rain, and water on the ground. We usually tried to hunt oak hammocks at this time because they were starting to drop acorns. It was also a time when a second rut started. Sometimes rattling and calling worked. It was also a time when mosquitoes could eat you alive. We used this to our advantage, as the deer like to stay in the swamps until mid-morning. They avoid mosquitoes by lying down in

The author on his climbing tree stand.

the water. We tried to place ourselves between known feeding strands and uplands because around nine or ten, the deer will move to the dry ground. It is hard to remain still because of the bugs and heat, but one must remain still to see wildlife.

We took lots of folks hunting. We took people hunting who had never been in the cypress. This was done because we like to take new folks and show them how difficult hunting is in the cypress. There are so many turkeys, deer, and hogs that you are hardly ever out of sight of their tracks. It always amazed new folks how they would always see game tracks but not see any game. It was difficult for them to understand the game was in the thickets and swamps. They could not look out across a mountain view and see miles of land and game. They found it difficult to believe that our deer had to have water and loved to live in it.

We learned how to use climbing stands to our advantage and as more people left the swamps and rules were enforced, we began to see more game. Game returned like we saw it when I first started Camp Red Bug. We grew older, lazy, and fatter. We did not walk around as much, or did we drive the buggy way off in the woods leaving camp in the middle of the night to go to a far-off hunting place. The result of this sitting was that we shot more deer and hogs. Each year, we would take more but never more than the legal limit. We also only took one or two bucks from any island. Thus, we would not over harvest the game in one location.

Denny and Wayne walking out of the swamp after a morning's black powder hunt.

Chapter Nine

◆ ◆ ◆

Everglades Ecosystem Restoration Work Begins with a Flood

The 1980s found many things happening. The first occurrence was the flood of 1981. This man-caused and nature-enhanced action caused the Big Cypress to fill up and the Everglades to overflow. The results of this were that we had a deer mercy kill, a deer rescue, and an animal-rights court case to stop the hunt. This was the first time the Endangered Species Act (ESA) was used to stop hunting. The result was the hunt was held, by then most of the deer drowned, and Governor Graham received bad press. He reacted by creating a committee to investigate what could be done. The committee was stacked with folks who had their own interests at stake if

A cow in East Henson Marsh during the floods of the 1980s.

the water was managed any other way than it had been. Thus, the finding of this committee was to have the FWC issue enough doe permits to collapse the Everglades deer herd. Freddy and I called the first FWC biologist for the Everglades. At this time, he was biologist for another game commission in a western state. We explained what had happened and what the FWC was planning to do. He said if they do that, they will collapse the Everglades deer herd. Freddy and I explained this to our club members and many club members would not shoot the does because they now knew what the FWC was up to. They bundled all their tags up and sent them back to the FWC. The FWC increased the number of tags they issued next year knowing that many would not be used. By increasing the number of tags, they would accomplish what the Governor wanted—to get rid of the pesky deer and deer-hunter. It was ironic that I had just asked the NPS to allow us to capture the Everglades deer and take them to the Big Cypress National Preserve. I was told the preserve is full of deer. However, in a matter of a few years, the NPS said there were not enough deer and had to reduce the number of hunters by fifty percent.

By now, the NPS had stopped all the camping along Loop Road and other popular places. They had started to close off entry locations and to jam folks into a few gates. This was done to reduce impacts over a larger area and funnel people into a few locations, so they said. This was done knowing that the increased level of use would cause greater impacts on the gate areas. But the NPS said they did not mind this as such an action would drastically reduce the impacts on many acres of land.

Also, by this time, the FWC had been able to get rid of most of the deer hunters in the Everglades. This was done when they collapsed the deer herd and only allowed very short hunting seasons. Before the Everglades deer management plan was implemented, the Everglades general gun deer-hunting season was ninety days long. Additionally, we would usually have five people on our hunting vehicles, and each could take a buck a day for the entire season. Before the doe harvest, the deer herd was not harmed by this level of hunting because the breeding season was over, and the herd population would bounce back each year. Every year, a few, large-antlered bucks would be taken. During these times, people would camp along S.R. 84 and the L-5 for the full ninety days. Some folks would even rent refrigerator trucks to hold their deer while they continued to hunt. But with the post early 1980s floods deer management plan in place, there were no deer so there were no deer hunters. Before the doe harvest, it was a normal day to see 100 to 150 deer during a day of hunting. Even when we sat on self-supporting ladder stands, we would see dozens of deer every day. But after the doe harvest, one was lucky to see one deer a day.

Also, by now, the NPS had moved their boundary between Everglades National Park and Big Cypress National Preserve to the north. They did not move this boundary by miles but in most cases by yards. By doing this, they were able to shut down the Stair-Steps airboat trail. At one time, this trail went from Homestead to Everglades City by following the salt-water freshwater line, just above the mangrove line. This trail was in place long before the creation of Everglades National Park and Stair-Step boundary. It had remained in place for nearly fifty years; the public could use the trail from Dona Drive to go to the western boundary of Everglades National Park and north to Loop Road, or travel the other way. It was a beautiful and long airboat ride. But by moving the ENP boundary northward only a few yards, they would close this trail and stop the public from accessing deep parts of the Big Cypress. They placed the ENP boundary so that airboats, which were legal in Big Cypress National Preserve but not legal in Everglades National Park, would have to ride on rocks. As you would suspect, airboats do not ride on rocks for long. Of course, Big Cypress National Preserve leadership did not complain but we did, to no avail.

The FWC had now killed off most of the deer in the Everglades so the miles of camps on the S.R. 84 were no more. The full three-month hunting season camps on S.R. 84 and L-5 were no more. The hunters were gone. The FWC had done what the governor's office wanted. They had collapsed the Everglades deer herd at the request of the governor via his committee. They had gotten rid of the hunters who were suing the state trying to make them manage the water correctly, to clean the water, and take back Florida's sovereign lands. Before the doe eradication program started, there had been 10,000-man days of hunting in the Everglades and probably the same in the Big Cypress. After the doe eradication program was completed, we were lucky to see 500-man days of hunting during the short, nine-day or less season, on nearly 700,000 acres of land.

Some of the older members, like Bobby Stossal Sr., knew that Florida law stated all waters below the ordinary high-water line at statehood belonged to the State of Florida and thus the people of Florida. They knew where these ordinary high-water lines were and that most of this land was being locked up by some landowners who placed fences around them. The largest amount of such land was in the Kissimmee River Valley.

Flood water on Fisheating Creek in the high campgrounds and under the old oaks.

Some of these sportsmen purposely went on these public lands, which were claimed as private land, by using airboats. This was the only way the land could be realistically accessed. The result of this civic disobedience action was that they were arrested. Some were handcuffed to fence posts for hours and some were locked in dog boxes in the back of pickup trucks. These cases went to court and their attorney had the case moved to a new venue because the judge and all the other folks involved in the case had some sort of connection to these big landowners. Not any illegal or clandestine connection, just the kind that comes with normal living in sparsely populated rural counties. In the end, these sportsmen won their cases and charges were dismissed.

However, the genie was out of the box and others were now paying attention to all this land that belonged to the people of Florida. This led to the State of Florida striking a deal with the landowners along the Kissimmee River allowing this river to be restored as much as possible. It also led to lengthy litigation against the Lykes Company over ownership of Fisheating Creek.

It was reported that this company had put up fencing and felled cypress trees across the creek to stop the public from using their creek. Then a group of interested and concerned people filed litigation against the company. The State of Florida under Attorney General Butterworth went to court with these citizens. In the end, another agreement was reached.

The landowner would not continue contesting their ownership of the creek itself, would sell to the state their property from the outside of the oak tree line and stop claiming ownership of the creek. They would also agree to consider a conservation easement on the rest of their vast holdings in a phased purchase program. As of 2004, the first phase purchase was reached but the other two phases had failed because of money and what was being or not being purchased. In the end, most parties were happy. The state and public got their land back. The sportsmen could access these lands in a managed manner to hunt, fish and camp. The landowner got a load of money and could continue their agriculture practices.

Soon after the 1980s flood, we had a huge national meeting in Port of Isle called Son of Big Cypress called by Governor Graham. Bob Brantly, Executive Director of the Florida Fish and Wildlife Commission, and the governor's office revived the Everglades Coalition. It was the kickoff for his second run at the governorship. During this meeting, he committed to working to de-authorize the Southern Golden Gate Estate, now the Picayune Strand State Forest, and to creating the Big Cypress Addition. Remember, we had already committed to Estus to help re-elect Governor Graham, thus we were seen as a part of the team and allowed into the rooms for planning sessions.

The Southeastern Governors Conference was sponsored by Governor Graham. Estus called me to ask if I could assemble enough airboats and operators to tour all the Southeastern Governors in the Everglades as Governor Graham was sponsoring their conference. He also wanted to know if I could find someone to cater this event. I went to the Everglades Coordinating Council, and they said they would. The clubs got all the airboats and drivers, and Dave Charland furnished the food. This was the kick off of the Save the Everglades program we have today.

The FWF board members in South Florida had already met with the Collier Enterprise Corporation folks in the FWC Palm Beach Regional office. They wanted to build a Ford Motor test track north of the Fakahatchee Strand State Preserve and did not want us to litigate because of potential impacts to the panther. In exchange for this, we were told they would donate their lands to the state to create the Big Cypress National Preserve Addition for what they would get from selling their access to S.R. 84 as

An FWF executive board meeting at Camp Red aBug.

it was converted to I-75. Remember, they had access from the road because they had donated 600 feet of right of way for ingress and egress for perpetuity.

We considered this to be a good thing because we would have more public hunting lands. We decided to not litigate their Ford Motor test track and considered the issue a done deal.

Our first indication of problems to come arrived right after the meeting in FWC's Lt. Col. Glen Kelly's Palm Beach office. He called me into his office and asked me if I thought the NPS would manage the Addition Lands differently than the rest of the Preserve. I said they could be but did not see why they would. Boy, do I think differently today.

All this was laid out at the Son of Big Cypress meeting at the Port of Isles and the rebirth of the Everglades Coalition. It was a grand plan to protect hundreds of thousands more acres and to allow hunting on them in the future.

Then things started to get interesting. (The Big Cypress National Preserve Addition had some folks who supported the original bill, creating the Big Cypress National Preserve and supporting this new bill.) They all said the right things about use and access. They were all working together. Then one day, I got a call from Carol Browner, Senator Chiles' assistant.

It is necessary for me to go back a year or two so you will understand

Cal Stone talking with Senator Chiles, Bob Brantly and Carol Browner talking with others looking on at a meeting in the Big Cypress National Preserve to address NPS management.

how Carol Browner knew me. Carol had met me at a meeting that Manley Fuller set up with the DOI, NPS, USFWS, Bob Brantly, and Senator Chiles. (Manley Fuller was the new President of the FWF and had been able to develop a meeting with Senator Chiles and others.) I worked on getting the local sportsmen leaders together and funding the trip. All these folks and many sportsmen would meet at Cal's camp to address concerns about the Big Cypress. It was fitting since this was where it all started. I was the primary organizer and as such worked through the Everglades Coordinating Council to get the food, transportation and other logistics set up. We would take the superintendent and his regional director from my camp to Cal's, which was some five hours from mine. We met there for two days, rode around, and saw the pine heart lands, then someone would take them on out to U.S. 41 and the Sportsmen Club. After all, neither NPS leader had ever been in the interior of the preserve, except by helicopter.

As the day approached, I got phone calls from a few media type folks who wanted to go. I did not refuse them, but I told them would have to provide their own transportation, they could not be pregnant, nor could they have a bad back. These are normal precautions that I would take whenever I took folks into the cypress on my buggy just because no matter how slow or well-built the buggy, it is not a smooth ride. Apparently, no media folks could find a ride as none showed up; of course, we controlled most of the buggies in Florida.

We met at Cal's, had great food, had a good social time, saw a lot of the Cypress, and saw how Melaleuca were taking over the area. Then, we met around a campfire and talked about the management of the Cypress. Senator Chiles, sitting next to me, told the superintendent this was not how they, Congress, wanted the area managed and he knew that. The superintendent made the mistake of pointing out that it was not the Senator's bill that passed. I said mistake because the Senator raised his voice over the sound of the tree frogs and hoot of the owl to tell the superintendent he knew better than that. The bill that passed was Senator S. Jackson's and was moved because he had more seniority than Chiles, but Chiles had authored the bill. By allowing Senator Jackson, as senior senator, to introduce the bill it would have more weight. Besides, this would be Jackson's environmental issue as he made a run for the presidency. Chiles was really mad and told both NPS leaders and everyone else that "he had not robbed the nation to pay for the cypress for it to be managed like this" (like a park as the NPS wanted to). The mood of the friendly outing never really recovered after that even when the Senator and Bob Brantly, Executive Director of the FWC, flew out the next day. The meeting atmosphere never returned to a party environment after the Senator spoke and remained a bit tense. I was glad to not have to take the NPS folks twenty-five miles out of the heart of the Big Cypress. I returned alone to my camp.

This meeting took place a year before the Big Cypress Addition bill was introduced. Now, let's go back to Carol Browner's phone call concerning the Addition legislation. She said, "Jack, we cannot get the western senators to support this action and she wanted to know if there was any way you could help." I said that I would try. What she did not know was that Dave Balman had a friend in his cypress camp who was a personal friend of Senator M. Wallop. They all hunted on the senator's Wyoming ranch. Dave's friend was as upset as the rest of us at the NPS and

Dave Blaman on his Model-A Buggy in the stair-steps.

was having Senator Wallop, the ranking minority member, hold up the bill. I called the NRA DC office and explained things to Mary Jolly who was working with me. I asked her who was the NRA's go to person in Phoenix, Arizona. She told me and I called Phoenix. I explained who I was, how I got her number, and what I wanted. I was told the Collier's had a land swap tucked into the Addition bill and that this would bypass public oversight and involvement. The Western Delegation would not support the bill until the offending language came out. I called Browner back and informed her of such. Two days later, Browner called me and said it was out and asked if I would go back to Arizona and see if they would now support the legislation. I informed Arizona: they checked and said they would support it as long as the language stayed out.

Carol Balman helping with a legislative outing.

Dave's wife, Carol, worked at the Loop Road eastern hunter check station each hunting season for the Florida Fish, Wildlife and Conservation Commission (FWC, previously the GFC). She would never become embroiled in the political issues of the day but always remained informed and was able to make many contacts with hunters as they came and went through this minatory check station. After working the check station, she made sure these sportsmen remained informed on the issues of the day.

We then had another hurdle. Sportsmen wanted the best language in the bill we could get to protect the interest of the FWC and sportsmen. We thought we had this until the NRA lawyer explained that "not more than three recreational access sites" could also mean none or zero. If we wanted three, then three should be stated. We wanted three in Broward and three in Collier because this is what Wes Sarvis's Everglades Recreation Committee had developed nearly twenty years earlier. Carol said I would kill the bill if I asked for this change. I said that was what the sportsmen wanted, and we had to have that. This was Chile's last year in office as he was retiring so there would be no more opportunities to act.

By then, these recreational access sites were supported by the Florida legislative Speaker of the House and President of the Senate. After all, Dave Charland, African Safari member, founder of the FWC Reward program, and ardent cypress hunter was a friend of the senate

Dave Charland on his big buggy.

president. These access sites were written into Governor Graham's Save the Everglades plan. (That letter, the National Audubon Society had used in 1971, appeared again.) When Johnny Jones retired from the FWF, we found this letter from the NWF to the FHWA explaining how this I-75 road was not legal (see appendix with letter). This time the Everglades Coordinating Council used the letter. The Council directed me to call Estus Whitfield, the governor's environmental assistant and chair of that Everglades deer committee.

I explained to Estus how the council was going to meet this coming Thursday night and would vote to file litigation to stop I-75 work as it crossed Florida because it is an illegal project. This was the last section of I-75 to be built in Florida. It would be the most controversial. Most citizens do not know that the state was awarded interstate funds in a lump sum and the state decides where to spend these dollars. Further, the state had to turn dirt on this last section of I-75 by a certain date or lose these funds. We had waited until the time was right to play this "card."

Estus wanted to know if he could come down and meet with us. We all agreed. After he read the letter, he wanted to know what we wanted to avoid litigation. We said simply that we want three recreational sites in Broward and three in Collier on public lands. At that time, only one location was on public land. He said OK, we would build the Broward sites small and inside the current project right of way to avoid having to do a new EIS. Then, we will build the big sites once main line construct was finished and EIS work is done on these sites. Again, we all agreed. Being one to worry about the budget and where the money would come from, Estus then asked how we would pay for these recreation sites. I said leave the toll on that part of I-75 interstate roads since other states had tolls on their Interstate roads. He thought that was a good idea. He wanted to know if we would help reelect Governor Graham. We agreed. We all shook hands and continued with the rest of the meeting. To this day Estus has lived up to his word.

I-75 continued to change Florida as FDOT had to purchase all the lands in the Big Cypress Addition that were not Collier Enterprise Inc. lands. This was done in the name of mitigation. They also had to sever access that landowners had to I-75. These two items amounted to more than $45 million in 1989. Not only did they have to take these private properties, but the state also had to change the law allowing FDOT to take property outside of the immediate right-of-way of a road even if this property was as much as six to seven miles from the road. This law was changed and FDOT began to take people's property via condemnation. It is said the Colliers got $21 million for their access rights. I know they had to be paid a lot of money for access because I received $31,000 for access to my acre and a quarter nearly a mile from the road. Then they traded this land-locked land for an Indian Reservation school site in Phoenix, Arizona, that is reportedly worth $400 million at build out. That was not a bad deal to get rid of swampland that would be very expensive to develop, if not impossible, under the ESA and CWA.

Let us go back to the Addition bill recreational access issue. At this time, Governor Graham was our U.S. Senator Graham, so he had to remember the history of these things. After Carol Browner calmed down and realized, I was not going to change my mind, Carol said she would talk with the environmental groups and get back. I said OK; I will wait. She called back in a few minutes with Manley Fuller, new President of the FWF and Ralph Johnson, Vice-Chairman of the Board FWF, on the line and said

Ralph Johnson with his grandchildren on his airboat. He is in the BICY addition lands south of I-75.

the language change I wanted would be done. Ralph and I directed Manley to work on passage of the bill as amended with no other changes. Manley did not know until then we were working in such a manner. We feared if we did inform him, we would put him in a bad situation and lose the issue. I said I would contact all the NRA state organizations to support the bill if it did not change. Carol Browner did not know all I had to do was call Dave Balman to get him to call his camp buddy to call Senator Wallop. However, I also called the NRA folks to make sure all was right and would watch the bill's final hours. That was done and the bill was moving again.

During this same time frame, the Collier Companies wanted to bring a road from Immokalee to S.R. 84 where there would be a major rest area. The rest area would require a bridge and thus this road would be able to go under I-75 and then run east along the south side of I-75 to L-28. This would essentially make sure their lands were open to future development. They would follow an old railroad grade so as not to create big environmental issues. Their plan had developed enough interest in Tallahassee that we were contacted and asked if we would support such a road. We said we would not and then pulled out the National Audubon agreement. This road idea quickly went away.

There was also a rumored ACoE plan to ditch and dike the BCNP south of I-75 to create WCA3. We made some phone calls to make sure ACoE did not even think twice about this idea. They were thinking of doing this under the concept of shared adversity as it would relieve having to stack so much water in the Everglades, which just came off a very well-reported and unpopular flooding. Additionally, they could provide more potable water for Naples.

Also, Dave Charland, who started the REWARD program to help stop poaching in Florida, was one of the members of the WD Ranch that was located along the south of S.R. 84 and had annual company BBQs. These were great times with good food. He would have three or four hundred people attend this activity. I would help by bringing my swamp buggy and taking his folks on rides. On one outing, I took Congressman Clay Shaw, his wife, kids, and grandchildren on a ride. Years later, while in DC working on the CERP bill I, Ms. Shaw found me in the big room full of people at the signing party. She acted like I was a long-lost family member. This made me feel really good that she would remember me from that one visit to the Big Cypress. Congressman Shaw, his wife, and I sat together during the ceremony. At another BBQ, I took some judges and the Governor of Rhodesia into the Cypress.

Dave Balman's grandmother was known as the Ft Myers Ox-Cart lady because she had gone from Tampa to Miami before Tamiami trail was built via an oxcart. There was a report about her in the *Miami Herald* in the 1980s. Years later, Dave's grandfather and mother operated a sawmill in the Cypress. It was located south of U.S. 41. His dad was a game warden for the FWC, and he grew up on Loop Road by Pinecrest. His wife, Carol, is an Indian princess in the family line of the Ray West Tribe from Georgia.

Carol and Dave Balman could really turn the heat up when they needed to. One-time Superintendent Hibbard had his plant people kill an old fig tree at Monroe station on U.S. 41. This tree was important to the Indians and sportsmen. Hibbard told me he would never cross her again as the phone calls, letters and political pressure was not worth the mistake he made having his folks kill that tree.

In 1985, Senator Chiles introduced the Big Cypress National Preserve Addition Act. We had done a lot of work to see that this bill was acceptable to everyone, and everyone had something in the bill they wanted; another 175,000 acres of the Big Cypress Basin were protected from ditches, golf courses and housing developments. The bill looked good and seemed ready to pass. To our surprise and dismay, it did not pass that Congressional session.

We went back to the next Congressional session with the same bill. Again, it was well-supported and seemed ready to pass. Of course, there were problems that were anticipated by Senator Chiles. I was invited to attend a meeting in downtown Miami at a lawyer's office in the tallest building on Brickell Avenue. The location was amazing and impressive. We could look out the north window of the office and see the entire east coast all the way to Ft. Lauderdale. I was really surprised to learn that Senator Chiles was there and prepared to lay out the legislative strategies to get this Big Cypress Addition Act passed this session. This was particularly important as this was the Senator's last session. He was retiring and even though folks knew that, he still had lots of clout because he remained the chair of the Appropriations Committee.

The Senator was extremely upset with President G. Bush Sr., because the president had been offered a trade for the Phoenix Indian lands in Arizona, the same eighty acres the Colliers wanted, by the Phillips family. According to Senator Chiles, the family had offered the DOI more than 360,000 acres of land in the west for those eighty acres. According to Senator Chiles, President Bush Sr. had considered the offer overnight, had not spoken to Chiles, and turned down the offer. Senator Chiles told us that this swap should have taken place and that they would have found the money to purchase the Addition lands, but they understood the Colliers were big Republicans and that their land swop had higher values for the Administration than the Democratic Phillips family. After the meeting was over, we talked a bit about the future of Southeast Florida and the tremendous quantities of potable water our exploding population would need soon.

In a few more months, Carol Browner called again. This time it was Monday morning of Thanksgiving week. She said she needed nine of nineteen senators to attend a meeting Wednesday morning and vote for Senator Chiles' Addition bill. I asked for the names of all nineteen and she gave them to me. I went to Ralph Johnson's shop in Hialeah, explained the issue, and used his company phone to contact SCI's main office in Phoenix, Arizona. I talked with Don Brown again explaining the situation and the need. I needed to know the name and phone number of two Safari Club International (SCI) members who were on breakfast terms with each of these nineteen senators. I had met Don a few years earlier at the SCI American Wildlife Leadership School in Wyoming, so he already knew who I was. He gave them to me, and I started calling. Each call required a brief explanation of who I was, what the problem was, how the solution would help hunters, and what I needed. They all said they would contact their Senator friends and that was it. Ralph's boss, Ray Schultz, was vice-president of Sister Cities International and knew a lot of people. He said he would make a few phone calls. Monday of the next week, Carol called again. I thought this was bad news that the bill had died, but it was not. She thanked me and said she did not know how I did it but all nineteen senators showed up, voted for the bill, and left. All this happened the day before Thanksgiving break.

I was also secretary of the North Dade Chamber of Commerce and an executive director of their board. This

Dave Powell at his sawgrass camp. We often used his place for legislative outings.

chamber was strongly supporting the Big Cypress Addition, not using public lands for storm water treatment areas, and not using public lands for reservoirs. These major business leaders of Dade County were strong on conservation and let all know this by including these issues in the annual legislative agenda booklet sent to the Florida Legislators and others.

The chamber also had a Development and Management of Water (DAMOW) committee that I chaired. By 1980, these businesspeople were concerned about our water supply, water quality and the environment. This concern was prompted by two incidents. The first was the droughts and fires of the 1970s. The second was a meeting attended by several chamber board members at which Art Marshall spoke. I think the latter concern is the one that really made the chamber membership wake up and take notice of what was going on. The chamber had a very progressive water position that included not using public lands to clean polluted water or store

water; to have a surcharge on excessive use; to stop the reverse charging plan where the more one used—the less they paid; and research for alternative water supply sources. This research was promoted by the SFWMD document "Desalination a Viable Alternative." For many years, the chamber carried this platform to the Florida

Harold Johnson on his airboat after a legislative outing to help save the Everglades.

Legislators, the governor, and the Florida Congressional membership. It helped but then there were not enough other groups working with them to make a lot happen.

Ralph was involved in the issues of Florida's environment and sportsmen long before me. He had been a founding member of many of southeastern Florida sportsmen-conservation clubs like the Broward County Halftrack, Airboat, and Conservation Club. He was also involved in politics to a greater extent than me. One day, Ralph shared with me that he had observed while attending a Cabinet meeting while Governor

Askew was in office. Folks had gone to Tallahassee to present testimony to the cabinet concerning the effects and impacts of increasing the size of the Everglades Agriculture Area (EAA). Art Marshal had chaired two Blue Ribbon Committees on this topic. Tom Shirley, who was the first to reach out to Cal Stone to save the Big Cypress from developers, told me the first report the committee created was extremely hard on this idea and on the EAA interest. Art had to reconvene his committee and develop a new report that was not so hard. Well, Ralph told me that while they were standing in the hall, a cabinet aide came out and told Art if he testified the way they thought he was going to (this testimony would be more in line with the first report), then Art would be looking for a new job. Art said it like it was and then he had to find a new job. Years later, I had Art Marshall and Paul Parks in the Big Cypress National Preserve riding my swamp buggy looking at gator ponds with cattails in them. They were interested in this matter as water from the upstream agriculture areas could not reach these isolated distant ponds, yet these ponds had cattails in them. Of course, the cattails had never, in the more than twenty-five years of my observance, spread beyond the nutrient rich water of these big gator ponds that had big bird roosts around them.

Tom Shirley working on his airboat after a legislative outing.

My uncle, A.C. Allen, was superintendent of a school system in Southeast Alabama, so he knew most of the Alabama legislative members well enough to seek their support and obtain it. A.C. also knew the Governor of Alaska because they flew bombers together in World War II. He was able to contact him and seek his support and the support of that state's legislative membership. It did not hurt that A.C. was a hunter and had hunted from Camp Red Bug on the few occasions he could get to South Florida. Of course, most of those he was talking with were also sportsmen and liked the idea of making sure the Big Cypress and the Addition continued to be hunted.

An uncle in-law of mine, Milton Gillespie, worked for a big newspaper company in Georgia and knew many of that state's legislative members. He committed to me to help get these folks on the bandwagon to assure the Big Cypress Addition was signed into law with the best language we could get to protect the interests of sportsmen. Again, it did not hurt that Milton and many of those he was working with also hunted.

Ralph and Peggy Johnson. Peggy lobbied in Tallahassee many years for the sportsmen and women of Florida.

Chapter Ten

◆ ◆ ◆

The DOI/NPS Show Their Hand, CERP Is Started, and More Good Times at Camp Red Bug

Camp Red Bug

∞

    With the Addition bill passed, taking only two years, the First Big Cypress Management plan approved, and the NPS I-75 recreational access plan done, it seemed like times were going to get easier. We had many good hunts during those years from Camp Red Bug. By the late 1980s, we had plenty of game around and within easy traveling distance of camp Red Bug. The only time we traveled very far from camp was to see old friends, to refresh our old buggy trails, and to remember how to get to a certain favorite place. We were really eco-tourists who were sight-seeing from a swamp buggy.

Not only was the Big Cypress National Preserve Addition being worked on but so was the Florida Panther National Wildlife Refuge. One evening, I received a phone call from a high-ranking DOI person in DC. I was asked if I thought they should make the nearly 22,000 acres on the north side of I-75 and west side of S.R. 29 a part of the Big Cypress National Preserve or a national wildlife refuge under the Fish and Wildlife Service. This was a no brainer as we were having real problems with the NPS on the Preserve; the Fish and Wildlife folks were supposed to be friends of the hunter. I said it should go to U.S. Fish and Wildlife as S.R. 29 would make a good natural boundary. I thought being a National Wildlife Refuge would be preferred because we were having such problems with the NPS management.

Boy, was I wrong about the U.S. Fish and Wildlife Service being friends of the hunter. They took this land from the Collier Company that had been one of the best hunting leases in South Florida and closed hunting and all human access for more than fifteen years. Then, when they did their first management plan, they made sure there would be no hunting, fishing, camping, or ORV use on this land for another twenty years.

A year after the Addition Bill became law, Manley Fuller, the new President of the FWF, had pulled together the National Wildlife Federation (NWF), National Rifle Association (NRA), Safari Club International (SCI), Wildlife Legislative Fund of America and several legislative aides. O.J. Monterry, who had worked on Senator Mack's campaign, made sure the senator had one of his assistants accompany us to this meeting with the Assistant Secretary. We went to DC to talk with DOI about the attitude and treatment of sportsmen by the NPS. I was cautioned by folks with a lot of experience in DC issues not to use the superintendent's name or attack his actions. I respected those who told me this and shared that with Sonny Nome's who represented the trespass camp owners. I learned later if this had happened, the superintendent would have been brought into the meeting and we would have lost control of the situation. As it was, the superintendent sat in the hall outside the Assistant Secretary's door for the entire meeting. Sometime later and back in South Florida, Superintendent Fagergren told me they—I took "they" to mean career NPS employees—did not pay attention to the Assistant Secretary as she was only a short-term political appointee. His statement must have been true because all that the political appointee had committed to was never done but the bureaucrats remained and continued their respective paths of actions.

We would spend twelve years working with the NPS to build a general management plan for the Big Cypress National Preserve. While meeting with the Assistant Secretary, a DOI lawyer explained to me how to construct a public response form that the DOI/NPS would have to accept, and which would support our desires. The ECC met every week for a good while to develop a unified position and comment response form. I contacted the NPS to see if we could copy their document and was told we could, so we did. We printed many thousands of copies, but we modified them as we were instructed by the Federal attorney. The end results were that we put so many hard copies into the process that the NPS had to hire people to evaluate these documents. I was asked by an NPS person why we took such an action. I responded by saying that in the past when we sent one ECC letter, you counted it as one so we decided to ask all our members to respond and many did.

During these early years of the Big Cypress National Preserve, the NPS and FWC produced a good number of surveys. For each survey, the Everglades Coordinating Council would meet and debate the pros and cons on how to respond to each question. We would then take these thoughts back to the many clubs' general membership and seek more input. Finally, the council leaders would meet again to create a unified position that provided guidance to all our members, friends, and family on how to respond and why. With most of these surveys, we were given permission to reproduce them or get as many as we wanted to handout. This strategy worked very well and allowed us to be sure to not make strategic mistakes in how we answered the questions that could harm our interests. The FWC deer survey in 2003 was not handled this way and it led the FWC to consider a trophy management deer program for the entire state. One simple question was a key factor in this action. The question was, "Would you like to be able to take bucks with larger horns?" Almost any hunter would say yes, and they did. I was told by many that they thought the FWC would go into a habitat improvement program and not a deer harvest reduction with private land harvest regulations. These folks had not debated the full implications of the survey.

The General Management Plan was not what we really wanted and not at all what they wanted. But things being what they are, we were about to get a General Management Plan (GMP) that all could live with. It was not long before we had a new superintendent. The new superintendent, Mr. Hibbard, stepped into the hottest NPS land unit in the nation and finished its first General Management Plan. There were local and national articles about how the NPS was treating the hunters and that there had been a major meeting in DC with the Under Secretary of Interior and staff. One particularly excellent writer went to the Cypress on several occasions with us. Steve Waters, the outdoors writer for a local newspaper, liked to hunt and went on a few trips over the years. He would write the truth about the Cypress because he had been there. While his editorial board was putting out propaganda driven by NPCA and Sierra that Big Cypress was a "pristine wilderness," Steve would let the world know the truth. It's too bad the editorial board of the Sun Sentinel, and many others, did not do their homework and study the history of the Big Cypress.

Barbara Jean Powell arranged a meeting with the new superintendent, Mr. Hibbard. She was now the president of the Everglades Conservation Club, Sonny's old club. At this meeting, Mr. Hibbard listened with all the training a good counselor would have. He heard how

Barbara Jean Powell running the Kissimmee River work day.

the only issue the NPS and we could agree with was limiting 2,500 ORVs to public permitting. Then the NPS changed their position and wrote 2,000 in the final GMP. He also heard how there was no need for airboats to be on trails in the southeast corner of the Stair-Steps. The NPS had put airboats on trails in this area because of the rocks in that part of the Preserve and they did not want their employees running their airboats into these rocks. Those who used the area knew where the rocks were and did not need trail makers or trails to navigate. The inexperienced NPS rangers did not know the area. At this meeting, the NPS plan writers did not say airboats had to be on trails in this area for the Cape Sable Seaside Sparrow, another ESA animal, but for safety. Mr. Hibbard, in his best diplomatic manner, said he saw no reason why we should not have 2,500 permits and would take the airboats off those trails. Hibbard also would allow us to set up tent camps in the backcountry before hunting season and leave them until the end of the season. Everyone left the meeting feeling very good. Little did we know that Mr. Hibbard was setting us up for future major litigations under NEPA violations.

I have mentioned the General Management Plan—which began nearly twelve years earlier just as the first manager left—for the original Big Cypress National Preserve area. This was another interesting battle. Sportsmen, and I assume others, received a letter from the NPS Denver planners. They said they were starting the planning process of the Big Cypress National Preserve and would like to meet with us to address our concerns. As Secretary of the Everglades Coordinating Council, I sent a letter to them at once with a range of dates we could meet. I invited them to go into the interior with us. I got a response saying they did not have time to meet with us. Naturally, this did not sit well with us, so I sent a letter and made a phone call to Senator Chiles.

It was not long until the Denver planning leader called to set up a date to meet with us. I made the arrangements. We met at our Council office of that day. It was a very productive meeting and we decided to take them to Cal's camp, Calusa Ranch, for a long, three-day trip. We had several buggies going and selected a good route. There were four planners, and each was assigned to a knowledgeable swamp buggy operator and another knowledgeable rider. This way we could talk about issues as we rode for three hours to Cal's.

We had a great trip and both sides learned a lot. We learned that the NPS was more worried about a full-blown oil project removing oil from all the Big Cypress than our activities. What I was told was, "you guys are not doing anything wrong, besides you are doing what you were doing before the law passed and had been doing so for many years." Too bad this statement did not hold true fifteen years later when the NPS locked up 80% of the Preserve.

I found out later from one of Senator Chiles' aides that when the senator heard how we had been treated, he told the NPS to get those planners to work with us or he would cut all the NPS funds. I suppose this got their attention because from that day on the NPS sent the superintendent, chief ranger, or other top managers to meet and discuss issues with us. We may not have agreed on all points and issues, but at least we were meeting and talking. This was what we had expected to happen since the Assistant Secretary had mailed his 1972 letter to Cal and Johnny.

All was working well until one day Mr. Hibbard just stopped coming to the meetings or sending one of his staff. It seems the recent litigation filed by Florida Biodiversity was preventing the NPS from meeting with us anymore. At least, this was Mr. Hibbard's reason for not attending.

Right after the Big Cypress Addition passed, the Wilderness Society moved a new leader, Jim Webb, into southeast Florida. Jim met with the Council, and we talked about a number of issues. One of them was the East Everglades. We did not want to see it developed nor did we want it to become a part of Everglades National Park. We were working to make the area a WMA under the FWC. However, Jim was a strong Park supporter and he wanted ENP to get it. He did a good job of lining up local support without us knowing about it. Why not?—While we were at work making a living and paying the bills, he was out beating the bushes with local leaders to get their 'buy in' to make it a part of Everglades National Park.

Governor Martinez appointed another committee to look at the East Everglades. Many years earlier, Freddy Fisikelli was on the first East Everglades committee that was appointed by Governor Graham. This time we had no one on it. Estus told me that Sam Poole, years later the Executive Director of the SFWMD, would represent the sportsmen. Mr. Poole, an Audubon person, would represent us? Anyway, Sam met with the Council and refused to consider any of our concerns. He would only support making the area a part of ENP. The hunter-conservationist had no representation on this East Everglades committee, a committee selected by Governor Martinez with a predetermined outcome.

We were shocked by what Governor Martinez had done with this committee because I was invited to meet with the governor at his first meeting with anyone from the public. A group of us went to Tallahassee for our fifteen-minute meeting in the governor's office. This meeting lasted for nearly an hour as we talked about the issues in the Everglades and the water issues we had. We had supported and worked for his campaign. We found the governor's betrayal unacceptable.

I shared our meeting with Sam with Estus Whitfield, the governor's environmental assistant, and I think this is why Estus supported keeping airboats in that part of ENP. At least airboats that were permitted at the time of passage of the law would be able to go into the area. Of course, ENP had no permits so the only permits that could be used were the ones issued by the FWC. As of August 2003, this issue had not been resolved because the ENP had refused to implement that part of the law. However, we should be able to get airboat use on designated trails, but we could no longer hunt or frog in the area. Additionally, only the airboats permitted as of the passage date of the enabling act would be allowed to use the area.

At the time the ENP Expansion act was being worked on, Governor Martinez's staff was telling people in DC that there was no wildlife in the area and certainly no huntable game. Somehow, a letter from Bob Brantly, Executive Director of FWC, which listed all the game, wildlife, and man-days of hunting, got in the hands of a friendly congressman. We started working the politics to stop this attack against sportsmen of the nation.

I had been the top fund-raiser for the Mayor of Hialeah, Florida, who was also chairman of the Dade Republican Party Environmental Committee. I was able to get him to take action supporting our cause. We had worked for several Democratic/Republican members of the Florida legislatures, local politicians, and national officials.

We were working our contacts real hard. As a result of this, I was invited to testify before Congress on the matter. This was a wonderful experience and an honor. I carefully prepared my testimony which had to be triple-spaced and submitted a week before I was to talk. I was also told I could not deviate from my presentation without permission.

On the plane ride to DC, I sat behind Nat Reed and John Ogden who I had read about and heard speak on the Everglades. I knew them but they did not know me. It was very interesting to hear them talk about the ENP Addition. I will never forget hearing Nat tell John it was time to stop compromising and the area must be a part of Everglades National Park. I knew right then we had a losing issue but I was determined to continue the quest.

During the testimony, I will never forget what I heard Nat tell Congress when Congressman Marlenee asked him about the hunting in that part of the Everglades. Remember, Brantly's letter was already there and Congressman Ron Marlenee who was on the committee was a real friend of the hunter. His aide had been to my camp a few years earlier. Well, Nat told Congress that the sportsmen had plenty of space to ride their airboats in the Big Cypress National Preserve just down the street a-ways; and besides, Congress had just given them another 147,000 acres to hunt on the year before, with the Addition to the Big Cypress National Preserve. It's too bad Nat would not remember what he told Congress at a hearing in the year 2003 (see his letter in the appendix).

Bob Brantly's letter cost the FWC a million dollars that year. Governor Martinez cut the FWC budget by that much. We are sure this was done to bring the FWC in line with his office. It must have worked because the FWC has not crossed a sitting governor since then.

We were apparently doing well at stopping this ENP expansion bill, because one night at one a.m., I got a call from a congressional aide. He said they could not help us any more as the Chairman of the National Republican Party had been talked to by Governor Martinez, who was also a Republican, and the party had sent word out to not oppose the governor. It was a done deal, and we were history. Of course, when Governor Martinez ran again, we did not forget and could not work for him. Chiles won by a landslide even with the NRA behind Martinez. Governor Chiles continued to support the sportsmen and the intent of Congress in the Big Cypress National Preserve; this made him a popular person for his next two terms as governor. Years later, I met and got to know Mr. Allison DeFoor and felt bad that he was not able to be Lt. Governor for Martinez's second term.

But then, someone in Martinez's team should have told him not to cross the sportsmen of Florida because they vote.

As a result of this East Everglades debacle, I was asked to be a member of Senator Mack's environmental committee. We never met but I was consulted about every environmental issue that came before Congress. There were no more park expansions.

I have already discussed the high water of the early 1980s. We had high water again in the middle 1990s. It was an exciting time because Governor Chiles had convened the Sustainable Commission of South Florida. I was fortunate to have been appointed to this Commission to represent the sportsmen of Florida. When I went on the Sustainable Commission in 1993, Barbara Jean Powell took over the duties of Secretary and Legislative Liaison for the Everglades Coordinating Council. She went on to help establish the Allied Sportsmen of Florida and the first Florida Legislative Sportsmen's Caucus.

The Sustainable Commission was a result of the litigations that were on going at the time Chiles came into office. I had some level of involvement

A foggy morning in the cypress was like the sustainable directions—unclear.

in most of these. The biggest was the one filed by Assistant Deputy U.S. Attorney Dexter Lehtinen. Pete Rosenthal, an ENP employee, worked to get Turner River restored and with that work well on the way, he had turned his attention to the issue of water quality and how it affected ENP. Pete was able with the help of Franklin Adams and others to restore the first river in America. Sure, it was 'short river', but it was restored. One day, I got a bundle in the mail. It was a bunch of documents from Pete. I called him and asked what they were about. He said it was water quality research and to hold it until the time was right to use it because he was leaving the NPS.

I also had documents from the SFWMD in which they stated they were polluting all the water in the WCAs.

Well, both Ralph Johnson and Freddy Fisikelli had fought for years to make sure the Everglades got the water it should and that it was of the proper quality. They took my documents. They went to David White, an attorney in Miami who had worked pro bono for us on other issues. David looked at the documents and said we did not have the money for this case, even pro bono. Ralph, who was on the NWF advisory board, went to the NWF and they said they did not have the money to run with the case either. He was told we needed an agency on this case. About that time, Dexter got his temporary assignment as Assistant U.S. Attorney. We knew Dexter was an old, swamp-loving airboater and would love to see our documents. They went to Dexter and the case against the State of Florida was filed because Superintendent Finely of ENP supported it and got credit for initiating the litigation, since a federal agency had to take this action.

In the early 1990s, I went to the Keys to watch a Congressional Field Hearing held by Congressman Vento. He was not one of our favorite congressmen because in our opinion he did not support sportsmen. He was also why I joined the Minnesota Deer Hunters' Association. Their support was required to make sure the BCNP Addition was as sportsmen friendly as we could make it. This created a real problem because hunters trap in Minnesota. We frog in the Big Cypress; we do not trap. My Minnesota friends had a real problem with us dropping out "trapping" and replacing it with

Freddy Fisikelli a real leader & conservationist.

"frogging." They were not going to support the bill because of this. After much discussion and education, they finally understood how we frogged by riding airboats like a horseman with a lance to gig frogs on many thousands of acres of swamp, since we could no longer trap in Florida; they decided to continue their support. The inclusion of frogging in the law became a requirement because since 1974 the NPS had banned the taking of all amphibians on their land units. They were moving to ban frogging in the entire Big Cypress National Preserve.

These field hearings would be interesting, and I wanted to see what was going on. Lt. Governor McKay spoke. During his presentation, he said that the governor was going to appoint a committee that would work to bring all parties together and investigate how to save the Everglades. A congressman from Puerto Rico presented a story about how local fisherman told a new hotel company not to build a pier in this certain location since a big wave would knock it down. The company built the pier, and you know what happened—a wave came along and knocked it down. This congressman said that the governor should have knowledgeable sportsmen on this committee. McKay said he understood what the congressman said and was sure there would be. Lt. Governor McKay sat down by me and said I would be on this committee. I said, "Ok."

I heard no more about this matter for a good while. Then one day, I got a call at school—from the governor's office. I was an Assistant Principal at North Miami Senior High. Governor Chiles wanted me to be on the Governor's Sustainable Commission for South Florida. I received permission from my employer to participate. Little did I know this would take two to three days a month for eight years. I did not know it would require tons of reading, editing, and debating on the floor on all sorts of issues that could make South Florida better or worse.

We were charged by the governor to develop a working relationship and trust among all the parties on the commission, to look at and evaluate all South Florida, to make recommendations to create a better place to live, to develop a plan to restore the Everglades, and provide for the needs of society and nature. The common analogy used by the commission was a three-legged stool: one leg was nature; one leg was agriculture; and one leg was urban needs. Without all three legs intact and working, the stool would not work.

We worked for a few years to understand the issues and to develop trust among the groups. During this time, no one was paying any attention to the commission. There were few reporters and fewer members of the public addressing us on their issues and concerns. Then, once we started to develop the plan and look at what really had to be done, folks started to come around and tell us what they thought needed to be done. The ACoE or some other agency came up with the bright and clever idea to break the South Florida Ecosystem Restoration into components. I am sure this idea came from a political operative.

Anyway, we worked up a long list of projects titled Critical Projects. Then, money became available to fund these projects and everyone became interested in our work. After all, if their pet project made the top ten, money would come their way to do their project. After much debate and lobbying by those with interests, we came up with a good list. There were many more projects than there was money, see the list below and the following map. In our opinion, if these projects were not done, then the Everglades system could not be restored or even repaired.

Critical Projects list as it evolved from the one created by the Sustainable Commission:

ACTIVE PROJECTS by Rank

1. East Coast Canal Structures (C-4)
2. Tamiami Trail Culverts
4. Florida Keys Carrying Capacity Study
5. Western C-11 Water Quality Treatment
6. Seminole Big Cypress Reservation Water Conservation Plan
9. Southern Crew Project Additions and Imperial River Flowway
10. Lake Okeechobee Water Retention and Phosphorous Removal
11. Ten Mile Creek Water Preserve Area
15. Lake Trafford Restoration

PROJECTS MOVED TO OTHER PROGRAMS

3. Melaleuca Quarantine Facility

7. Southern Golden Gate Estate Hydrologic Restoration

8A. South Miami-Dade Agriculture and Rural Area Retention Plan

8B. South Biscayne Bay Watershed Management Plan

12. L-28 Modification Report

13. Loxahatchee Slough Ecosystem Restoration

14. Geodetic Vertical Control Surveys

16. L-31E Flow Redistribution

20. North Fork of the New River

The author resting at a turkey "fly" camp.

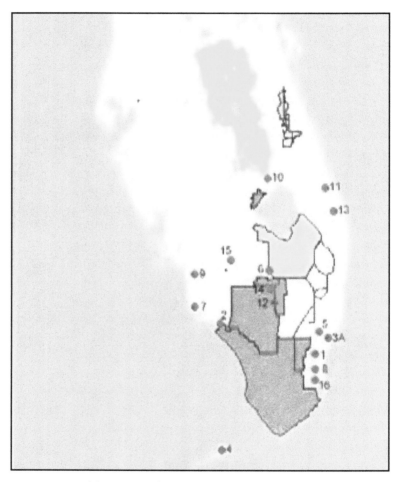

General location of the critical projects to restore the Everglades. These are not budgeted as a part of CERP.

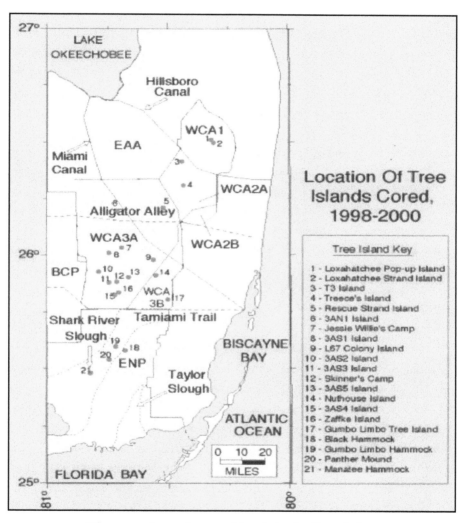

These are the major tree islands in the Everglades.

The governor had called together all the interested parties involved in the Everglades litigations and those who would be impacted by any actions to Save the Everglades when the water delivery philosophy and infrastructure were changed. There were forty of the most hardheaded, distrustful folks in one room you ever saw. But after beating up on each other and with some skillful mediation and leadership by Chairman Richard Pettigrew, we began to work together and develop a conceptual plan that would go to the governor and Congress. It was pretty good and by 2003 much of what we recommended had started to come about. However, there was much to be done before the entire plan was finished.

Once our report was done, The Governor's Sustainable Commission for South Florida was sunsetted and a new Everglades Commission was created. It did not meet too many times since the real work was in DC where everyone was working to pass the Comprehensive Everglades Restoration Act (CERP). The Everglades Coordinating Council hired retired Congressmen Marlenee to lobby for us and our CERP interests. I went to Washington representing the council on a few occasions to push CERP's wildlife needs over too much water and sportsmen's issues. We were somewhat successful.

Sportsmen found the restoration effort extremely interesting in that those responsible now wanted to undo what we had tried to stop many years before. For example, the L-29 canal is a canal that runs beside U.S. 41 in the Shark River Slough area, the eastern part of what is now the Everglades. We had tried to stop them when they wanted to make this canal deeper and wider and make a very big levee. Now they wanted to push in this levee, and backfill the canal. Another quick example is the Miami Canal. For years, this canal did not go all the way to the L-5 pumping station, the levee on the county line between Broward County and Palm Beach County. Before the canal was dug to the station, it would pump its water down a short stub canal, and this would cause the water to spread out onto the Everglades to sheet flow on south. When the canal was finished, which we tried to stop, the water would then rush on south to Miami and beyond. The sheet flow was stopped at the northern end of the Everglades. Thus, this part of the Everglades dried out and burned badly when we had fires in the spring. We lost many acres of uplands and higher ridges in the north end of WCA3-North.

Sportsmen also, before my time, stopped the creation of the world's largest pumping station at the gap. This was an area between L-28 as it runs north from U.S. 41 and south from S.R. 84. This pumping station was intended to send water via four big canals to the East Coast. The water would come from eastern Collier County and Hendry County. Thus, it would become a flood control structure and allow for urban development in this part of Florida for big landowners like the Collier Corporations and ALICO. However, under CERP, this pumping station without the four big canals is to be built. The ACoE says it is needed to allow them to bring the necessary water from the new reservoirs being built and Lake Okeechobee to Everglades National Park via Shark River Slough. I say this is true but, also, because they are not removing the L-28 Interceptor that goes north of I-75, they are installing the necessary infrastructure needs to allow for urban development in North Eastern Collier County and Eastern Hendry County.

By developing a CERP plan that included this new pumping station, the ACoE/SFWMD made sure they could circumvent the wishes of Broward County's citizens and their elected leaders. After the early 1970s flood, ACoE and SFWMD pointed out that whenever there is a lot of rain, a large area of cattle land in Hendry County was flooded to a depth of ten feet. This was because they built the L-1 and L-2 in the wrong places. The water from this part of Hendry County flows into the Everglades, to the southeast, and not to the north or west where the levees are trying to make this water go. Their new 1970s Hendry County plan was to pump this polluted water into the Everglades in Broward County. We got wind of the plan and the public hearing to be held in the Broward County Commission chambers and packed the building with sportsmen conservationists. In the end, we were able to get the Broward County Commission to take a stand against this plan and state that none of this water is allowed to be pumped into Broward's Everglades. The bottom line is that in the end when CERP is done, this part of Florida will have flood protection suitable for development and more dirty water will be pushed into the Everglades.

At the same time Tom Shirley and Lee Chamberlain created a book using their old photos, newspaper reports and documents from the SFWMD. This book was to show how the water depths being sought in CERP at that time would not repair the Everglades but destroy it. It would destroy it because the Everglades only has eighteen inches of water in it for a part of the year. The rest of the year, it has much less water and for a part of the year, it must be dry. While I was on the Sustainable Commission, I

Lee Chamberlain at Camp Red Bug.

was being told by Tom and other sportsmen who were hired to take experts out to study the Everglades that these folks wanted to put too much water in the Everglades. I would bring these issues up and most people would ignore them. Dexter who now spoke for the Miccosukee Tribe, was bringing up the same issues.

The Council determined that since none of the decision-makers were listening to me, Tom and Lee's book needed to be created and sent to Congress. Lee mailed them in bulk to subcommittee and committee chairs. We think most were held until after the bill was heard. But a few got through because I carried them there and Ron used them. These few were enough to wake folks up and make a difference.

At the same time the Sustainable Commission was working, there was a Lower East Coast Water Supply Committee. Freddy Fisikelli was our primary member and B. J. Powell and I were his backups. This committee started before the Sustainable Commission and lasted a year longer. The reason for this committee's existence was the water supply to the Gold Coast of Florida. This was the real driving force behind the Everglades Restoration. The public water supply people—developers and major landowners—wanted to make sure that the Gold Coast had plenty of cheap fresh water. Without cheap fresh water they would stand to lose money and development would become much more costly. After the Sustainable was over and CERP was a law, this committee made sure that their report would key into CERP and provide cheap water to those who needed it. While Freddy did his best to keep the committee's report from being extremely harmful, he was but a minority on the committee and like me was not completely successful in his endeavors. Also, because he was a volunteer as well, he was at a real disadvantage.

We know Tom's book made a difference because of negotiations with the Airboat Association of Florida (AAoF). Their club property sits in the middle of Shark Slough that is in the East Everglades. In the days of the legislative battles over Everglades National Park expansion, we were able to get Senator Graham to draw a line around this property. The club was not in ENP. It was not an inholder. It was the only non-Indian private property on the South side of U.S.41. Well, the ACoE had contacted the AAoF president and wanted to survey the property to develop plans to pay for water damage. The club met with ACoE folks. I was invited and asked not to be introduced so I could hear what these ACoE folks had

Bruce Brock—another real leader and conservationist—from Minnesota.

to say about their needs and impacts of water. This was before Tom's book was sent out. I heard the ACoE lands people explain that there would be a need to raise the entire property and all the buildings four feet to keep them from being flooded due to CERP. Mind you, this club had been there since the very late 1940s and had never been under water. Sometime after Tom's book was out, the ACoE lands people decided they no longer needed to raise the AAoF property as much as they first reported. This could only mean one thing—the water would not be as high as initially reported.

We know hiring Congressman Marlenee, at $20,000 to help us in DC as Bruce Brock suggested, was working as well. These investments were showing up in presentations being made by ACoE folks and others.

It is a matter of time to see if these investments pay off in the end with a repaired Everglades that sportsmen and others can enjoy. We had the concepts of no increased flood damage caused by CERP, no legal water user cut off from their water, and base lines studies needed for authorized and unauthorized recreational uses and how these would be replaced. All this is tied into CERP. Most of the environmental people and water supply folks consider the statement about no legal water user cut off from their use of the water until a replacement was made available as only applying to potable and agriculture water needs. They did not think that the statement would also apply to the sportsmen's use of the water as canal fisherman or duck hunters or deer hunters. But these words in CERP do apply to the interest of sportsmen's activities that require water.

Flooding on Tamiami Trail was evident of how deep they wanted to make the water when CERP was done.

The ACoE employees explained how the water would go over the top of U.S. 41 once CERP was done, and three trillion gallons of water would no longer be pumped annually into the sea but sent back into the Everglades. They were now saying just what I was saying in the Sustainable Committee and the council was saying all over the USA. The advent of the computer allowed us to get the message out fast—ACoE wanted to put too much water in the Everglades. Tom's book went on the Internet to be seen by the world.

Our message was simple and easy to follow: Half the Everglades are gone north of U.S. 41. All of Florida Bay is there that God created. You cannot put 100% of the pre-drainage water in the Everglades that is left and restore it. If you place 100% of pre-drainage water, which is what Everglades National Park and Florida Bay needs, in the 50% of the Everglades that is left, you will drown the remaining Everglades. Everyone could understand this.

The AAoF land became a focal point regarding how sportsmen would be treated in Everglades Restoration. To help one understand how this would happen, I have to go into a bit of the business of the Sustainable. While meeting in the Omni Hotel in Miami-Dade County, we received a report from a group called "The Man in the Biosphere Project." The presenters had a good sales pitch and made the project sound great. Then someone on the commission let it slip that they, all the federal representatives and some selected other commissioners, had met in a secret place in the northeast for a weekend meeting. Since all these folks were either federal or state employees, I am sure their expenses were paid. Anyway, at this meeting they investigated the Man in the Biosphere project and thought it was a good thing for the Sustainable to adopt. This statement set off a lot of red lights. In short order, one of the commissioners who had not attended this secret meeting asked if this was not a potential violation of the Florida Sunshine Act. (This was an act passed by Florida to make the government stop operating behind closed doors.) The Man in the Biosphere program essentially made all the current public lands that are undeveloped off-limits to all human access. No scientist, no hunters, no camping, no fisherman could enter because the land would be locked up. Chairman Richard A. Pettigrew, being the good leader he was, quickly made a chairman's decision that this was not an issue the sustainable would act on and stopped the presentation. After all, Chairman Pettigrew had stated at our first sustainable meeting that hunting would remain a part of the Everglades.

This one action set in motion a change of attitude by many that the federal people really wanted to get people out of the Everglades—all people, not just those living in the 8.5 square mile area of the East Everglades.

Keeping this in the back of my mind many sustainable meetings later, I made a motion that was really needed. I moved that we support the "raising of U.S. 41 across Shark River Slough and provide access for the private landowners along the road." It was seconded and then Superintendent Ring really surprised me as he amended the motion to include access for the public-to-public land. I accepted this as a friendly amendment. Actually, I had planned on amending my own motion in the same way if needed.

There was no debate since the NPS and the hunters were now on the same page. The motion passed with unanimous approval.

Years later, we reviewed our draft and final draft that would create the final document. In both the draft and final draft, my amended motion on raising U.S. 41 and allowing for access to public and private property was included. Then to my shock at the last sustainable meeting, this motion had been butchered. The motion that went to Congress and the state only listed raising the road. All the people's stuff had been cut out.

These two incidents were the first that caused us to realize that the real intention of the DOI/NPS/USFWS was to remove all people from the Everglades via Everglades Restoration. From then on, there was a continual battle to keep the people in the Everglades. The one thing all the Sustainable Commissioners could agree on—they all enjoyed the Everglades in some form of recreation—was the one thing the Feds wanted to stop.

The conspiracy (I call it this as I do not think Federal agencies are stupid, ignorant or negligent) to get rid of the Airboat Association of Florida continued. Rock Salt had a job title change from Executive Director of South Florida Ecosystem Restoration to "Director of Stake Holder Concerns for DOI Lands in South Florida." At least, that is the title we gave him. What this made-up title means to me is he was now paid to handle the sportsmen's interests and concerns and any other group that could be considered a stakeholder in Everglades Restoration and would be impacted by DOI land decisions. I can truly say the Rock looked for solutions

Cape Sable Seaside Sparrow in the hands of an ENP researcher. The bird that destroyed the Everglades under USFWS single species management policies.

and understood the love sportsmen had for the South Florida ecosystem. He is more in our corner then many in the federal government.

Rock asked me for recommendations for a subcommittee to the Federal Task Force that would address the Cape Sable Seaside Sparrow issues around MOD Waters. I suggested Barbara Jean Powell who was Co-Chair of Allied Sportsman and Secretary of Everglades Coordinating

Council, Freddy Fisikelli who was a commissioner of the newly chartered Southwest Ranches City of Broward County, and Joel Marco from the Airboat Association of Florida. Rock did not put Joel on the committee because he thought Joel's issues would be too narrow. Why not be narrow as he would be representing the only private landowner on the south of U.S. 41 in Shark River Slough that was not Native American Indian? Could the answer be the federal government really wants to take the AAoF property? It sure looks like it at this point, but time will tell.

There are two tribal camps along this part of Tamiami Trial. Neither the Army Corps of Engineers nor the DOI/NPS could take these lands; therefore, they paid many millions to raise them above the expected high-water line that would be caused by Everglades Restoration. Rock explained to me that the ACoE could not do this for the AAoF lands. They could not treat the club the same as they did the Indians because they were neither agency nor Indian. This strikes me and many others as a discriminatory act and a violation of the U.S. Constitution. In further conversation with Rock, it came out that ACoE had not included the AAoF lands in their proposal to Congress, so their needs were not funded. I explained to Rock that it sounded like either ignorance, negligence, or conspiracy. Rock said he would talk with Dennis Duke about the matter and get back. Time will tell what happens with this long-standing sportsman's conservation club.

In 2004, I learned that leaving out the full motion I made was not a mistake but an action by the NPS. Bob Johnson, ENP employee, told the CSOP committee that the AAoF was an inholder in the ENP and would be purchased when the last member died who belonged to the AAoF at the time of passage of the ENP Expansion act. Further, he reportedly said they could not have any new members. I do not understand how the DOI/NPS/ENP would know who a member was when the Expansion act was approved. I also do not understand how he could consider the club property as being an inholder when the map we received from Congress clearly had the ENP boundary drawn around their land. The acts of the ACoE, SFWMD, and NPS are clearly directed at taking this sportsmen club from the members who supported the saving of not only Everglades National Park but all the Everglades. The State of Florida had already named WCA3 Wildlife Management Area after Franny Taylor who was one of the founders of the AAoF.

The most amazing information presented by modeling experts to CSOP was that the models were not accurate. CSOP members were told that these models had a plus or minus error of one and half feet (+,-, 1.5 ft). That is a lot of water when one considers the models are covering all the remaining Everglades. This degree of error is disastrous to the health and sustainability of the Everglades. There is no way these models should have any bearing on the projects because it is really useless when one knows that a mere few inches of water elevation mean life and death to the Everglades fauna and biota.

While I was on the Sustainable Commission, I put my archeological work into play in the debate about water depth. I pointed out that there were large oak trees in the Big Cypress that had been girdled by the Seminoles before Florida became a state and before the four main drainage canals were built in the 1800s. These areas were dry before statehood or they would not have grown 100-year-old oak trees on them. The man-caused 1994-95 floods is a key event for water depth measurement as it was the first time we saw how much water they wanted in a restored Everglades. This level of water was covering these oak tree islands with water. They had put water over these Indian farm areas long enough to kill large, living oak trees. If ACoE and SFWMD planned on putting that much water in to the Everglades, then they would be destroying a good part of the Big Cypress.

Right, the floods of the 1990s were man enhanced. Though the rain had been excessive, the real problem was how the ACoE and SFWMD were operating the sixteen-county drainage and flood protection system. It was explained by Dexter to all on the sustainable that even though the SFWMD knew massive amounts of rain were on the way, they would not drop the water table in the canals and the system. The water was not lowered because they did not want to interfere with Modified Water Deliveries Experimental test iteration number 7. This work is commonly called MOD Waters and was a part of the Everglades National Park Expansion Act of 1988. The ACoE, DOI/NPS and SFWMD were directed to test different scenarios of delivering water to Everglades National Park. They were to test the system in a manner that it had not been designed for.

Dexter went on to point out that all the water gauges on the East Coast were six inches above their maximum schedule, yet the SFWMD would not drop the water. Thus, they caused millions of dollars' worth of damage to farms, urban areas, and the economy. Just as bad, they continued to expedite the destruction of Lake Okeechobee, St. Lucie estuary, Caloosahatchee estuary, and the Kissimmee River basin. Right, to test a system that was not physically ready for more water they turned off and/or turned around the pumps to stop water from being pushed to the ocean. In short, they destroyed the Everglades that belonged to Florida (this is the area north of U.S. 41) to see if they could save the Everglades that belonged to the DOI/NPS. They also showed everyone how much water they really wanted in the Everglades north of U.S. 41; this was not going to restore or repair the Everglades but continue its destruction. The really sad thing is most of the environmental groups, who lacked the real-world experiences we had in the area, thought the DOI/NPS was correct. These well-meaning but misdirected groups were now working to destroy the Everglades, a wetland, and make it a littoral zone. Some years later I obtained via a FOIA all the documents from the ACoE on their MOD Water testing. After reading these sixty pounds of paper, I learned that Dexter was correct. These floods of the 1990s did not have to be as bad as they were if only the ACoE, DOI/NPS and SFWMD had stopped their testing.

We pointed out that the elevation of the land south of U.S. 41 in East Slough where the Cape Sable Seaside Sparrow (CSSS), an endangered species, lived was a certain elevation while U.S. 41 and the land north of the road was a higher elevation. If they put the amount of water they said they wanted into the Everglades, the CSSS could not live, the Tamiami Trail would be under water, and all the uplands would be destroyed. Further, they would make the Everglades a littoral zone as Arron Heiger, USGS, told Tom and I right before he retired from that agency. According to Dr. Paul Gray of the National Audubon Society, by definition a wetland has to have an annual drying. He made this statement when talking about the health of Lake Okeechobee. Yet, the wetlands in the Everglades were not going to dry out for many years if CERP was completed as was being planned.

By now, knowledgeable people realized the ACoE and DOI had learned how to use water as a weapon. By this, I mean they have learned that if they only stalled the implementation of MOD Waters as Congress and the nation had directed them to, they had a tool to remove people living in the 8.5 Square Mile Area of Miami-Dade County. This was an area located on the west side of the last levee in western Dade County. We had an ACoE engineer explain to us that development was not wrong, the levee was built in the wrong place. No matter, the DOI and their support forced the issue by keeping the water high and drowning out these people.

Not only did they use high water as a weapon against the 8.5 SMA, but they were also using it against the Miccosukee Tribe. They knew that every year they stalled implementing MOD Waters and brought about infrastructure changes to U.S. 41 in the Shark Slough area, they were destroying the uplands and islands of the Everglades north of U.S. 41. These islands were where many Miccosukee Indians lived. The logic was simple; no islands, no Indians; no Indians, no funding of legal work by Dexter Lethinen.

In an email, Joette Loraine stated the following: "The Source (addressing where the figure of 200 acres per years of lost uplands) is the Final 8.5 Square Mile Area EIS/GRR. I don't have the document with me and will double check the following, but I think the loss of 8 tree islands equates to a loss of about 200 acres a year. I know they estimate a cost of $50,000 to $500,000 dollars an acre to attempt to restore and/or rebuild. As you know, tree island restoration is in its infancy. It may be that we can never get back what's been lost. The loss to the Miccosukee Tribe's culture and way of life is, of course, incalculable. Dennis Duke testified at a deposition in the Interim Operational Plan case that it would take more than the entire $8.4 billion dollar restoration cost to restore the tree islands lost in WCA 3A (50%) since 1947. In my opinion, it is short-sighted not to count these environmental costs before deciding on an alternative that will delay Mod Waters and cause more tree island loss. It is equally short-sighted to be advocating that water above CERP levels go through WCA 3B as part of Mod Waters, since that would obliterate tree islands there. I think my major concern is that certain folks have lost the ecosystem restoration perspective. We will never get the Everglades restored without it. Thanks for asking. Joette" Her statement sort of places the issue in proper prospectus when one realizes that we are losing eight tree islands a year or about two hundred acres of uplands in the Everglades with more than 50% in one of the Water Conservation Areas already gone.

Not only were they using water as a weapon against the people living in the 8.5 SMA they had realized they could also get rid of the pesky hunter with the same weapon. They soon realized that hunters would stop raising money to file litigation and to become involved in the political venues to save the Everglades if they had no game to hunt in the Everglades. Thus, by not doing MOD Waters and allowing the Everglades to regulate their water depth and duration naturally and properly, they could drown the wildlife or destroy the uplands it needed to survive. This strategy was working because while there were many hunters living in South Florida, they were leaving the area and the state to hunt. They were comminuting to Texas, Alabama, Georgia, and South Carolina in droves to enjoy the outdoors. Not only was their money leaving Florida and South Florida so were their political contacts and interest. This was the major objective of those who wanted to use the WCAs, the Everglades, for water supply and water storage reasons.

From the minutes of the CSOP committee created by Rock Salt there was data sent to these committee members with an explanation from the DOI about how they had harmed the Everglades during their testing for MOD Waters. They also stated that Test 7 was stopped because of the Cape Sable Seaside Sparrow litigation filed by NRDC and supported by the FWF. If it had not been for this litigation, they would not have stopped Test 7 and there would be no uplands in the Everglades because MOD Waters testing was destroying the remaining uplands. I once again remember what our ACoE neighbor had told us forty years earlier about how water would be stacked up like a lake all the way to the northern end of Broward County one day. This would be done by the building of the S-12 facilities on U.S. 41. It sounds like his prediction will come true.

Again, within a few weeks of Tom's book getting out, the ACoE decided they did not need to raise the ground levels and buildings on the AAoF club property. The water was no longer going to get that deep. Imagine that these folks decided they had planned to put too much water in the Everglades. Only time will tell if this holds true for the duration of this thirty-five year $8.5-billion water project. Others will have to continue this battle if they want to protect the swamps and stay in them. I had spent thirty-five years fighting a *Road That Changed Florida* and the nation that led me on many other roads; I was moving to Texas and becoming a grandfather.

Years after Dexter filed his litigation, Governor Chiles said the state was wrong and resolved the case by settling it with the U.S. Attorney's office. I was summoned to a meeting in the SFWMD office in Palm Beach to talk with Cabinet aides about this matter. There were but a few people in the Storch Room to listen to the aides talk and the U.S. Attorney who had taken Dexter's place. We listened but did not like what we heard; since we were only friends of the court in this case, we had no real power. Besides, we did not have millions to pay our own attorney to keep the fight going until we had a full win. After this meeting, we were invited to an EAA reception at a nearby restaurant. My friend, Pete, who had worked for ENP, was there and we developed a conversation about where to get money to pay for the needed water infrastructure changes.

At this time, Florida's leaders were talking about raising the tolls on all toll roads. This idea stuck with me, and I almost jokingly told Pete we should raise the toll on the Alley by a quarter and use that quarter to help pay for the water infrastructure needs. Pete thought that was a great idea, so he pulled the governors cabinet aide and his bosses together to hear this idea. I shared it with them. As usual, ideas are beat up before they move on to reality. The aide said she was concerned about the political fallout for raising another toll on other toll roads. The EAA folks really liked the idea until I said that money could be used to support bonds and purchase their land. Pete did not like this too much, even if I was kidding.

The idea was liked, and a state law was passed that took surplus funds from the current $1.50 (seventy-five cents on each end) Alley toll and applied that to water infrastructure needs. The next year, the idea went to Congress as a Sustainable idea, and it became a federal law. One never knows when a simple idea at a party will become the law.

I also found out later that Mr. Hibbard had given up his share of these Alley tolls for the three recreational access sites in the Big Cypress National Preserve. He told me Estus had called and wanted to know if Hibbard needed these funds. Hibbard said he did not because he thought there was money in the NPS budget for these now federally required projects on I-75, but as expected, the NPS had no money so the sites are not built.

In the meantime, I-75 was built, and Broward had their three recreational sites. There was one site built at the 71-mile post where the old main buggy trail crossed S.R. 84, long before that road was built. This buggy trail can be traced back to the 1930s when used by Baxter as he took his Yankee eco-tourist to Baxter's Island. It is also where the real estate company built their road, Cypress Lane, into the Baxter Island area that later the oil company improved. It was also where I could access my property. In Collier County, all three recreational sites are located where there is either a very old, well-established buggy trail or other ground disturbances like L-28.

During the building of I-75, I talked with the road builder. His foreman needed some advice about land matters to the west. We met at Camp Red Bug and I told him what I knew. During the conversation, he wanted to know if his boss could visit me at camp and if I would take him for a buggy ride like we had done. Being one to always take new folks into the cypress, I said sure, and we set a date.

During this trip with the owner of White Construction, I asked him when he was going to close the fence gap to Cypress Road from I-75. He said he could leave it open until the very last day. Thus, I had access to my camp for the entire time I-75 was being constructed in the middle '80s. This was great and we stopped maintaining Cypress Road as we were the only ones in the woods and did not want to make it too easy for others to

get in. We had a 4x4 truck with big tires. The NPS considered this road "as my private drive" as it was built on the deeded right-of-way of the land project, see the letter in the appendix. Well, we came and went from I-75 until a week after hurricane Andrew.

Kathryn and I climbing a mountain of dirt used to build I-75 on Alligator Alley

During this time, I had asked the foreman if I could get some dirt from his road job to put around my citrus trees. This would help keep their roots out of the water when it rose each year. Since the NPS had acted to restore Turner River based on Pete's work, the water in the Baxter Island area had become higher. The water table stayed so high that the bottoms of the sloughs did not dry out anymore. They always stayed damp even in the driest time of spring. The action of plugging Turner River Canal made me haul in tons of ready-mix concrete for the barn floor. It was good to be able to do this without having to go across country or unload and handle eighty-pound bags of ready mix a number of times.

The foreman told me I could get the dirt I needed while I was at camp for a full week during spring break. This would allow me plenty of time to shovel dirt. I got one load, and it was too much work so I stopped. One day during my week at camp, the foremen stopped by. He said, "I see you got some dirt" I told him that was all I was going to get. He said don't worry, "I will take care of you." Well, before they closed the gate, he had a big sixteen-wheeler dump truck drop a full load in my front yard. Denny and I shoveled dirt for many days. By 1995, I wished I had several more loads as the SFWMD flooding of the Everglades was backing water up onto my property.

Camp Red Bug on Baxter Island, 1980.

Chapter Eleven

◆ ◆ ◆

The Big Cypress Returns to Its Wilderness Character, Building Swamp Buggies

Since 1971, I knew the day would come that there would be a fence by I-75, and I would not be able to get to camp that way unless I could get public access. But to prepare for not being able to get this public access site built, I did what other camp owners had done. I built a big buggy. The first one was a Model A: Poke-A-Long. I did not build this one from scratch but rebuilt it as needed. I also started to learn how to get to camp from Turner River Road and from US41 at Monument Lake. During off-season when it was dry, I would drive to these locations and remember how to get there and where deep water would be or where soft ground was. This was done before GPS units were available. It was done before computer maps were available. We had to learn the country

Pepe Rosenthal and me on Poke-A-Long— a Model-A buggy.

and remember each stump, rock, hole and turn. It was exciting and not many could get as far back in as I did. After all, it was fourteen miles from Turner River Road and thirty-five miles from Monument Lake. The shorter route was only four hours away if all went well. The longer route was six hours away and again that was only if all went well. We never saw others in the woods until the walk access parking lot, vault toilet, and gate were built on I-75.

Before the recreation walk gate was open, I took Pete Rosenthal and his son to Camp Red Bug. On the way back to Wiggin's landing on Turner River Road, fourteen miles from camp, the buggy broke down. Right then,

I decided I needed a buggy built out of more modern steel. We were riding along in the spring of the year when the water was down but not completely gone as I shifted the four-speed transmission the shift lever came off in my hands. There we were with me holding the gearshift in my hand and the transmission in neutral. I know Pete thought we were in real trouble.

Poke-A-Long coming out of East Crossing.

The main reason one should build one's own buggy is to be able to handle these types of problems. I took off the floorboard center section. It was built for just such a case. Then the top of the transmission came off. I put the buggy in granny and the top back on. I told Pete we would get on, but it would take some time. We were about four miles from the Wiggins landing where the truck was parked. He and Pepe, his son, enjoyed the slow pace and walked most of the way in as we crossed Copeland Prairie. They would come back to the buggy to get a drink or ride a bit then get off again to go look at something else. We had a real good time.

Later that year, Dave Balman gave me an old two-wheel drive Model A which had two transmissions. It was just what I needed to leave at camp and use to hunt. It would be a good back-up as Poke-A-Long was getting old and I feared more problems since the breakdown with Pete. It was easy to rebuild the buggy Dave gave me. I asked Kathryn, our daughter, what color to paint the new buggy and she chose pink. I do not think she really thought I would paint the buggy pink, but I did, and we called it the Pink Panther. It worked great; the back tires were four feet tall and twelve inches wide. It had a fully welded, locked rear end so it could not get stuck unless both tires went down. Then you could place it in reverse-reverse wrap a cable or heavy rope around the axle hub and let it wind itself out of the hole.

One weekend, Denny, Debbie, Stu, Burney, and I went to camp, on Poke-A-Long. Burney had his ATC stored in the barn and ranged out looking for deer and hogs. He found a lot of signs several miles to the southeast. We decided to go there in the morning. For

Pink Panther Model-A two-wheel drive

some reason, Poke-A-Long was not working well. It would run awhile and then stop. After it sat for a few minutes, it would run again. I thought it might be an electrical contact breaking down. Because of this problem, we took the Pink Panther. While going down Cypress Lane, one tire of the locked rear end gripped more than the other pushing me into a big pine tree. In the blink of an eye at four a.m. in the morning, we rolled over and were in the canal along the road. Luckily, we were not hurt, and no guns damaged but the Pink Panther was dead.

That weekend, for the first and only time ever, we had other hunters camped near camp Red Bug. Ben Rowe and his son heard the crash and came over to help us. They took us and our gear back to camp. We dried off, calmed down, and drove Poke-A-Long back to drag Pink Panther to camp. Over the next year, I cut up Pink Panther with cutting torches and pulled big parts under the fence to take home for the new buggy. I gave the engine and rear end to Wayne, my woods neighbor. Nothing went to waste as we even burned the wood body for a campfire.

A year after the Pink Panther wreck, 1988, I got a phone call from Pete Rosenthal. He said he had four tires they did not need and if I wanted them to meet him at Oakalanta on Saturday. He cautioned me that they were big tires, and I would need a big trailer to get all four matched tires. I was excited, as this is what I needed to make my modern cross-country buggy. I already had a big rear end in the back yard. The tires were big 24.5x26 R2 tractor tires that were just what I wanted to build a nice two-wheel drive buggy. I traded two tires with Dave Charland for the steel to build the buggy, bought a 1971 in-line, six-cylinder, Chevy engine, had a 350-turbo hydromatic reworked for low RPM high torque application, and rebuilt a big Ford dump truck 4-speed transmission and rear end. I took the back tires from the Pink Panther and put them on the front of the new buggy—BIG GREEN. I paid Robert's Radiator to build me a four-core three-eighths fin copper radiator that was twice the size of the stock car radiator. Pete Theis of Miami Drive Line rebuilt both of the second transmissions; one went in the buggy, and one was for a spare. He also rebuilt the Chevy 2-ton truck rear end and put a 7 to 1 ring and pinion in it. This would give me an awesome gearing capability. In the lowest gear, I would have 3.76 in the automatic, 7.5 to 1 in granny (first) gear second transmission and 7 to 1 in the rear end for a total reduction of 197.4 to 1 at the wheels. Richard Larkin built the wheels after I gave him the rims, which were obtained from Long Wheel and Rim in Jacksonville, Florida.

By now, with I-75 fenced, we were putting more than a thousand hard miles a year on the buggy as we went to camp and hunted or explored out from camp each year. These trips were like going on a safari to a far-off country or another state. We had to have everything we needed with us and be able to handle all sorts of problems and be totally self-reliant. There was no one else in the woods once we got past Camp Wet Foot except those who used Camp Poor Boy. These were good days, but they were hard on

Big Green on Copeland Prairie headed to camp.

man and machine. We did break down on a few trips and/or became stuck. All of this added to the mystique of going to camp.

I built my buggies at home in the garage. The city did not like them in the yard and more importantly, neither did my wife. Thus, all of them had to be able to drive into our double-car garage. Big Green and Poke-A-Long both had an inch of clearance when the air was let out of all the tires.

I frequently asked those who hunted with me to come over to help with the design, holding parts, or painting of a buggy. We worked together on these projects. One day, I could not get anyone to come by to help and I really wanted to install the big, new tires on Big Green. Kathryn was in high school, and I figured even with her small stature she could work the handle of a high-lift jack. She had never done this before, so I gave her careful instructions on how to make it go up. I got the buggy up to almost the right height for me to slip, pull and winch the big tires onto the lugs. The only thing was the buggy, being a narrow 80 inches wide when the tires were on it, had other ideas. It started to slide to the side every time I pulled or pushed the big tire. I was afraid it would fall on me and on through the wall ending up in the living room. I started telling Kathryn to let it down. She did not. Then I realized I had not told her how to lower the jack. This was a very close call and one of the closest in all the years I built buggies at home. pull and winch the big tires onto the lugs. The only thing was the buggy, being a narrow 80 inches wide when the tires were on it, had other ideas. It started to slide to the side every time I pulled or pushed the big tire. I was really afraid it would fall on me and on through the wall ending up in the living room. I started telling Kathryn to let it down. She did not. Then I realized I had not told her how to lower the jack. This was a very close call and one of the closest in all the years I built buggies at home."

Big Green was good to go in five months. I had one heck of a machine. It would carry all I could put on it and almost as many people as I wanted at camp and their gear.

It took from 1971 to 1999 to get one gate built so the public could use their land from I-75. This one walk gate is required by the Big Cypress National Preserve Addition Act along with two others to the east. The NPS-approved I-75 recreational access plan had been done for many years and the FDOT plans for these other facilities had been eighty-five percent finished and on the shelf for many years. All the public wanted to do was to have access from I-75 to their land as established in Governor B. Graham's Save the Everglades Program.

It sure was good to walk through this gate and to enjoy the Big Cypress National Preserve.

With the gate now available and only a two-mile hike on my driveway to camp, I no longer needed Big Green, so it was sold to one of the leaseholders on the Lykes Ranch. This meant I had to build another buggy. Thus, the Gray Ghost was born from a 1971 Jeep Gladiator truck.

A lot of folks do not know it, but as the Viet Nam war phased out, Jeep used their military spec. parts to build this truck. Those built after 1971 are not likely to have these stronger parts.

Thus, I had a great vehicle to put the 12.5x24 tractor tires on and only had to remove the old body and build my own. The entire project only took four weeks. We had a great buggy up until the time I sold it with Camp Red Bug.

It only took 28 years of work to get a gate for the public to access their land from I-75. October 26, 1996, was the first trip we could legally make it through this public access gate!

From junk to buggy in four weeks. Denny is saying we are going to do WHAT?

Denny, Bill, and Ross with a palmetto fattened hog.

Some years, we had an abundant crop of palmetto berries. This was great as there would be a lot of food for the deer and hogs. They would eat them until they could hardly move, particularly the hogs. Sometimes late in the berry season, there might be enough still on the plants that the heat fermented them. I know some who have not seen this will not believe this, but it does happen every now and then. When it does happen, the hogs are fat. They will eat enough fermented berries until they become drunk. When this happens, they are likely to stumble around all day and night. If one is careful and quiet, he can walk up on the hogs as they stumble around making loud grunting noises. We experienced this on two occasions.

Kathryn on her camp swing, five years old.

Chapter Twelve

◆ ◆ ◆

The DOI/NPS Make Their Move to Turn the Preserve into a Park and Good Hunts at Camp

In 2000, we had new ORV regulations and new ideas about how the cypress should be managed. Nothing was new; it was just more of the same—LIKE A PARK!

I thought it best to work with the NPS as they built their management plan and put in many hours developing a thoughtful ORV primary and secondary trail system. I took the NPS folks to the woods to show them what I was talking about. I drove the eighty miles to their office to work with them. They used a good bit of what I suggested, but they still had it in their mind that we should not move about in their land by way of buggy or airboat. Their trail system was much too restrictive and eventually locked up about eighty percent of the Preserve; this did not include the Addition that we had not been on since 1986 when it was hunted as leased land.

The NPS continued to press on with making their rock road ORV trails. We nicknamed them the Yellow Brick Roads or YBRs. This was because they cost so much to build. Not only did they cost a lot to build, but they will cost more to maintain. As one would expect, when lime rock is soaked and/or under water and vehicle rides over it, that rock will dissolve and float away. This was evident the first-year roads were installed.

NPS Rock Road (YBR) and fill for more road building without a 404 permit.

The Army Corps of Engineers (ACoE) was notified that superintendent Donahue was placing miles of rock on the wetlands of the Big Cypress

National Preserve. The superintendent stated he did not need a 404 permit to do this. Yet, the ACoE sent him a cease-and-desist letter calling him a "knowing violator." We figured this was good because a few years earlier the ACoE had fined the FWC $30,000 for de-mucking a lake without a 404 permit. Further, we thought this ACoE action would get the NPS back to the original plan. This plan was to rock the buggy trails for a mile or so back into the woods from the highway entrance points. This would relieve some of the pressure on the ground at these points of concentration. The original plan only few years earlier had the NPS stabilizing trail areas that were particularly soft or across marl prairies where there were no routes around. But the NPS took a good idea and turned in it to a multiple-million-dollar 400-mile road-building plan that would eat up a lot of O&M money forever. The outcome of all this paperwork and legal work was nothing. The ACoE sent the issue to the EPA in Atlanta. The EPA then had to administer disciplinary actions. Their actions were to require the NPS to do more restoration of old house pads and canals faster. This was the very thing they were supposed to be doing during the last twenty-five years and to allow them to continue building their roads was the very thing the state's Big Cypress Basin classification of Area of State Critical Concern was supposed to stop.

What their Yellow Brick Roads would also do would be to take the excitement and unexpected out of riding these trails. They would also allow anyone who did not have the right equipment or experience to travel all over the backcountry of the BCNP. All these things would be counter-productive to keeping the wilderness character in the Big Cypress. All these roads would not comply with the charge given the NPS of returning the Big Cypress to its wilderness character. The NPS was turning the Preserve into a Park. The sense of exploring the

Ed and Dad taking on the challenges of the Big Cypress in our Onan buggy. Gone are these challenges because of the NPS rock road system and maps.

unknown was gone from in the Big Cypress because these mapped roads removed this element of the unknown.

Equally as important, these roads would allow the NPS rangers to speed to the backcountry. Without these rock roads, the rangers had to know and learn about the country and trails. This means they had to stay in the Preserve for a very long time to accomplish this educational task. I was told by NPS staff that they could not keep their buggies running. This was due mainly to the unacceptably short time frames rangers were assigned to go into the backcountry and come out. Remember the archeology issues I shared earlier. The same thing was happening with the rangers. They were expected to go to Stone's, twenty-five miles up and twenty-five miles back, work the area and be back at the Oasis Ranger station in eight hours. This is not possible without the Yellow Brick Roads. One of these roads will go right to Stone's where for some reason the NPS has built a new modern cabin. I am also sure the NPS did not pull the first building permit for these new structures.

Another example of how the NPS rangers did not know the Cypress was made clear to me when the rangers assigned to the northern part of the Preserve asked me how I got to my camp after the I-75 fence was installed. The ranger said he had tried to get there from Wiggins' landing but he either got lost or stuck. I said it is easy; leave the landing, go over the railroad tram, turn north, keep the cypress on the left and the oaks on the right. Where these two systems meet, there is one buggy trail, and it goes right to my place in a few miles. It sounds easy but it is not. Try this at night and it becomes even more difficult.

I know it was hard for those without experience or proper understanding and knowledge of the area to get to my camp this way because I had some of the same experiences. One of the first night trips found Denny and me doing circles, in between the railroad bed and the northern end of the prairie most of the night. We drove for hours in what we thought was the correct direction, but soon we crossed our tracks and realized we had taken the correct turn at the wrong island. Once the realization that we were lost set in, we shut down and spent the night on the buggy. At dawn, we went hunting and then figured out where we were and went on to camp.

On more than one occasion, we became stuck and had to winch our way out of the marl, which is like wet mashed potatoes. This was why I carried more than 300 feet of cable, plus 100 feet of logging chain and then a long snatch strap. On several trips we spent the night on the buggy rolled up in our rain gear to stay warm or out of the mosquitoes. But we were always able to eventually get out and get into camp. Getting to camp has always been the first challenge of going to the Big Cypress.

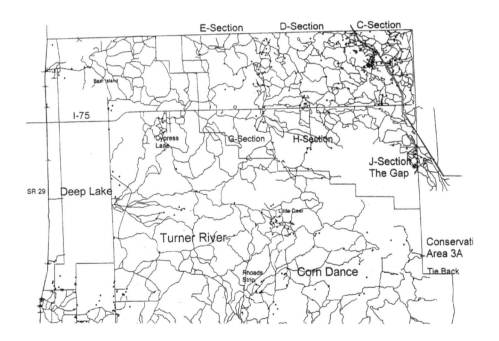

A portion of the NPS map of the original ORV trail system that was on the ground in 1974.

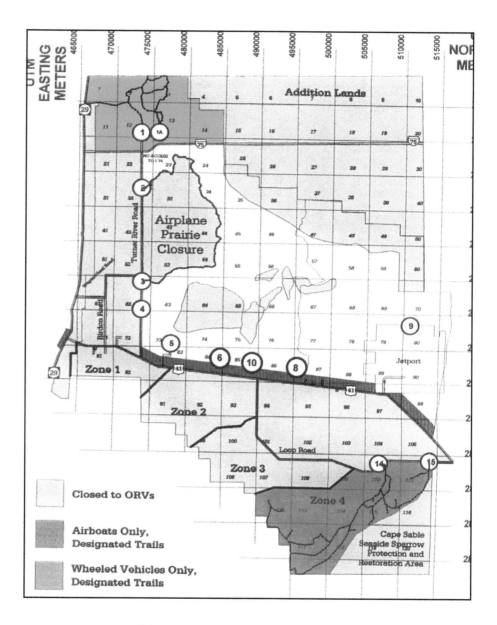

A copy of the NPS ORV map showing how much of the preserve is no longer available to the public because of the loss of ORV historical and traditional ORV trails to these areas. This is 880 square miles of public land.

My last hunt from Camp Red Bug was with Rick. We went to an area we called the oil pad. I had been there several times that year and had seen a lot of deer and hog sign. It was an area of heavy cypress but with plenty of high ground, good mast crop, and plenty of thick palmettos. We saw a lot of deer there and heard hogs on almost every trip.

Rick and I arrived about thirty minutes before daylight. We walked off from the buggy to the west. I put Rick in a tree I had been using and he overlooked a real good set of game trails in the cypress swamp and a stretch of open grass between the cypress strand and a big hammock. There had been no people in this cypress strand other than

Pine trees pushed over, and game trails made by hogs and deer.

us. There were only deer, hogs, bear and turkey and no cows so all the trails in the swamp had to made by game. During several earlier hunts, I had seen many deer and heard big game animals walking in the swamps around my tree.

I went on through the deep cypress with my IZH-308/12, climbing stand, and backpack. We were set to stay the day if need be. I was in an ideal location that was situated by a big hammock with game trails going into it at four spots that I could see. There was the big cypress strand I had walked through; there was a cypress sawgrass area behind me; there was a deep-water cypress strand to my left and then one of the biggest oak hammocks in the area. I was overlooking a small flat with many game trails in it and pines pushed over by hogs.

Around eight o'clock I heard something walking in the water to the north and it was moving my way and using a well-worn game trail. It would take a few noisy steps and stop. It did not act like a deer but more like a person, a bear or big hog. The second time it moved, I knew it was big hog because I could see ten-foot- tall cypress trees moving when it would rub them. Then I could hear the bark tearing as he hooked them with his tusk.

My heart was beating hard as he moved several yards at a time toward me. I could not see him because the sawgrass was much too high and dense. Would he keep coming, or would he turn toward Rick? Would he turn to the west behind me and disappear in the heavier sawgrass or walk

The author in his climbing stand, a mile back in the cypress swamps from his buggy.

down the middle of the big cypress strand between Rick and me and neither of us would take him? Would he keep walking or sense something was wrong and start running? Would I need the 308 or the buckshot? As all these thoughts rushed through my head, I saw his ugly face materialize from the sawgrass. He was looking over the little flat with a great deal of scrutiny. He stood there for what seemed like a long time and I had to fix my eyes ahead of him, make no eye contact, and hold my gun at the ready. I could not cause the small pine I had climbed to move because he would see this and be suspicious. He then started to walk on toward the open flat. As he went behind a small myrtle bush, I raised the gun. I hoped he would not turn into the cypress and disappear. Had I raised the gun too soon and I would have to hold it for a long time? Should I have snapped

The last hog I took from Camp Red Bug

a shot at his head with a shotgun when I first saw him? I had questions and more questions, but I did not really have time to ponder them because he stepped out from behind the myrtle. My crosshairs found his ear and he was down in the shin-deep water.

I sat in the tree watching him and listening for other hogs or deer to move about. Hogs often travel in groups and deer will frequently be near them because the hogs provide another warning to help them avoid the ever-present panther. It was a cool December day, and the meat would not turn green for a long time because he was in the water and the shade of the big Cypress trees.

After a while, Rick raised me on the radio and wanted to know what I had, if anything. I told him I had a big hog and asked him to please come and help me get him out. The work was just starting as two nearly sixty-year-old men carrying lots of gear had to drag this huge hog out to the buggy almost a mile away. We were no longer young men of twenty! It took us two trips to get everything to the buggy. We were wet to the waist and exhausted but satisfied.

Back at camp we weighed the field-dressed hog in at 175 pounds. Many folks will not take these big boar hogs as they think the meat will be tough and strong tasting. We do not hesitate because we soak the meat in ice water for a few days and allow it to age. Before doing this, we remove all the fat and tallow. Then we always slowly cook the meat. This meat is great, and you cannot tell the difference from domestic pork.

175 pounds of pork on the hoof.

This was a fitting hunt for my last one at Camp Red Bug. I had been with a good friend—a friend who helped me build the camp. I had experienced the Big Cypress and its diverse habitat. I had hunted where during this one season I had seen deer, hogs, squirrel, and turkey. A pair of wood ducks had flown by each morning as they went from the roost to their feeding area. I had seen no other hunter or even heard one. I had driven my swamp buggy in tough wet country and not on a Yellow Brick Road. What an experience it was, and it was all on public land!

A few years before I sold the camp, I started to investigate the use of a canoe or gator boat. I thought of carrying it on a swamp buggy mounted canoe rack. I would be able to drive as close as I could on the NPS trail system and then take the boat and get to where we would hunt. It seemed the NPS had put most of their ORV trails where folks would not find game or be able to hunt. Maybe this is what superintendent Hibbard had in mind when years earlier he said they might need to know more precisely where we took game.

Homemade gator boat on wheels and loaded for a three-day hunt.

A three-day gator boat camp.

I finally developed a good design and talked it over with my neighbor Rick. He was very knowledgeable about such things. I made some changes and went to Mike Herndon to have one made. I gave him a simple design: 14 feet long, 28 inches wide at the bottom, 30 inches wide at the top, up sloping bow with a pointed bow, square stern, flat bottom, and ten-inch sides. He built it out of 80-thousands aluminum. I put several coats of steel flex on it to make it slick as glass. It was a one-man modern gator boat that really worked well when there was water. When there was no water, I had a tall heavy-duty bicycle-tire carriage the boat would sit on. It worked well, too. Except it did not work well in muddy marl. I no longer could roam all over the Big Cypress with the freedom to go where I wanted to. I could no longer take off and head to places far off and unknown.

After I sold Camp Red Bug and built my gator boat, we began to explore the cypress in another way. For years, we had looked for high ground; now we were looking for water, the deeper the better. We studied the computer interactive maps to get an idea of the best places to look. No longer did we have to get out into the swamps to see these spots. We could do this from the comfort of our air-conditioned house. We already had a good knowledge of the water where we had been going for years with the buggy. We decided to camp at a place called Mincy; it was so named after the landowner who had dug a nice lake. This would be base camp as we would have high dry ground and water much like the Indians needed.

Rick and I went into the area during archery season. We had few problems moving since the water was high. We both had to work together to pull each boat across the marl flat by Crazy Mary's. Once beyond that, we had deep water to within 100 yards of our camping site. By the time we reached the camping location, we were both exhausted from working for hours in the nearly 100-degree heat and high humidity. The next day we poled our boats to the other side of East Crossing. This was easy as the water was a foot-and-half to four feet deep. On this scouting trip we saw several deer and two fine bucks.

Rick with his last buck from Camp Red Bug

When black powder season came along, we were good to go. We left the road about two hours before dark and barely got to Mincy's by dark to set up our tent camp. We had a comfortable place that allowed us to enjoy a good camp. We were going to stay on until Monday so Denny would come in Saturday night.

Saturday morning, Rick went to his favorite stand to the south-southwest. I went to one of the ladder stands on the far side of Chair Camp. This was a bit far, but I figured it was a good place. I was able to get the boat to Dick's stand and I walked the rest of the way. That morning I had several deer sneak in behind me and run around the island I was sitting by. From the sound they made, I guessed there were four or five deer. I never saw them; I just heard one snort and they all ran, stopped, ran, stopped ran and so on.

I called Rick on the hand-held radio and said I was moving around to the other side of East Crossing near the Duck Pond. We had seen two bucks there in the middle of the day fourteen days ago. More than an hour later in the heat of the middle of the day, I reached my designation. I was now more than two and half hours out of camp and five hours from the road. I found that someone else was there as they had driven through in a swamp buggy. The NPS designated swamp buggy trail went right by where I had chosen to hunt. One thing I learned a long time ago is that buggies do not bother deer. All one has to do is sit still and shortly after the buggy goes by, the deer will be back out. I had seen cases where the deer actually followed the buggy eating the tops of the bushes knocked over by the buggy.

I climbed a cabbage tree with the climbing stand and settled down by putting my tree-stand umbrella up to provide shade from the intensity of the Florida sun. Once again, I was hunting by ear as I started to doze off after eating a bag of tuna fish. A deaf person could have heard the deer coming. There were nine deer walking and jumping in the ankle-deep water. I watched three does come near me. They kept looking back as the rest of the deer moved along the cypress pond. I soon saw a nice buck moving on the edge of the cypress pond. Some other does went by him as he looked back around a cypress tree. I fired the .50-caliber black powder Ruger. The buck disappeared as the other deer ran off to the west. I feared I had missed since I had taken a hundred-yard off-hand shot at the neck—the only shot I had. Besides, the cabbage tree where I was sitting fifteen feet up had a slight sway in the hot breeze.

One thing had I learned over the years of deer hunting is to go look even if you think you missed. Marking the tree and taking a compass reading from my stand, I got down and eased over toward where the buck was last seen. In the knee-deep water lay my last Big Cypress buck. It was not a buck to brag about as far as antler size was concerned. But the four-point was a real trophy. With deer in hand, it was time to skin him and get the meat in the cooler of ice in the gator boat.

By the time I was done it was 1:30. This is the time of day when

The author returning to their gator boat camp with a 4 pt in the cooler.

the afternoon sun made the temperature its hottest. My body was steaming from the heat and work. I was exhausted. I had been wet, muddy, and working hard since four a.m. that morning. I was glad to have a gator boat to get the buck back to camp and on to the road. It was even better to float slowly along as I poled through East Crossing with my four-point in the cooler, knowing this was my last hunt from the Camp Red Bug area and it had been a good one.

While I was floating along, I could not help but think of the Indians and those who would follow me. In the not-too-near future this type of hunt would no longer be possible because the trees would take over this hundred-year-old buggy trail. I was seeing and doing things that in ten years could no longer be done. I was no longer sure that anyone would be able to use the recreational access site since the new superintendent was regularly throwing out the general management plan that we worked twelve years to create. The NPS could just as easily continue ignoring the enabling acts and not allow people off I-75.

I had seen a full cycle of wildlife at Camp Red Bug. When we started there was an abundance of game, but we could not sit still long enough to take any. Then there was very little game and now at the end of my time with Camp Red Bug, hunting had become less challenging because on almost every outing someone would take game. Not bad!

No longer did people have to get out and explore the Big Cypress; they could not because the NPS had put everyone on a few trails. They did not need to explore because of new computer technology, GPSs, radios, cell phones and marked NPS trails with maps to boot. The frontier culture of southwest Florida would be no more. With CERP and South Florida Ecosystem Restoration online and billions of dollars going into studies of this system, there would soon be no more mysteries in the Big Cypress Swamps or Everglades. They might even find the skunk-ape that had been seen along Tamiami Trail. The map below is where I shot my last deer, a four-point. I did not have to go there to know if the habitat was good or how far it was from one side of the grass flat to the other. All this information and more can be gleamed from this one map.

We did not realize it, but the Big Cypress and South Florida had been taken over by a new movement. Thanks to the computer age and time to research issues, we learned that the South Florida Ecosystem had been captured by the Wildlands Project. The project that the Sustainable Commission would not address was alive and well. It was being implemented by the DOI/NPS and other organizations supporting the NPS. This action was clear in the ORV management plan created under President Clinton and Vice-President Gore. The plan had a half-mile of ORV trail or road per square mile of land that is just what the Wildland Project prescribed. This seems to be a sign that most other restoration projects will end up in the same condition.

This is a copy of the Collier County Tax Appraisers interactive electronic map. I could scout the area for good pick off places without having to go to the area and learn it.

Chapter Thirteen

◆ ◆ ◆

Camps/Cabins and Industry and Cultural Cleansing of the Big Cypress

I have shared some information about a few camps. Before the NPS arrived, there were many camps, cabins, and houses in the Big Cypress National Preserve. I am sure there were a lot more than Congress was told and people considered possible. Because my friends and I were mainly interested in the Cypress as a way to escape from people and to hunt, I purchased all the USGS photos of the day to see where there were few cabins or campsites. Most of the time, you could not see the structures on these documents. But what you could see was the telltale buggy trail or road going to a hammock or pine island. This was a sure sign that the location was well used, either with a permanent structure or a permanent tent camp. I did not want to spend a lot of time getting to a location only to find out that someone was staying there.

There were many old and well-established places. These places had been built as far back as the 1940s and '50s. The structures were usually big or had several smaller structures associated with the property. One camp was Camp Wet Foot. One of the owners told me that their grandfather had established the camp during the Florida deer eradication program. This conversation, with Chuck Hampton, in the middle of the Big Cypress National Preserve during the 1970s, intrigued me and led me to get the minutes concerning the deer eradication from the State of Florida.

This was a program that had been designed by the 1937 cattle industry that existed in Florida. Cattlemen convinced the Florida Board of Trustees (BOT) that deer carried a tick from Texas that caused a disease in cattle. They also encouraged the development of a lot of cattle dipping vats. These holes in the ground were filled with water and some kind of poison to run cattle through and get rid of ticks. These vats would have water pumped into them by the cowboy pumping a pitcher pump that was attached to a shallow well. Of course, the pump would pull up water tainted with the poisonous dipping solution. Frequently, cowboys became sick from drinking water from this pitcher pump. Some of these vats are in the Big Cypress National Preserve. But they could not run the deer in them. The logic was simple—the deer were the reason this tick was continuing to cause problems so get rid of the deer.

Because cattlemen were very influential and the cattle industry was important to the state, they were able to get the Livestock Sanitation Board of Florida (now the Department of Agriculture) and the Game Commission, which was under the BOT's control, to start a program to eradicate all the deer in Florida.

They hired hunters to shoot these deer. They could shoot them all year, night or day. They were not supposed to sell meat or by-products. The state paid hunters $100 per month, a bounty per deer ear and supplied carbide light, fuel, munitions, and supplies. Remember these were poor times and hard times. They had no problem hiring people to do this task and they did it well.

It was not long before they had killed all the deer down to the "deer fence" line or quarantine line. This was a high fence that separated the most intense cattle country and the range with "wild cattle" on it. This is what Raleigh Burney told me they called all the cattle south of the deer fence—wild cattle. This was an undrained, unimproved area known as the Big Cypress. Today, there is a deer fence canal that is along a highway in Collier and Hendry County that is going to play a major part in CERP.

As I said, it was not long before all the deer north of the Deer Fence had been killed off. The cattlemen were not satisfied and wanted all the deer out of Florida and particularly out of the Big Cypress. They wanted to run their cattle there even if it was swamp. It would make a good cow-calf operation area. The Big Cypress Indian Reservation was the last stronghold of deer in Florida. The cattlemen had to get on this area to finish the job. They went to Washington, DC, and brought back an Indian Agent from the

DOI on February 6, 1940. Then they went from Ft. Myers to Immokalee to the Brighten Indian Reservation during the spring of the year when it was low water time and cool. The minutes described how they traveled in 4x4 jeeps and trucks. They also had teams of oxen to pull the trucks out when they became stuck or drowned out from the deep water on the route.

To get a better fix on the location of this Deer Fence line, I asked Richard Hilsinbeck, who is one of the most knowledgeable people in Florida about such land matters. This is what Richard told me: "The Deer Fence canal starts about five miles E/NE of the old Sunnyland Station, heads E and then runs into a N-S running portion of the Deer Fence Canal where both come together in Lard Can Slough before it (the canal) runs southward into the W Feeder Canal that cuts through the Big Cypress Seminole Indian Reservation just to the NE of Cow Bone Island in the Big Cypress. Most maps also show another canal (perhaps another leg of the Deer Fence) that cuts NE, then E from the southern end of Lard Can Slough (from where the latter drains into the Kissimmee Billy Strand). This leg roughly follows (i.e., made possible the construction of) the old Government Road, south of where C.R. 833 turns into the Josie Billie Road—within the Big Cypress Seminole Indian Reservation."

This Indian Agent trip did not go quite like the cattlemen wanted. The Indian agent sent in his report and stated it would be cheaper to build a deer fence around the Brighten Indian Reservation than to pay for all the deer to be killed. The Agent stated, "One accepts if all the rest of the extermination will have been in vain if the Seminoles' deer are not also exterminated, one must ask: why did not these agencies (State and Federal) obtain clearance in advance with the Seminoles and the Department of Interior? Florida has neither jurisdiction over the Seminole Reservation, nor does the Department of Agriculture." The State Attorney General had even ruled that the Seminoles had to pay for the eradication and restocking of all these deer at some future date. The Agent's final decision was to have the State of Florida erect a double six-foot fence around the entire Brighten Reservation as this would be cheaper and keep the deer on the reservation. The DOI Office of Indian Affairs issued an order that closed the Brighten Indian Reservation to all traffic or trespassing. The order was signed by

Dwight R Gardin, Acting Superintendent Seminole Indian Agency. The cattlemen could no longer go on the reservation and that was that.

Also, at about this time, World War II was causing an increase in employment and rising wages. It was becoming harder to find people to go into the swamps and shoot deer. At the same time, the Florida Wildlife Federation and a group called Deer Hunters United had taken the issue to court. The outcome of this court action was deer eradication was stopped and the state had to turn loose $25,000 worth of deer in southwest Florida. Public outcry moved the Game Commission out from under the BOT and made them a Florida Constitutional independent agency. This meant no longer would the Board of Trustees, the governor and cabinet, have control of the Game Commission. This is an important concept that will be important to remember years later. This issue also brought about the first environmental litigation in Florida—the Florida Wildlife Federation and Deer Hunters Unlimited suit to stop the deer slaughter. Their actions contributed to the settlement and independence of the Game Commission.

Wet Foot folks from Arcadia, Florida, had opened a new line of thought for me—*if we had that many deer back then and had shot all of them except on the Indian Reservation, could we still have a problem of too few deer for panther to feed on in 1970?* Not likely, my biologist friends told me, since deer will multiply quickly when there is good habitat and we had that.

One of the buildings at Wet Foots Camp.

There are several small cabins at Camp Wet Foot and right next to them on the same palmetto ridge is a cabin that was owned by a Judge Evers of Immokalee. It too is still there though the judge is no longer with us.

Judge Ever's camp next to Wet Foot Camp

Camp Poor Boys

Wet Foot Camp with all this long history remains in the Big Cypress National Preserve and should be considered as a National Historic site, as should many other places, and not burned by the NPS. These locations should be protected by the NPS as they are charged under their cultural resources regulations to do.

While I read the minutes about the deer kill, I found the last names of many people I had met and would meet. At least, their parents or grandparents had been in the Big Cypress since the 1930s hunting, running cattle, or developing their property as best they could.

Another camp I mentioned was Poor Boys. This is the camp of Joe Garrott today. His dad and a few others started this place in the early 1950s. They would come down from Immokalee on Monument Road just as many others would in those days. In fact, one of the founders of Poor Boys, Smokey Smith, had built my Poke-A-Long many years earlier. The camp was used by many generations of Garrotts. One time, I had supper with Joe, and he had five generations of his family in camp. If we count his father, who founded the camp, but has passed away long ago, there were six generations who used Camp Poor Boys. Most camps in the BICY have this sort of history.

Joe shared a story about how his dad, Mr. Garrott, who loved to hunt and spent all his waking hours in the swamps. His dad knew there were panthers around his camp and learned that Ross Allen wanted a panther for his Silver Springs 1950s show. A friend of Mr. Garrott's knew Ross Allen and decided to catch a panther alive. A western panther hunter with his cat dogs was contracted to come down and work with them. They arrived at Camp Poor Boys, and it was not long before the dogs struck. Off

Lloyd Austin's house before the NPS burned it.

they went on a chase through the swamps and across the big palmetto thickets. Finally, the cat treed. They managed to get the cat down from the tree but not like they wanted. The cat jumped down as one of the cat hunters went up to place a lariat on the animal. The cat landed in the dogs and began to do real damage to the dogs. BOOM! The cat dog owner had shot the panther. Well, that ended cat catching and they all went home the next day.

I mentioned Lloyd Austin's. This camp was a working cattle operation. I have been told that he had ten sections fenced. He never seemed to mind folks hunting on his land since the gates were never locked nor were there any posted signs. Most of the gates were wire gates, which was a post with barbed wire tied to it and held in place by two wire loops on the fence post. There was one wooden swing gate that I knew of. This was on the eastern side of his property on Monument Road.

Cal Stone told me a story about the first time he met Lloyd Austin. Cal said he was sitting on the site where he would eventually build his cabin. He chose that location because it was the highest ground as determined by the size of the big trees and the depth of the soil. Cal looked around the island and found an old campfire rock circle. He had his tent set up and was just starting supper on the opening day of hunting season when he could

One of the barns at Austin's.

hear a buggy coming and dogs barking. Mind you, this was in the late 1950s. It was not long before this buggy drove up with a very large man driving it. The man said, "I am Lloyd Austin and what *!*/! are you doing at my camp?" Cal responded, "I own this land and you ***#@!@* better get off it!" From then on, they had a good understanding and shared coffee and dinner. Cal invited Lloyd to stay the night, but Lloyd decided to move on.

I am sure Mr. Austin was a big man. If you ever visited his spread before the NPS burned it, you would have been impressed with all the work he had to do by hand. There were miles and miles of three-strand barbed wire fence all held in place by hand-dug fence holes with hand-chopped liter pine post. He had a huge cattle-holding pen that was well-built to keep the wild cattle in that he used for his cow-calf operation. He had outlying cow pens and line-cabins built as well.

Old timers who grew up in southwest Florida told me that not only did Austin live at his homestead but so did Concho Billy. Concho Billy was a deaf-mute Seminole. Billy would live at Austin's in the summer months while Austin was in the city of Immokalee. Then, in the winter, he would move to one of his two other camps. I took the archeologists to one of his other camps. This Indian campsite still had several partially standing chickees. These structures were assembled with old, square,

Some of Austin's range cattle.

hammer-forged wood nails. This was not the only location that I showed the archeologists that had some remains of Indian camps.

There was a big cattle pen on the main buggy road that went onto Weller's Bamboos. This, too, was an extremely well-built corral that was more than ten feet tall, with very close posts made of trees to hold up thick cypress plank fencing. He had two story barns, chicken houses, and a hog house. He had a real frontier home that was miles from the nearest county-maintained rock road and even farther from the nearest paved road. But sadly, under Superintendent Fagergren's "make it a Park" policy all of these improvements were burned. This site should have been listed as a historical site but instead it was burned by the NPS as soon as Mr. Austin died. It should have been protected by Florida's Department of Historical Resources.

I was told that Mr. Austin would round up his cattle each spring to cut out the calves. He would then carry them to Turner River Road, the nearest dirt road about five miles away. This was done in the spring because the water was low and the soil across the prairie would be the hardest. I

Weller's Bamboos, 1979, before the NPS burned it.

do know he used sweet feed to attract his wild cattle and spread it by using a Model A swamp buggy. I know this because the cattle would follow Poke-A-Long when I drove it in his pastures.

Lloyd had some very big, modified, 6x6 military trucks with huge airplane tires on them to take the calves to the road. He also knew how

Wiggins' back country camp and sawmill.

to read the vegetation so he could ride where the rock was closest to the surface. In my opinion he had a real operation and was the sort of man who founded America. How did the NPS recognize this? They burned all he had done.

There was a dirt trail that went north of Austin's cattle pens on Monument Road. Some of it

was pushed up and maintained. Some places had shallow holes that were dug to get fill for the road. In some places there were corduroy roads built. It was a good woods road and went to the pine heartlands of the Big Cypress.

Burney told me Lloyd died in one of his line camps.

Going north on Monument Road a few miles from Austin's corrals was Weller's Bamboos. I neither knew Mr. Weller nor did I ever meet him. By the time I went by his place, he had gone. But it was still standing, and we camped there sometimes to hunt hogs that would come to his mango grove. He had a huge grove behind his house. I was told that he had taken a very large front-end loader and moved an Indian mound to make his grove. The grove was built on high furors and produced big banana mangos that dropped during black powder season. This, in turn, attracted hogs and that brought us.

Donny Powell, husband of Barbara Jean Powell, told me that he watched Weller take this huge, front-end loader and literally put the bucket on big pine stumps. He would then push the stumps into the ground. That was a big machine to use in the Big Cypress.

There was a very large two-story house sitting in front of a big patch of bamboo. This bamboo was the kind that grew tall and was six or so inches in diameter at the base. It was a big stand of plants. He also had a very big, two-story, generator equipment barn, a chicken coop, and another small cabin on the property. Weller had an African American husband and wife who lived in a small house. They were caretakers for his property and farm hands who worked his mango grove.

If you went to the west of Weller's, you would come to Wiggins' sawmill in a few miles. This gentleman had two places. One camp was on Turner River Road, and one was about four miles east of this road. It was a nice place in the backcountry of the Big Cypress National Preserve. I am not sure when he built it or how long he was there, but when I read minutes from the Animal Sanitation Board in the 1930s, I found his surname listed as attending the meetings.

He dug several rock pits and built a good number of equipment barns and working areas. His house was a finely built place and it should be as well because he would cut cypress in the wet season, saw it into planks and then take it out in the spring. Like Lloyd he, too, had modified 6x6 military trucks with very big tires on them. He would cross Copeland Prairie and go to his Turner River Road place. This was a small house trailer with an open-air shed to park under. From there his timber would be taken to town.

Wiggins leased some of his land to others to build cabins on. This was apparently done before Wiggins sold his land to the NPS. I say this because these places remained until the leaseback agreement Mr. Wiggins had with the NPS ran out. I met one of these men and helped him as a good swamp neighbor would. Dr. Collins lived in Arcadia. He was a dentist there and like many he liked the Cypress. He had a place to the south of Wet Foots, Corn Flake I and II but after it burned twice, he leased land from Wiggins and built a nicer place.

On one of my trips, I was showing an Audubon leader—remember I took lots of folks and even contracted with National Audubon to guide them and work on their base line study for the NPS—around the backcountry of the Cypress when we came on a 4x4 Jimmy Chevy. It was stuck and really good. Doc had been able to get down Monument Road from I-75 and south of Wet Foots to the first marl prairie where his truck sank. His dad, who was in his late '80s, was with him. They had spent the night not more than a mile from their Camp Corn Flake II. Doc was sure glad I came along with a hi-lift jack and a chain fall. Shortly after that, his camp was burned,

Doc Collin's Corn Flake III Camp.

and he moved to Wiggins. Doc and a hunting friend were killed when they were pulling his buggy to camp from Arcadia. A semi-tractor trailer truck ran into the back of his buggy while it was on the trailer and they were reportedly burned to death.

There was another cabin to the east of Wiggins. I visited it a few times but never knew who owned this place. It was also located in a good place to hunt, with a huge cypress swamp nearby and a bigger pine ride to the north and east.

In fact, between Wet Foot, Weller's Bamboos, and Wiggins' sawmill, there was some of the best hunting habitats around. It was a mix of big pine ridges, dense cypress strands, and open marl flats with ponds in them. Further, because of the logging work done by Wiggins, it was open and easy to walk in or drive a buggy through. I would try to go there every spring gobbler season and camp well to the north of Wiggins' sawmill but south of Wet Foot. We took a lot of birds from there. I never did get that far from Camp Red Bug to deer or hog hunt. These animals were there in abundance, too.

Another really nice place that I saw but never met the owner was Balchom's. If you left Weller's Bamboos and went to the south and east for several miles, there was an island out on the northeastern part of Wind Mill Prairie on the north side of Monument Road, as it turns to the east toward Austin's. This was Balchom's. He had a house bigger than mine, a big equipment barn and a chicken coop. There was a real citrus grove there. His place was there in the 1960s and was a nice house. To the east of him across a few hundred yards of prairie was a big cypress ridge loaded with small oak hammocks and pine islands. We tried to get there to hunt at least once a year. This was so far from my cabin that we would have to camp out. We had a well-established tent camp location on a chunk of high land in thick palmettos on the

Balcom's camp after the NPS got rid of him.

side of Monument Road. No one could see us unless they stumbled on our camping place or saw the big pine trees reflecting light from our campfire. It became a place where we stopped when had to drive to Camp Red Bug from U.S. 41.

To the southwest about three-quarters of mile in a big oak hammock, Balchom's brother had a house. This was a high island and was well-hidden from the casual observer. I never did see the house, but the remains of his establishment indicated he, too, had a real big place with a good number of out buildings. There is a good grapefruit tree on this island. There are many islands in the Cypress with one to dozens of citrus trees on them.

The absolute furthest we went deer hunting from Camp Red Bug was Stump-Camp, owned by Mr. Bodinham (Bodie). I mentioned this place earlier. It was north of Mud Lake by about three miles and northeast of Wet Foot about four miles. We would usually get there by turning on the old main buggy trail as it left Monument Road, northwest of Wet Foot. This was a challenging route for all my small buggies, but not Poke-A-Long, because there were a few really deep-water cypress strands to get through.

To get to Stump Camp we had to go by Raw Hide Camp that was tucked into a dense and large oak hammock about a half-mile southwest of Bodie's place.

Stump Camp, as I said, was owned by Mr. Bodinham who also lived near Arcadia. I met him years after he had sold out to the NPS, after they

Stump Camp, kitchen owned by Bodie.

told him he had to. According to Bodie and his wife, the NPS did not tell them they could have kept three acres of the forty they owned and the building. She said it was just as well because they were so old by then that if something happened to Bodie, she would just have to tie a rope onto Bodie and drag him out of the swamps like an old hog. This statement caused me to realize the NPS will, one day, own all the camps in the cypress because if the current owner does not sell to the NPS, then someone will in the future. Time is on their side.

Stump Camp had a huge pine tree stump in the middle of the eating area that was made into a table. Bodie told me they would get to the camp in the 1930s by leaving Clewiston with ox carts. They would hunt all the way in and then stay several weeks eating what they shot. The last day or two they would shoot some deer, smoke the meat with green pine smoke,

and then start out. He told me I could have the two oxcart wagon wheel steel rims at his place so I relocated them to Red Bug Camp.

Stump Camp had "dog box" bunks to sleep in. They were better than sleeping with the bugs. There were also several small two-man size bunk wagons on the island.

Dog box bunks at Stump Camp.

These were early camper trailers. These camper trailers had just enough room to slide in beside the bunk beds and one man at a time could change his clothing.

From Stump Camp there was a buggy trail that led to the northeast and north. It crossed the Alley about where the big rest stop is today and went onto Clewiston. There were a good number of camps and houses between I-75 and Stump Camp. This route to I-75 would go by Turkey Foot Camp, Wagon Wheel Camp, Horse Camp and some that had no name. This trail would cross Osceola's Rough. This is a large oak ridge on the south side of Mullet Slough. We did take a three-day deer-hunting trip from Camp Red Bug to hunt Osceola's Rough. Years later, we would bump into another hunter with one arm who shared an interesting bit of history about Osceola's Rough.

This conversation happened somewhat south of Camp Red Bug. We heard a model A and some ATVs coming our way. I got down from my

Raw Hide Camp to the SW of Stump Camp.

stand and went over to Poke-A-Long. I met a gentleman driving a smallish two-wheel drive Model A buggy who said his name was Summerall. I found his family name in the records of the deer kill. This was after I-75 work had started and our gate site was the only way into the backcountry. Summerall said he was looking for Osceola's Rough and left the NPS ORV access site south of I-75 on Turner River Road. At this time, this was Wiggin's landing. They had a camping site at Osceola's and were trying to make it by dark. I noticed he had one arm missing from the elbow down. We shared a Coke and talked some. He soon told me he had lost his arm as a boy while hunting with his dad at Osceola's Rough. He said they had just dumped the deer dogs out of the buggy. He had his shotgun leaning on the ground and as the dogs took off, he pulled the gun up by the barrel. Somehow a stick caught the trigger and discharged the gun. The buckshot took off his arm below the elbow. This was in the early '50s and there were no phones to call for help or helicopters to get him out. The only way out was by slow, rough riding, swamp buggies and many miles to the nearest town. I told him how to get to the main buggy trail and which trail to take to the east to get

The author at Mud Lake with the Bandits across the lake.

to Osceola's. I doubted they would get there by dark that day. I never saw him again.

A short distance south of Stump Camp on the buggy trail going toward Mud Lake is a watering hole dug by the lumber railroad men to recharge their boilers. This hole is on the west side of the trail and Cal told me this was called the "African American Hole." The reason for this name is that reportedly there was an African American who was working in the timber business who died and is buried there under the mound of dirt.

South from Stump-Camp several miles lies Mud Lake. By Cypress standards, this is a big lake that always has water in it and plenty of gators. On the northeastern side of the lake is an oak hammock. When I first visited this lake with Cal, he told me, pointing to a hammock on the northeast side of the lake, that the oak hammock was called the Bandits.

The author with a black bear eaten ladder stand.

That was because in the '50s when there were good enough roads a street legal car or truck could be driven deep into the Big Cypress where some men lived. According to Cal, these fellows did not work but lived off the land. When they wanted something or money, they went to town and stole what they wanted. Then, they would run back to their hideout on the edge of Mud Lake.

Going on to the east by way of the northern trail out of Mud Lake, you will go by Buckholtz, then Drakes, then to the south to Boar's Den camp and then Stone's place. In the area of Stone's, because of the number of camps, a small community remains there.

By 2000, we were having problems with the bears eating our ladder stands. In 2000, Tommy Buchholtz, who has a camp a little to the northeast of Mud Lake, was also having problems with bears; they seemed to like to scratch and eat his barn post.

In the 1980s, bears started to make a real comeback. One day, I went to Camp Red Bug and found a mother bear had visited my place. I could tell it was a big bear and cub by the tracks on the porch and windows.

They had gone through one section of the screen porch, stood on the couch, leaned on the glass windows where they left prints and then went out another section of screen. Then she went to the back and ripped open the back door to the inside hall. There, she again leaned on the window, leaving prints that I never removed. She then went to a back window that was nearest the refrigerator in the kitchen. She ripped the entire window out of the wall and stuck her head in. I kept the house really clean with no food left that would attract bears. There were canned goods and some bottled food in the gas refrigerator

Camp Comfort was raided a number of times by bear.

that I always left on. I figured she smelled the gas flame and no food that was easy to get so she did not go in the house. I heard that many other camp owners were having trouble with bears tearing up their houses. There had even been one shot on Turner River Road because the bear came into the house while the family was there.

I went to Immokalee and bought a replacement window and a solar-powered electric fence box with wire. I would fix that bear! I put an electric fence on the wall and around the entire house. I put a grounding wire a few inches below the bottom electric fence, figuring if a bear stuck its nose to the bottom wire, it would also touch the grounding wire and get a shock. It worked; I had no more problems. That same bear attacked my neighbor Wayne's, Camp Comfort. The she-bear went into his place and lived there. She dropped cans out the window to her cub. His windows were high off the ground. To get in she had eaten halfway through a 4x4-corner post and plywood siding and had pulled the aluminum-framed window out far enough to get in. She then proceeded to eat through a wooden closet door and consumed gallons of cooking oil, many cans of food, glass jars of Gator Aide, and flour. She made a real mess of his house. A year later she came back and raided again but this time she went in via another window and then out the back door. Of course, she did not open the door as we would but instead tore it off its hinges.

On my last trip to Camp Red Bug as a guest, I looked at the barn and was shocked to find a bear had located some termites. He then proceeded to tear the tarpaper off and eat the plywood. He left large paw prints on the tarpaper.

A black bear was digging into Camp Red bug barn looking for termites.

Most people did not know it but there were a good number of airports in the Big Cypress. Sure, everyone knew of the big one that started the entire process—the Dade-Collier Jet Port. What they did not know was that many landowners had built their own. There were some south of Loop Road, but most were north of U.S. 41 and north of S.R. 84. One of the best ones was Poppenhager's. This camp and airport were purchased by Tim Griffin. His family enjoyed the use of it for many years. There were also a few natural ground land strips. These locations are hard to find today because there was no ground improvement. Most of the natural ground landing strips had more than one direction for landing and takeoff. These approaches can be found because of the trees cut down by the pilots that would facilitate their needs. The ground at these locations is always hard sand with low wiregrass.

To the northeast of Poor Boys was Les Gray's. His camp was on a

BJ Powell, Donny Powell & Mr. Ellis at Poppenheiger's camp airport, 1996.

big, high pine island. One time, when Larry and I had been backpacking off the Alley, we walked south as fast as we could. We would make it a practice to walk as fast and straight as we could from the road for four or five hours to set up our first camp. We figured from there, if we hunted for four or five days, it would take us all day to hike out because we would be tired. In the morning, we heard a buggy start up and knew they had not driven in there during the night. They had been there when we set up camp 300 yards off on a small cabbage hammock. They drove over to our campsite and were sure surprised to see us that far back in the swamps.

As it turned out, they were going back home that afternoon and asked how long we planned on staying. It was Thanksgiving weekend and we planned to stay through Sunday. Mr. Gray asked if we would mind staying at his place since that way, he would have someone there who would be camp sitting. We said sure, broke camp, and high-tailed it over there really fast. We were in hog heaven; the camp had beds, screens, a stove, high dry ground, cut firewood, and well water. This was great. We said goodbye as they left.

The next morning, we had no idea where we were or if other camps or people were nearby. This was long before GPS and good maps. We walked out and separated to find a place to hunt. By noon, we both set up looking at the same island-cypress junction. We started to go back to Les Gray's, but you know what, we did not know where it was. Dark found us seeking our footprints in our flashlight beam. We followed these tracks in the mud to get us back to Les's. We arrived there around 10 p.m. We were never lost but that camp sure was. From then on, I was responsible for knowing where we were, where we had been, and where we needed to go to get back to whatever it was, he had to get back to. This was in the late 1960s and we did not know Poor Boys was a few miles to the southwest. Years later, Larry went to the University of Florida and Les Gray's son was one of his roommates.

Farther to the northeast of Les Gray's place, there was Frank Tanner's camp. He had a small cabin on a low, wet pine island. This island was well out in Mullet Slough. All the water in this big marl and cypress slough came out of Little Marsh in Bear Island and drained into the Everglades far to the southeast. Mullet Slough was low and wet. We stopped by Frank's place a few times in the 1970s as we continued to seek that really hot place to hunt. The Tanner name is also on that list of state deer killers from the 1930s.

Between Poor Boys and Wet Foot and about a mile to the north of Monument Road, right where the NPS designated trail takes a hard bend back to the southwest, about a mile north, is Albritton's place. He had a really nice, low wall, all-tin house on a high knoll of a big pine ridge. This ridge was the last big one before the ground drops off into Mullet Slough. His family name is also on the state deer killer's list. After

Albritton's camp torn down and left by the NPS.

he died, his family no longer appreciated the camp and hardship of getting there. The NPS got it, pulled it over with their swamp buggy and left all the building material right where it fell.

To the southwest of Wet Foot and more to the west than south, right where the buggy trail goes out onto Copeland Prairie, take a hard left and another and in a short distance you will arrive at Pot-Leg camp. I never knew who owned this place and only went there once with the archaeologist who found a clay pot leg that looked like it had come from Mexico. This was an exciting find for them since they could envision trading around the rim of the Gulf of Mexico. Mind you, this, like all the artifacts, was removed from several inches in the ground.

Northwest from Poor Boys you would go through some of the most difficult terrain yet. This buggy trail went through high palmetto roughs with deep solution holes in them. You would be in deep-water ponds with soft soil between these roughs and would have to climb four to five feet up an almost straight drop-off edge. Once you went through a few miles of this terrain you would arrive at some big oak ridges. Some of these oak trees had barbed wire fence imbedded several inches into them. Cattleman many years ago had nailed the wire to these trees and they had grown over the wire by several inches. As soon as you left these hammocks, you would be on the most northeastern part of Copeland Prairie. From there, a buggy trail to the northwest leads to Big Opossum Camp owned by Elmer Alterman, so the camp sign said. Big Opossum was tucked into the East Crossing Strand

Elmer Alterman's Big Opossum Camp.

on its southeastern side. This was a huge, all-tin house. It was easily twice the size of mine. Judging by the old model A parts and old jeep parts around the yard, they had been there for many years, by the time I stumbled on the camp in the 1970s. We seldom got this far to hunt because the terrain was just too tough on my equipment, but we did hunt a lot on the eastern side of the palmetto rough country and took a good bit of game from there. The NPS also destroyed this historic structure.

There were two cabin sites on the other side of East Crossing strand. The one on the southwestern side was called Miami Boys. It was a nice, huge, screen house with bunks and a kitchen. The builders had cleared out under very big oak trees with wild sour oranges all around. Some called this the Orange Grove Camp. There is a huge grove of wild oranges trees that had to be started by the Indians. The NPS burned this place.

Miami Boys' orange grove camp before the NPS had it removed.

Going south from Miami Boys Camp along the the eastern edge of Copeland Prairie is Nash's camp. A little farther south would be the turn to the east to Wiggins. If you do not take this turn and go south, you would arrive at Stop Sign Camp. Dave Charland purchased this camp in the late 1980s when he lost his lease and camped on the WD Ranch to the Big Cypress Addition. He then allowed Donny and Barbara Jean Powell to use it if they maintained it, which they did.

One day, Dave Charland called; he wanted to know if my big buggy was working. I knew something was up. After all, a year or so ago, I had called him at six a.m. offering to pay for his trip to the Big Cypress so he could pull me out. As it turned out, someone from Wet Foots Camp came along

Dave Charland's Stop Sign Camp rented by BJ Powell and her husband, Donny.

and helped me. Anyway, I told Dave it was working great. He then wanted to know if I would help him take some building material to his Stop Sign Camp. I said, "Sure why not? The water was down, and the soil was only a little muddy." When I arrived at Wiggins Landing, I was surprised to see what a little building material was. It was a ton of lumber and all the tin needed to place a new roof on the camp. I sized up things and figured if I was the only person on Big Green, took the back seat off and put the front seat's back down, I could carry all the tin. It worked and we went all the way to Stop Sign across Copeland Prairie without a problem. I was a bit surprised by the ease with which we traveled Copeland Prairie because it was a bit too wet and that Prairie had been known to swallow buggies.

If you travel on up to the northwestern side of East Crossing strand where it joins Copeland prairie, you will find Carter's camp. Carter's was straight north of Miami Boy's camp. This old man would run Copeland Prairie

Big Green loaded with the roof and wood for repairing Stop Sign Camp on Copeland Prairie.

in a highboy farm tractor. At Carter's, there were several big house trailers under the oak trees. They had pulled these trailers in during a drought in the late 1960s. There were also some other small tin houses. This was a large camp with many people in it. Carter's was due east of the Jockey Club. The NPS burned these places, too.

The old trail to the north toward Camp Red Bug goes by a camp we called Chevron Island. Summerall and Bondurant built this small place in 1937. This camp was located on the very northern side of East Crossing strand as the buggy trail left the deep water. Nearby is Chair

Camp that was built by Bondurant in 1940. According to Summerall, the one-armed hunter, his grandfather and his hunting buddy had a falling out, so they separated, and the latter built a new place about three quarters of a mile away. Two other camps were nearby to the southeast of Chevron Island that were built in the late 1940s—Bear Camp and Dead End Camp. On farther up the trail to Red Bug Camp is LBJ's Camp, Skinner's camp,

Camp Comfort

and, finally, you would get to Camp Red Bug. All of these camps are gone except Camp Red Bug and Camp Comfort.

LBJ or Lowell B. Jarvis had a nice house and was a partner with Mincy, of Mincy Bonding agency. They owned a section of land. LBJ was a bounty hunter for Mincy. When Mincy needed some bail jumper to be collected, he would go get LBJ who then went to work. Before the Alley was built, LBJ would leave U.S. 27 in western Broward by airboat, stop at the cypress-sawgrass line, and then go on by swamp buggy. This was a very long trip but he and Mincy did own the land and they were going to enjoy it. Leaving an airboat or swamp buggy parked in the woods or along highways was a common practice until about 1972. Then, it seemed like the prisons opened up and even overnight parking became risky. But we had no other choice than to leave our trucks and trailers on the side of the highways. We no longer left buggies there but carried them back and forth from town or paid someone who lived out that way to allow us parking rights.

Southeast from Red Bug Camp toward Poor Boys is Cleat Rock Hammock. The first turn to the south after going south of Cleat Rock Hammock (Dark Hammock) and the second turn to the west led to a camp we called Porno Camp. The name gives away why we called this camp that. The walls were papered with such pictures as only could come from men's magazines. This camp was very old in that there was equipment there used

Porno Camp after it was abandoned and waiting for the NPS to burn it. This location had been used since the 1930s as a logging. camp.

to remove trees from the deep swamps to the west of the camp, during the logging heydays.

On S.R.84, about five miles to the east of my place, was Red and Billy Davis's Camp. They built on a big island to the southwest of where the major rest area is in Collier County. This was a place used by the Seminoles. It was a very high and hidden island in the cypress. Red and his wife lived there. They would allow people to park their buggies on their land for a fee. They charged $90 for a year's rent or $10 a month for short-term renters. In 1975, they had about 300 buggies in there, during the height of the hunting season. Sometimes, they would have BBQs where all attended and had a great time. Red's general house bunk area had hats all over it. He collected hats from those who missed deer or hogs while hunting in the Cypress. When I-75 was built, he was not protected by the Big Cypress National Preserve enabling act and FDOT took his land. The sad thing about this is, he did not get much money because most of his improvements were not own his land but someone else's. They were broke when they left the Big Cypress.

These camps and cabins cover but a little of the Big Cypress. They are all in the northeast part of what is known as the Turner River Unit. As you can see, the area was far from pristine as many liked to claim in 2000 and told Congress in the 1970s. The media with all their resources refused to state the area was not pristine when Congress approved taking 700,000 acres of private land; this was done so a few connected folks could make billions developing their property on both coasts of Florida when I-75 opened up. I am also sure I left a lot of camps and property owners out of this brief trip around the northwest part of the Turner River Unit.

Many who were run out of the Big Cypress Addition were fortunate enough to get recreation leases on large private ranches. The landowners were happy because they were making good money doing nothing and those in the lease were happy but poorer. Dave Charland was a close friend and a big supporter of the Big Cypress enabling act and addition act. He was able to get into the Lykes' Ranch lease.

One year, the water was so high the deer and hogs could not get to the creek swamps to feed in the winter. This is the time when the palmetto berries and acorns are gone. While the deer were not seriously harmed by this high-water event, the hogs were. I was invited to hunt on this lease and take some hogs and doe deer. The deer were so plentiful that the landowner had the lessee take a bunch of does with the permission of the Florida Fish, Wildlife and Conservation Commission. I took two does that were nice and fat. We then turned our attention to hogs. After taking two hogs, I would not shoot anymore because they were so poor, they had no meat on them. They were healthy enough but a hog that should have weighed 300 pounds was lucky to go 120 pounds. They had no food on the pastures and could not get into the deep-water swamps along the creek to feed on the bottom-growing plants. Thus, they were slowly starving to death. Later that year, my friend, Dave Charland, told me that they found many dead hogs on the lease.

Dave had a really nice place on the Creek. He and his close friends would spend many a weekend at their hideaway on the Creek. They would invite many to the Creek to enjoy this part of old Florida.

The NPS had found a new weapon to finish off their cultural cleansing of the Big Cypress that would enable them

Dave Charland's Fisheating Creek Camp

to complete their destruction of a community of people that started with the removal of the trespass camps. This new weapon was the installation of a superintendent who would not directly challenge sportsmen but appear to get along with them and allow the public to do whatever they wanted with their ORVs. Sure, Mr. Hibbard did manage ORVs as he would close the area when there was too much water, he stopped the use of PWC at

the request of the author, and he outlawed the use of go-devils in the Big
Cypress National Preserve. What he did wrong was to not make an ORV
management plan! He did not create the required ORV plan, he did not
complete the required recreational base line report to Congress by 1990,
and he did not complete the required Wilderness study that was due to
Congress by 1993. When he was forced by the courts to do his ORV
management plan, he brought in a group of demographic experts to do a
study titled the "BICY OFF ROAD VEHICLE RECREATION AND
ITS BENEFITS."

After a rough start these University of Tennessee experts were able to
get the sportsmen to talk openly with them. These research people created
a really good document—a document that all thought would help the NPS
create a good ORV management plan. But what the NPS did was to change
the superintendents and send in one who did not like hunting or ORVs. He
thought the Preserve was to be a PARK, right back to the same old blue
blood NPS attitude. He and his writers used this ORV Benefits report that
exposed those who had used the Big Cypress for generations as "culture"
against the sportsman community. The final ORV plan took a position
against everything we said was important to us. By doing this, the NPS had
accomplished what Pete Rosenthal told me he and his fellow NPS peers
were directed to do right after the Big Cypress National Preserve enabling
act passed; that was to figure out a way to get rid of the ORVs and hunters.
It only took the NPS a little more than twenty-seven years to implement a
set of regulations and new visitor attractions that would assure the eventual
complete removal of all hunters and ORVs. The NPS could then do what
their Wilderness study conclusion stated: "Once the mineral rights and
inholder's interest were identified then the issue
of Wilderness would be re-addressed." This
twenty-year-old document would eventually
become true, and the Big Cypress National
Preserve will become a Wilderness Area Park
like Everglades National Park.

*Cal's camp with new
NPS buildings and the
end of one of the YBRs.*

Chapter Fourteen

❖ ❖ ❖

Litigations, Civil and Regulatory Actions to Save the Everglades

A fiery sunset in the cypress is symbolic of how the issues in South Florida are.

∞

Long before Dave got on the lease, I received a phone call from a sportsman. Many sportsmen would call me when they found a problem in the backcountry where they liked to go. This person, not one who is mentioned in this book, told me the Lykes were digging a hug ditch that is already miles long. The ditch looked like it would cut the water off to Fisheating Creek. The Everglades Coordinating Council put an airplane up and surveyed the area. The work was photographed and, sure enough, it was extensive and appeared to be designed to do just what was reported. Knowing of Ralph Johnson's relationship with Attorney General Butterworth, I took these pictures to him.

Many years ago, the sitting Attorney General's children were fed by wild game provided by Ralph. The Attorney General's children had a genetic condition that did not allow them to eat food with chemical additives either from food supplements or otherwise. The Attorney General of Florida (AG) did his own investigation and there were major problems for the Lykes. It was reported in the papers that the company had an employee who was using their equipment without their knowledge, and they did not know what he was doing. The employee was reportedly dismissed. Their fines and the FWC fines were not like the fines the NPS got for doing illegal dredge and fill work.

By 2000, Ralph was feeding the poor and people in distress nearly 10,000 pounds of processed game meat a year. This was being done through the South Florida Chapter of Safari International. He also presented a sensory safari for the blind. The sensory safari was held on one day and at one of their conventions or schools. He and other club members took their trophies to the meeting hall and set them up. Then blind folks would come back and feel the mounts while we would tell them about the animal. Everyone involved appreciated this activity.

Another time, I had been driving my swamp buggy along the northern boundary of Bear Island's northeastern fence line. I found a large new ditch cutting off the water from flowing out of the privately owned marsh that fed Little Marsh, which in turn went into Mullet Slough and on to the Everglades. I had not seen a public 404-permit notice. I got all of them for the State of Florida. I made a few phone calls and work stopped. A few months later, Ralph and Wes wanted to know if I had taken action to stop the ditch digging along Bear Islands northern boundary. I said yes, why? They both laughed and said they tried to go to their lease and could not get there because all the locks had been changed by the landowner whose property they had to cross to get to their land. It appears the landowner who was digging the ditch thought Ralph and Wes had busted him. I also learned that the road being built with the ditch spoil was intended to allow oil removal along that part of Bear Island. The oil company backed out not wanting any part of the non-permitted ditch. I also learned that the Big Cypress National Preserve helicopter pilot had been on vacation when the work started and thought nothing of the work when he returned so he took no action.

Another time a sportsman called me after going to the Holely Lands, scouting for deer. He found the oil companies were doing seismic work there. They were driving large drill rigs all over the area. There was no real problem with this, but they had done something that should not have been done and we knew this. The oil company had driven through a large maple tree island. We had worked for many years to get regulations approved to prevent any ORV from driving in this type of habitat. If the sportsmen could not drive on these islands, then the oil companies could not either. I made some phone calls and learned that FWC did not even know there was work going on in the area. The SFWMD was in the dark just as much as the FWC. I found this interesting since both had employees working in the area every day. The company had received their permit from the DEP that had not been checking the work being done nor did the DEP even know there were such islands in the area. My actions resulted in the company getting a substantial fine. But it also led to a new DEP person starting an initiative to take the sportsmen out of the Everglades. This employee figured if oil companies could not drive on an island, then certainly the use of ORVs in the Everglades by sportsmen hunting deer was worse. She did some work and we ended up having another big committee that met for a day or two. Manley Fuller helped make sure this committee was constructed in a balanced manner. The outcome of the committee was that location specific regulations pertaining to the use of ORVs should be followed. We were left alone for now.

I heard stories from many of those much older than me and who had been involved in actions to protect the Everglades about how some took the law into their own hands. One such story about a mayor of Hialeah was that he had a hunt lease in what became the Southern Golden Gates Estates or the Picayune Strand State Forest. He and many in the group did not approve of the new canal being dug to drain southwest Florida for the huge General American Corp. land speculation plan. The company was building the world's largest community and to do this they had to dig the

Faka-Union canal and others. The Faka-Union canal would drain all the water from this part of the system and allow the building of roads and houses without the expense of dealing with the water. It was said that the mayor would shoot out the lights on the dragline to slow the work down while others worked politically to have this massive project shut down. These activities went on long enough and regularly enough that the sheriff stationed a man on the dragline around the clock.

Years later, in 1999, during an Everglades Restoration meeting held in the area in which Vice-President Al Gore told all that they were sending $25 million to Florida from the Farm Bill to purchase land on the east coast of Florida for CERP, Barbara Jean Powell took a stand to get this money applied to Southern Golden Gates Estate and it was. This resulted in the USFWS maintaining oversight of the land management plan and in the FWC backing out as the lead managing agency for the State of Florida. This resulted in the area not becoming a WMA as we set up in the 1980s, but a State Forest with the Division of Forestry State of Florida (DOF) the lead managing agency. DOF lands are not hunted as much as FWC lands so this created a lot of hunter backlash to CERP.

Another story I heard several times was that the first time the SFWMD had the WCAs boxed in by canals and levees, they closed the system and held the water back. This happened in the late 1960s and when it did, it caused unacceptable levels of flooding. It was said that a few well-meaning Everglades lovers had obtained a significant amount of dynamite and planned to blow up all the flood gates and pumps from U.S. 41 to Lake Okeechobee. Some calmer heads were able to prevent this from happening and most of those with the explosives were never captured by the authorities. But at least one was caught, charged and found guilty of conspiracy against the State of Florida.

The very first litigation I was involved in had me acting only as a member of the Dade County Halftrack Conservation Club (as of 2004 the name is Dade County Fulltrack Conservation Club). It was on this issue that Johnny Jones, President of the FWF, instigated to help restore Lake Okeechobee and the rest of the Everglades. The issue was simple in our minds; the water being back-pumped (back-pumping is the process of pumping water into Lake Okeechobee from locations that it would not flow into naturally) into Lake Okeechobee was so polluted that it was destroying the ecology of the Lake. The other issue was that the dairy farms around the northern side of the Lake were allowing their cows to use the drainage canals and creeks as bathrooms. This waste along with that coming from the feedlots and dairy processing areas was running straight into Lake Okeechobee. The Lake had too much phosphorus and nitrate in the water column. This resulted in excessive growth of algae. The alga was destroying the oxygen content of the water and therefore the fish were dying. All this additional vegetation and dead fish were furthering the speed at which the lake was changing from a clear water lake to a mud pie.

We won this case and many things happened. The first thing was the hump in the Miami Canal was removed. This canal runs from the south side of Lake Okeechobee all the way to Miami. At the time of this litigation, it only went a few miles south of the L5. About two-thirds the distance from Lake Okeechobee to the L5, the canal bottom was elevated. This hump caused water to be pushed back into Lake Okeechobee instead of running on south and into the Everglades. This polluted water was going back into the lake.

I have already mentioned the back-pumping issues. The judge ordered this to stop, except during times of emergency. He did not define emergency, thus years later, we often saw back-pumping for high water and low water because these conditions were declared emergencies by the authorities. However, most of the back-pumping was stopped for a long time. With changes in leadership in the FWF, we did not continue to monitor the no back-pumping order on a regular basis and lost control of the issue.

Another thing that came out of this litigation was the creation of the Lake Okeechobee Advisory Committee. This group was appointed by Governor Askew to study the lake and to make recommendations on how to properly manage it. They did and their study went on the shelf with none of their recommendations implemented.

The litigation and resulting removal of the hump brought about some unwanted actions. One of these was the connection of the Miami Canal south to the part of the canal that ran out of Miami and one to a little north of Alligator Alley. This would allow the water managers to make sure they could move water from the EAA into the Everglades and provide the water management needs of the EAA. It would also allow Lake Okeechobee to move from a lake to a reservoir. The canal completion work caused serious problems with over drainage of the very northern parts of the Everglades. The muck lands in the northern end of WCA3N would become exposed, oxidized, and burnt away. In the 1971 fires, we lost thousands of acres of ridges and up-lands because of this over drainage and dry muck condition.

The results of this muck loss in 1971 lead the SFWMD to install weirs in the Miami Canal. These weirs starting about 5 miles south of Alligator Alley and then one about the same distance north of the alley would cause the water in the canal to increase in elevation five feet at each control structure. These structures did help slow the draining effects of the Miami Canal, but it did not completly stop the over drainage.

As already mentioned, it is interesting that years later the ACoE/SFWMD in their attempts to restore the Everglades via CERP are going to push in the Miami Canal so that the northern end of WCA3N will not dry out. They are going to move water into this part of the glades via new canals and structures to allow sheet flow to start at the L5. All this expenditure of tax money could have been avoided if they would have listened to the sportsmen in the 1970s.

This was also the first time a satellite was used to fight for the environment in court. Eros was sending good pictures back to earth showing how the algae bloom was expanding and the results of this growth was harming the lake.

The resulting Lake Okeechobee Advisory Committee report was huge. When I read this report, I became very concerned that there was an anti-hunting and anti-fishing bias in our Florida leadership—no intrusive activities. Right in the final executive summary, I found the term 'no intrusive activities' would be allowed in the Everglades. I obtained the full report and all the back-up material that the committee produced. I was looking for someone who recommended that the position of no intrusive activities be a final recommendation from the committee. To my surprise, I could not find any information in all these documents that allowed me to determine whose idea this was and why they thought this should be the management direction for the Everglades. There was no mention of this concept in any of the documents, data, or motions found in the committee's portfolio. I never found out who or why this position was in the executive summary, but it concerned me for many years. I was concerned not only because of what this idea would lead to, but because if this was the belief of our leaders in Florida, it would not be long before hunters and fisherman would be out of the Everglades ecosystem. I was also concerned because of the process by which the executive summary was produced and allowed to have unsupported positions recorded in it.

During all these years of exploring the Big Cypress and Everglades, I became involved in a number of litigations. This happened mostly via the Florida Wildlife Federation but also via local sportsmen's conservation clubs. I have already laid out the big Everglades litigation that was still on going in 2003, but others included litigation against oil companies to protect the Big Cypress. The first one in which I was a named plaintiff ended in money for the first Florida Panther fund, extra FWC staff funded by the oil company for the Cypress, and development concessions.

The funds from our truck pulls and bass tournaments did not only go to fight Everglades and Big Cypress issues. They helped fund litigations against big folks like ARVIDA, ITT, and the City of Jacksonville-Durden Dump. These were all successful in helping save parts of Florida for sportsmen and wildlife.

One particularly contentious issue had been Holely Lands. This is a small parcel of land, bigger than Brown's Farm, located in the very southern side of Palm Beach County. For years the EAA wanted to use this area as a place to store their water. Much of the land was obtained during the establishment of Everglades National Park via a land swap for Educational Sections in ENP. The department of Education was given land in Holely Lands, and they are to be managed as conservation lands not reservoir lands. It is called Holely Land not because it is sacred as some think but because it was a live bombing range in World War II. In several court actions, the area has been set aside for the intended purposes of conservation and recreation and not as a reservoir. Yet under CERP concepts it may well become a pond for the EAA. The Dade County Full-Track Conservation Club was recognized by the National Wildlife Federation as one of their clubs of the year for their work to save Holely Lands.

There was a long, drawn-out battle for those who owned trespass camps in the Big Cypress National Preserve like many of those I described above. The judge took many years to rule on this case. It was rumored that the judge had at one time been a member of a trespass camp and hunted deer with dogs. It could have been true because many of South Florida's judges once used the Big Cypress.

During one of the high-water events in the Everglades, sportsmen-conservation clubs filed suit against the SFWMD for destroying the Everglades. All was going well until a sugar company entered the court on the side of the SFWMD as a friend of the court. A field trip for the judge was arranged to the Everglades. This was needed because the SFWMD experts said the water was only twenty inches deep and not three feet deep. We knew better. Well, the judge went with us and said we were right. Later, in the courtroom the judge ruled against us because our attorney had filed under the wrong law. Then a real shocker came. The SFWMD sent our club president a letter stating in so many words that we owed them $10,000 for our club's share of the court costs. We responded that there was no way we were paying. They came back with another lengthy letter that basically meant pay up or the executive board goes to jail. Here we were trying to save the Everglades from our own agency, and they were making us pay them for killing it. Further, we heard that the sugar company had requested a million dollars for their high-priced attorney. Thank goodness the judge disagreed with them since they were not named by the plaintiffs. We held truck pulls and bass tournaments to raise the money to pay for the SFWMD.

Thank goodness the judge denied the U.S. Sugar Corp's claim we owed them $1,000,000 for their legal fees. They had joined the litigation on the side of SFWMD in order to bring in better attorneys.

It seemed that every litigation ended with a committee, a commission, or a council being formed. One committee was formed by a judge who had an animal rights case before him. This animal rights group sued the FWC over their handling of an early 1980s flood. The FWC wanted to have a mercy deer hunt instead of allowing all the deer to drown and the entire herd to be destroyed since they would over-graze their limited habitat caused by flooding. But this animal rights group sued under the Endangered Species Act. They claimed hunters would harm the panther and the indigo snake that supposedly lived in the flooded Everglades. The judge appointed a blue-ribbon committee to evaluate the conditions. The committee ruled in favor of the FWC actions, and the hunt went on. The animal rights group then went after the chair of this committee by getting big donors to contact the university where the chairman worked and threaten that they would no longer donate if the university did not get rid of this scientist. We went to work and found big donors to thank the university for allowing their employees the latitude to do unencumbered scientific evaluation of South Florida environmental conditions without concern for job repercussions. We won this battle, too.

Another time, there were two Lake Okeechobee Technical Advisory Committees (LOTAC). This time, a company that purchased major quantities of fertilizer reportedly contacted the employer of one of the scientists who sat on this committee. This company threatened to purchase their fertilizer from some other provider if the scientist took a position that would harm this company's water interest. We went to work again and found major buyers of fertilizer outside Florida, and they delivered a message that basically said if the man's company interfered in the free workings of LOTAC, they would go someplace else for their fertilizer. We won this issue too, good reports came out, and no one lost his job.

One year we heard that Senator McPherson was speaking at the Everglades Coalition meeting and that he was not going to support the mission of Saving the Everglades. So, we went to one of our members who owned a T-shirt and hat business, John DeNunzio. John printed 500 white, baseball-style hats with green letters on the front—FOREVER GLADES. This was the first time this term was seen outside the Everglades Coordinating Council. We rented several buses and took 300 sportsmen to this Everglades Coalition meeting. When these folks started to slowly infiltrate the meeting, it was not long before everyone started to notice and looked around. The good Senator asked for one of the hats, put it on before he spoke, and gave a good speech about the importance of the Everglades and how it needed to be restored.

The next legislation session found the Forever Glades bill in the hands of Florida's legislators. Again, we went to John and had him create enough hats for both the Senate and House. It was our plan to have these hats on the seats of each member for the opening session. However, someone in the system blocked our hats from being placed on the seats along with the gifts from other groups. We then sent someone to Tallahassee to hand-deliver a hat to each member, which turned out to be more effective.

Brown's Farm was an area that remained a great place to hunt as it, too, was a drained Everglades habitat. It was on the boundary line between Broward County and Palm Beach County several miles east of U.S. 27. Brown's had been drastically reduced in size from the times when I rode my Dad's friends' swamp buggies as a boy. But, nevertheless, there were lots of deer and hogs on these 4,000 acres. With the press to Save the Everglades, which eventually came to mean Everglades National Park, the realization was growing stronger and stronger that there was too much water going into the Everglades that contained unacceptable amounts of Phosphate and Nitrates. This level of polluted water was causing the Everglades to become choked with cattails. The need to store and release clean water into the Everglades led to the creation of Storm Water Treatment Areas (STAs). Each STA had to go through a long permitting process before they could be built. Once the first series of STAs were approved, there were no more created because the idea was too slow and costly. It was cheaper to create reservoirs that would accomplish almost the same result.

The STAs were approved and one of these was Brown's Farm. The powers that be also wanted Ray Rottenbergers and Holely Lands as STAs or reservoirs. We were able to prevent them from using the latter two because we could generate enough popular support to keep them as Everglades suitable to restore and use for recreation. But we could not generate the same kind of outcry about Brown's Farm. Brown's was a walk hunt WMA only and its users did not care. Thus, Brown's became an STA, and this habitat was lost forever. The decision makers paid no attention to the fact that Florida Panther used the area and that the USFWS Florida Panther Recovery plan called for the continuation of connective corridors between the Big Cypress Basin and the east coast. This was one, if not the only, such corridor south of Lake Okeechobee. Anyway, today it is an STA with no upland wildlife habitat and no place for the panther to hide as they move along the levee from the Big Cypress to J. W. Corbett and on.

The loss of Brown's farm was a not a total loss because these public conservation lands had to be replaced. Barbara J. Powell tirelessly worked to obtain as many new huntable acres as possible. She was able to obtain enough land to create a new wildlife management area in Hendry County—Okaloacoochee Slough. This is a great area and still used today. However, it is farther from Dade and Broward County.

During the year before the Forever Everglades legislative session, we targeted the voters where important legislators lived. We went around to the chambers, cities, league of counties, condo associations, homeowner associations and other civic groups. We had two resolutions approved that basically said that public lands were not to be used to store or clean water from the EAA and that polluters were to pay to clean up their pollution. That legislative session, not one legislator would cross the line and support anything that went against these resolutions. It was the first time that the citizens had beat big sugar. It was also a sign that these agricultural interests had to make some changes in their operation, and they did.

Many years later while driving on U.S. 41 to camp, I noticed a lot of ditching going on beside the road. Then, I found that a cable company was running a cable down U.S. 41 and Loop Road. I also knew I had not seen an ACoE 404 public notice for this work. Being on the Sustainable Commission, I had access to all those responsible for such dredge work. I asked them about the work, and each said they knew nothing of it. It was not long before a newspaper report came out about the work being done in the Big Cypress National Preserve; the preserve staff said they did not have any knowledge about the activity. This seemed strange as the work was going on within the boundary of the preserve and it was miles long. Well, the company did have to get its 404 permit and the NPS rented them a building the NPS had purchased from Mr. Golightly on Loop Road for some kind of support needs. No wonder the cable company was going down Loop Road and the NPS did not know anything about it since the NPS was going to make big money from the cable company. It would pay the NPS not to know too much.

Another civil action that worked against the sportsmen involved the FWC regulation to stop the use of ATCs to hunt, fish from, or use to access the Big Cypress for these activities. It was the custom of the FWC to hold public hearings like town hall meetings when they were going to change their regulations. They called for such a meeting to be held in Milander Hall in the City of Hialeah, Florida. There were so many sportsmen there that the entire hall was full and there was standing room only. Not only did the FWC have their officers there, but they also called in some City of Hialeah police officers. The meeting was going as expected—a bit loud and a bit hot but under control. Then, after one sportsman gave a particularly good speech and the audience liked the presentation, a group of animal rights folks in front of Ralph, Bruce and me started to hoot and holler. We knew they were animal rights by the PETA T-shirts they were wearing, and we did not recognize them. Before they did this, they motioned to another group of four sitting in another section. This hooting tripped the lever and the entire group of people started to hoot and holler. The FWC folks did not like this behavior and I could not blame them. After a while, order was restored, and the meeting continued. The results of this action, since the FWC did not know the crowd was set off by animal rights folks, was that the FWC changed their rules-making process and did away with these town hall meetings; instead, they went to mail-out surveys and meetings with small groups. This change did not allow the average man to participate in the rules-making process. This change continues today.

Another interesting litigation occurred when the Tosahatchee State Preserve was changed to a State Reserve. On a 'State Preserve' there is no hunting allowed. On a 'Reserve' there is minimal hunting allowed. I did not go but Rick and Denny drove the several hundred miles to the Tosahatchee and arrived just in time to learn that Charles Lee of Florida Audubon had walked up and served the FWC with a judge's order to stop the hunt. It seems that Audubon considered hunting as something that would harm their members' ability to see game. This action resulted in another long series of meetings on the topic of visability of wildlife. After all was said and done, the committee decided that the act of hunting did not affect this issue but that other factors like weather and lunar cycle did. Any hunter knew this.

In the late 1990s, nearly twenty years later, this issue of visibility of wildlife again surfaced. The Florida Biodiversity Group and a bunch of other anti-hunting groups used this as one reason to attack hunting in the

Big Cypress National Preserve. Also, the Florida Department of Forestry was using this to limit the amount of hunting on their state lands.

As I mentioned earlier, Florida Biodiversity, a new group of five members only, entered Florida and filed litigation against the DOI/NPS/Big Cypress National Preserve/ACoE/USFWS for failure to create an ORV management plan. They alleged that the use of swamp buggies and ATCs were violating the Clean Water Act (CWA), Tullock Rule, and the Endangered Species Act. They claimed that the use of ORVs required a 404 permit from the ACoE for each trip an ORV made to the Big Cypress since this equipment moved dirt and that was violation of the Tullock Rule—a rule developed in North Carolina to stop logging in that state. They also claimed the use of ORVs was causing the Florida Panther to be stressed and, therefore, harmed and that the use of ORVs was causing harm to the Indigo Snake and the Red-cockaded Woodpecker.

I took Colonel Rice, who was head of the Jacksonville ACoE office at that time and on the Sustainable Commission with me, some of his staff, John Hall, who was head of the permitting department, and a lawyer from the Department of Justice on a field trip to the Big Cypress. We rode around the area on the highway and looked at some swamp buggies and they rode with the NPS behind the Oasis Ranger Station. This took all day, and we had many good conversations. The ACoE people did not think the use of ORVs required a 404 permit. The DOJ man, who wrote the Tullock Rule, thought they did and even went so far as to tell me if a tree fell in the wetlands or waters of the USA, it would need a permit. We had a real problem!

On returning to town and reporting the results of my field trip to the Everglades Coordinating Council and FWF officers of the day, it was determined that we had to get into the litigation, not as a friend of the court but as full-fledge participant on the side of the NPS. We did and the following were accepted as co-plaintiffs: the FWF, the ECC, me, John DeNunzio, Barbara Jean Powell, Dave Charland, Franklyn Adams, and a few others. We proceeded to select a lawyer and went through the FWF to get the most for our investment.

Bob Apgar was our attorney of record, and we produced many documents, photographs and affidavits for his use in defending our interests.

But most important by now, we had received word from within the NPS that they were not going to defend the Big Cypress National Preserve Amended enabling Act but would roll over to satisfy the plaintiff. We had already figured out that this litigation was a friendly litigation coming from the DC level and was a part of President Clinton's move to remove vehicles from Federal lands across the USA. This is where the plaintiff's attorney's office is located.

The friendly case pre-case talk must have gone something like this: DOI/NPS to plaintiff attorney, we cannot get rid of those pesky hunters and their ORVs. The law and popular political pressure have been too much on their side. Can you come up with an attack that will do this and if so, we will not really defend the case? Further, since you may use the CWA and ESA, you will receive a boatload of money from the taxpayer. Enter the five members of Florida Biodiversity with their attorney. The lawsuit was then filed.

Additionally, they all knew the litigation was filed on faulty legal premises. This is because there was nothing in any scientific work to substantiate their position. Further, they all knew the Tullock Rule was not legal. This was proven later by a similar lawsuit filed by the mining industry that went all the way to the Supreme Court and they threw out the rule. The Court stated the rule went far beyond the intent of Congress and if Congress wanted this rule to exist, they had ninety days to pass one. Mind you, this was during the Clinton Administration. Congress did not act to create a legal law like the Tullock Rule. Of course, we did not have the funds to take our issue all the way to the Supreme Court.

Further, both the CWA and ESA were up for reauthorization and funding. Thus, the environmental community really did not want a full-blown court case over this Big Cypress issue. In the opinion of many, the case was predestined to be settled out of court and it was. The plaintiff won nothing since the settlement left us with our 2,500 ORV permit numbers. Remember, Superintendent Hibbard had changed the general management plan years before from the plan that approved 2,000 to 2,500 ORV annual permits. Because of this, the plaintiff also alleged there was a violation of NEPA when this was done. The other thing that the NPS had to do was create an ORV management plan. For years, we had tried to get this done as we knew the NPS had to have an ORV management plan, or the activity could not be allowed (See appendix.) On each attempt to get this plan made, the DOI/NPS said they did not have enough money. Now that they were sued over the issue, they agreed to do one in three years. They did not complete this plan on time because Mr. Hibbard claimed to have lost too many people to NPS cutbacks and no funds. Yet, he was spending his planning money on changing the Florida Scenic Highway the Sustainable had approved to the National Scenic Highway and on developing safety amenities that turned out to be visitor attractions in the form of unneeded and excessively large boardwalks. He was also planning to build a new visitor center in the heart of category one panther habitat.

At the same time, he was supposed to be doing his congressional required recreational baseline study, his Wilderness Report to Congress, and a biological assessment on the wildlife in the Addition lands. The latter had to be done before hunting could be allowed.

Mr. Hibbard had actually started the Addition lands biological baseline study by hiring Dr. George Dalrymple. While turkey hunting with me, George told me he worked a year and was doing well with the expectation and indication that he would receive the second year of this two-year project. He did not nor did anyone else since these funds were being spent by Mr. Hibbard to do the planning for the new National Scenic Highway on U.S. 41. Thus, hunting has not been allowed on the 175,000 acres of the Addition land since the Addition lands act passed in 1988.

In June 2005, after Frank Denninger worked as volunteer concerned sportsmen-citizen for nearly eight years, the City of Everglades voted to not support the National Scenic Highway classification. Then, a few weeks later the Collier County Metropolitan Planning Organization (MPO) put this bad NPS project in its grave. Their plan would have led to the entire U.S. 41 across South Florida becoming a Park Road like those in Yellowstone National Park. The NPS had already contacted the people in Yellowstone to learn how they accomplished the takeover of these roads many years earlier.

However, during the eight years Frank fought his one battle to stop this road, the Florida Department of Transportation had been able to convince the Federal Highway Administration that this road was or would be a National Scenic Highway, thereby getting nearly $10,000,000 in grant money. This money was only for use on National Scenic Highways. The interesting thing about this money is that not one dime of it went to any Florida property, any Florida agency, or was it used to improve the safety of the highway. What it was used for was the creation and building of NPS Big Cypress National Preserve and U.S. Fish & Wildlife Service projects. Most of the money went to the NPS projects. I suppose since Mr. Hibbard came up with the idea and went out on a limb to get the title plan up and running, he was entitled to most of the money. Further, when Assistant Secretary Nat Reed addressed Congress in 1972 about the future funding needs of the Big Cypress and infrastructure plans, he told Congress there would be little development or improvement, and it would not become a destination NPS unit. Essentially, it would remain as it was when purchased, like the Big Thicket National Preserve in Texas—minimal improvements. Thus the $8,000,000 in visitor attractions and amenities Mr. Hibbard wanted and Superintendent John J. Donahue built would not be funded by Congress. Thus, Mr. Hibbard figured out he could dupe the Miccosukee Tribe of Florida, mislead the State of Florida, plus mislead the citizens into thinking this National Scenic Highway classification was a good thing.

Frank reported to us that there seemed to be violations of the Florida Sunshine Act because there were no minutes, no notices sent out, and there were members of different groups and agencies attending this meeting that would advise the Secretary of Florida Department of Transportation, FDOT. He also explained how the vote was taken during one specific meeting of the Corridor Advisory Committee. Mr. Hibbard had a bunch of NPS employees show up from his office and from Atlanta. The hired consultation had some of his employees there. During this meeting, a comment was made that Sustainable had only supported the State Scenic Highway Classification. Mr. Hibbard reportedly said they only advise. It was reported that someone else commented on the new people in attendance and wanted to know if they were going to vote, too. It was stated that meetings are open to all, and they can vote. They voted even though it was their first and last meeting and they did not live in the community. This Corridor Advisory Committee was supposed to represent the

Community and provide local support and reason for Florida Department of Transportation to justify the National Scenic Highway Classification.

Well, as we have seen, the true community did not support this idea and eight years later it was dead. However, there is still the question in many knowledgeable people's minds. What about the way this money was obtained? Was it legal, should the conspirators be looked at for some violation of law or trust of the public? This document was received by Mr. Brian McMahon from the FDOT consultant who orchestrated this entire project.

Grant Source	Year of Funding	Amount	Total
National Scenic Byways Discretionary Grant: Interpretive Plan	1999	$36,930	
Public Lands Discretionary Grant: Visitor Center--Big Cypress Preserve	1999	$2,100,000	
Department of Interior, Visitor and Safety Amenities (for the Big Cypress National Preserve on Tamiami Trail): Welcome Center	1999	$5,000,000	
National Scenic Byways Discretionary Grant: Master Plan	2000	$240,000	$8,641,930
National Park Service-FDOT Statewide Enhancement Funds: Historic Preservation Project at Monroe Station (Collier County)	2004	$785,000	
US Fish and Wildlife Service-FDOT Statewide Transportation Enhancement Funds: Ten Thousand National Wildlife Refuge Trail and Scenic Overlook (Collier County)	2004	$480,000	

Many lawyers thought we should have gone after our expenses, too, and have them paid by the Federal taxpayer as the plaintiff did. Manley directed our attorney not to do this.

Many lawyers thought our attorney had not really taken the battle to the plaintiff because the environmental folks did not want the issue to get out in the press to such a level that Congress would pay attention to it. This would have caused problems with getting the CWA and ESA funded. They did not get reauthorized and have never been reauthorized since passage, yet they have been funded.

My reason for thinking this litigation was friendly is that years later via a FOIA, we found documents sent to the plaintiff by the USFWS that were blind copied as the documents were mailed to the NPS.

A picture of a corduroy road presented to ARC by Richard Hillisnbeck, TNC, as a reason to purchase land in North Florida. Roads like this were destroyed by the NPS in the Big Cypress National Preserve.

All this litigation led to the overly abusive ORV management plan and a serious distrust of the environmental community by sportsmen in Florida and many in the nation. It is a real shame because at the time we all needed to pull together, we were moving apart.

This management plan lead superintendent Donahue to build the Yellow Brick Roads and, in his haste, he destroyed more of old Florida's historical artifacts. This corduroy road above is an example of what he destroyed with his bulldozers. The corduroy road picture was shown to the state's Acquisition and Restoration Council by a TNC representative as a reason why the state should spend millions to purchase a piece of property to protect it from the bulldozers. ARC recommended that this purchase move forward.

We were thoroughly familiar with how the federal folks work together and do not want to challenge each other's authority. Many years before this, the Air Force in Homestead Air Force base wanted to use the

Big Cypress as a hot-fly zone. This meant they would fly mock air battles at low altitude over the Big Cypress. Superintendent Fagergren had the Air Force consultant contact us. She sought a meeting with us. At this meeting, the first question the consultant from England asked was, "How high do airboats fly?" The second question was, "How do the props chop up Manatee?" We knew we had a real problem—if this was the person doing work to create a document for the Air Force. We spent many hours talking with the lady and at least one field trip was taken with her on an airboat. In the end, we prevailed, she was educated, and there was no hot-fly zone over the Big Cypress.

All the time I had Colonel Rice and his folks out, I could not help but recall the hunting documentary that ACoE wanted to make with me. Many years before my field trip with Col. Rice, I had taken their field inspector to the cypress at the request of the President of Johnny C. Jones to see how the removal of the oil roads was making a shallow ditch. A few TV news folks at the request of Superintendent Fagergren had also interviewed me about oil work that might be done in the Big Cypress. Thus, I had become known by the ACoE. They, in turn, contacted me and said they would like to have one of their people go with me to film a documentary about hunting in the Big Cypress. Because we were setting up a trip for the opening weekend of the next hunting season, the initial contact was made around February. Over the year, I spoke with them several times. The last contact was two days before the season opened and we made final arrangements for where and when to meet. In this phone conversation, I told the person I wanted editorial rights and that no shot game would be in any video. The next day, the person called me back and said he could not go as his wife was in the hospital giving birth to their baby. I said OK. However, I found it strange that at no time during our numerous conversations did the subject of his wife's condition come up. Still today, I firmly believe they were going to do a hatchet job on hunting in the Big Cypress with this video and my last-minute stipulations but a kink in their plan.

Early in the history of the Big Cypress, I had another run in with Clean Water Act 404 public notice process. I received all the ACoE notices for Florida. One day, a notice came to me that was a real surprise. The Hendry-Collier Cattle Company was going to develop more than 7,000 acres to the east of Bear Island. They were applying for a permit to build a road from S.R. 84 to the north. In addition to this road, they wanted to build drainage ditches and extend the hyrdro-period of Little Marsh. This marsh was up-stream from Camp Red Bug. They would flood my property. I filed a complaint on this permit and got others to join in the process. Superintendent Fagergren called me, and we had a good talk about this development permit. In a few days, the company's environmental consultant called from Tampa, and he was not as pleasant to talk with as the superintendent was. He tried in his best engineering jargon to convince me that they were not going to flood my land. I only responded then you will take out the part in the permit that says they will extend the hydro-period of Little Marsh which was in the Big Cypress National Preserve. He said they would not. They would not so I did not drop my concerns. The company did get their permit from the SFWMD to build their road from S.R. 84, but the permit also stated this new road could not impact the construction of I-75. The company never did any of their canal and ditch work, so I suppose they did not get their ACoE permit. I never saw a land sale sign and in a few years the land was made a part of the Big Cypress National Preserve via the Addition Act of 1986.

Chapter Fifteen

• • •

Fire & Flood

Camp Red Bug after the Turner Ten wildfire

South Florida is fire and flood. That is, it is either flooding or too dry and burning. In the late 1960s, the SFWMD completed their levee system and could impound water in the Water Conservation Areas, WCAs. These areas are also Wildlife Management Areas, WMAs. When they did this, the 1960s sportsmen took their equipment and money, caught the deer, and put them over the levee into Ray Rottenbergers and Holely Lands.

This established a very strong deer herd there which provided many hunters great hunting for a long time. Baxter Island had water going over it in this 1960s flood. This was the first and only time I ever saw it flowing over the island. Some say that the water operations in the WCAs will not impact the Big Cypress, but it will. I will explain this later.

The early 1970s had serious fires that burned all of the Big Cypress and some of it twice. The Florida Division of Forestry (DOF) drove their bulldozers with plows all over the Cypress chasing the fire. They did a good job around all those structures I listed above and many more. However, I do not think they extinguished or slowed down the advance of the fire. The area is too big and wild.

In 1971, the FL DOF cut hundreds of miles of fire breaks.

After this 1970s fire, I attended a seminar sponsored by the state on wildfires and the Everglades. As a science teacher, I could use the information in my classroom. It was interesting and they decided that it was wrong to use the plow in the Everglades because this turned the dry muck up allowing air to get into the soil. The fire could burn into the muck and go underground thereby doing more harm than if only the surface vegetation burned. They never put the plow in the Everglades again.

During the serious fires of the early 1970s when a lot of land burned twice, those who owned camps in the Everglades not only carried water out in 55-gallon barrels to help put out the wildlife fires, but they also drilled wells on the islands where their camps were located. Almost everyone had a small one-and-half-inch or two-inch well, but these would not allow enough water to be pumped on the island to keep it wet. Therefore, they drilled four and six-inch wells, brought out big diesel pumps, and prevented these islands from being consumed by fire. Not only would the vegetation have been burned but the muck soil as well. In essence, the island would have been no more. The island map in this book indicates where only the very largest islands remain after years of fire and erosion by flooding.

Not only did many islands without camps on them burn. The large, high myrtle ridges burned down to rock (Years later I would spend several days and one field trip working with Dr. Chris McCoy and author Ted Levine talking about the loss of the ridges in the ridge and slough area of the Everglades). Because these ridges were much higher than the nearby sloughs, they were drier and when their muck burned off big shallow lakes were left. When the water returned, there was sterile soil and rock on the surface and no muck. This loss of elevation and flattening of the ridges would create real problems in later years as the Everglades restoration program was being planned. The pre-drainage amount of water could no longer be placed in the Everglades without drowning the remaining lowered uplands. Thus, the water needs downstream in ENP and Florida Bay could not be fully met without completely destroying the rest of the Everglades north of U.S. 41.

After the flood and the 1970s fire, the FWC decided they should do a wildlife survey of the WCAs. This was a good idea and the sportsmen worked with them to do this. Sportsmen, at their own expense and time, worked with the FWC by carrying their employees on our equipment. The area, which covered nearly 700,000 acres, was zoned off and each group worked their zone. All wildlife was counted and reported and FWC staff recorded all this information. I always thought this should be done every year and suggested so to the FWC, but they did not like the idea, and it was not done. There was no hunting season that year in the Everglades. There was too much water and not enough vegetation because the water came up too fast and drowned most of the plants. Sawgrass will grow about an inch a day and if the water rises faster than that, it will die after it is burned. The SFWMD can put the water in the area much faster than an inch a day.

During the 1980s, we had high water, low water, and fires. The Everglades became a place that one might or might not hunt in because of these environmental issues. However, there was one flood that stemmed the start of today's Everglades Restoration actions. This was the early 1980s flood in which the FWC held a deer mercy hunt. This was on national TV and in worldwide papers. Coverage of drowning deer and men having to shoot them to save the few that could find high ground and food was good television stuff. This led to Governor Graham's deer committee and

Save the Everglades plan that required deer populations to be maintained at twenty (20%) percent below carrying capacity at high water. Never mind that they did not know how much high ground there was and thus did not know what the carrying capacity was. The deer herd was collapsed by over-harvesting of the does. There was one flood that stemmed the start of today's Everglades Restoration actions. This was the early 1980's flood in which the FWC held a deer mercy hunt. This was on national TV and in worldwide papers. Coverage of drowning deer and men having to shoot them to save the few that could find high ground and food was good television stuff. This lead to Governor Graham's deer committee and Save the Everglades plan that required deer populations to be maintained at ten percent below carrying capacity at high water. Never mind that they did not know how much high ground there was and thus did not know the carrying capacity was. The deer herd was collapsed by overharvesting of the does."This 1980s flood was the real beginning of the Save the Everglades Program (CERP) we have today!

In this early 1980s flood, I had an experience that could only happen in the cypress. I was traveling in the north part of Bear Island and the buggy trail went between two small cabbage islands. They were about three feet out of the water and the water was nearly three feet deep in the trail. Well, just as I got between these two islands, a covey of quail broke and flew over me. I stopped to admire them and looked down to see a school of pound size largemouth bass swimming under the buggy.

In the 1980s flood, it was estimated the SFWMD drowned 40,000 deer in the WCAs, which were also WMAs. This Everglades deer never came back. This was not only our thought but was put on the Internet by the University of Tennessee in their CERP work. They developed the ATLAS to be used in evaluating the impacts of CERP projects on the wildlife and other natural system attributes.

The FWC mercy deer hunt saw two different management ideas come head-to-head. The first idea is that it is necessary to take as many deer as possible out of the area before communicable deer diseases break out and the entire herd dies. The other idea is to leave them alone and only the strongest will survive. The FWC allowed deer to be caught, evaluated and treated by a veterinarian from the north side of Alligator Alley. (This was the idea of animal rights supporters' side.) The FWC had hunters go in, take a deer, and get out as fast as possible. The deer heard on the south side of the road fared well. The deer herd on the north side did not fare well and most died even though the north side had more high ground and lower water levels. Jack Kasawitz ran the rescue. He got some airboaters from the different clubs to help him. These folks captured thirty-three deer and only one survived at Jack's ranch. The Dade County Fulltrack Conservation Club helped Jack by collecting the native vegetation his deer needed for food. These sportsmen also gave him money. They gave him more money than the animal rights groups did. Once the media show was over, the national animal rights leaders were gone—out of town—good-bye. They had their press and day in court.

A few years later, the FWC got another one of their harebrained ideas. It came from Texas where deer were being raised and studied in big holding pens like cattle. They decided that hunters all wanted to shoot bucks with big racks and that the long-standing hunting regulations had caused the gene pool to skew toward bucks with small racks since they were the only bucks left to pass on their genes.

For years, we had a five-inch, minimum spike antler rule. Therefore, the FWC said any buck with a hard antler could be shot. This idea was neither accepted by sportsmen nor the NPS. The NPS used this as a reason to do their first deer study and hired Dr. Larry Harris of the University of Florida. Larry was a member of the FWF and called us as soon as he had met with the superintendent. He was very upset and talked for an hour about how the superintendent directed him to do a study he could use to stop hunting based on the deer harvesting regulations of the FWC. His report supported our position, which was to not take bucks with less than five-inch spikes. Shortly after that, the FWC wised up and went back to the five-inch rule. In 2003, FWC started going the other way and saying hunters could only take two bucks a year: one with three-points on one side and one buck with five-inch spikes. Again, they were getting their management concept from Texas and the philosophy that people only hunted for big-racked trophy deer.

Some tried to convince us that water management in the WCAs did not affect the water level in Big Cypress National Preserve except along the eastern interface line. We had always known better and the high-water events of the 1990s illustrated this. The U.S. mail carrier who traveled Tamiami trail every day could always tell when the water was raised in the WCAs, by the time he reached Turner River. He told me that when the SFWMD increased the water elevation in the WCAs the water in the Tamiami canal would flow to the west. The water was pushed up the canal to the northwest against the natural flow. This was because the water to the east was higher than the water's natural elevation to the west. Thus, water was seeking its own level and going into the Big Cypress National Preserve.

I also had conversations with the FWC biologist who had worked on the Big Cypress for most of his career. He explained that when the water level in the WCAs was raised during the 1990s, water would flow northwest, upstream against the natural flow, in Mullet Slough a long way before it turned back south through cypress strands and over low pine islands. Essentially the SFWMD/ACoE/ENP were killing the Big Cypress with too much water because they were experimenting by sending more water to ENP. That year, many big pines and century-old oak trees died from rotting roots.

In 1981, the Big Cypress burned. It was not as bad as the 1970s fires, but it was bad. It has been said until the massive Yellowstone fires, this was the worst wildfire in the history of the NPS. This Turner Ten fire, as it is called, led to a very aggressive burn program in the Big Cypress. They reportedly burn more acres than any other NPS unit does. Today, they still do a lot of burning. The only difference is that the fire is so well- controlled that it is not very hot. This is allowing the prairies to become dominated by myrtle. However, it is a good thing they do such a good job of controlled burning. Most years, they exceeded their desired target number of acres to burn.

In the 1990s, there were serious floods. These floods were worse in many ways than the floods of the 1960s and 1970s. Not only was the water higher than before but the high water lasted longer. This was because the SFWMD under Sam Poole was hand in hand with ENP to implement Experimental Water Deliveries to ENP under Modified Water Deliveries. Therefore, the water was not only extremely high, but it stayed high for months. Thus, according to the Indians, the owls were eating songbirds on the islands in the Everglades. They also pointed out, as well as knowledgeable sportsmen, that everything was dead in the Everglades, including the rats. Not only were the uplands dying from this experiment, but the willows and large areas of sawgrass were also being drowned. In short, the area was in its worse shape ever while we were talking about restoring it and spending billions to do this.

After the early 1970s flood, some of the hunters with track vehicles that were developed to traverse the Everglades placed blades on the front of their machines. This made the machine look like a strange type of bulldozer. The hunters, at their own expense, pushed up small mud islands. These islands were to replace the islands and ridges that had burned away from the fires that followed the floods. These islands were so successful that Franny Taylor was able to get the Board of Trustees, under Governor Askew, to fund hiring a contractor through the FWC to build more and bigger islands. A later study by the FWC stated the islands would work but first the water management practices would have to be changed to stop the disastrous flooding and excessive drying of the Everglades. The floods would erode the islands and then fires would burn the muck they were built out of. In short, as long as the SFWMD/ACoE were allowed to continue their operational practices, it was a waste of money to build these islands. Not only did Franny make uplands for terrestrial wildlife but he also made gator holes for aquatic wildlife and birds.

An interesting side story to Franny's work is that one day Allen Currelli, then president of the Everglades Coordinating Council, received a phone call from the ACoE about the illegal dredge and fill work Allen was doing in the Everglades. Somehow, they thought Allen was doing this work. Allen told them he had not done any, but that Franny had and was in charge of this program. They asked how to contact Franny. Allen said they should go to heaven because Franny had died.

Chapter Sixteen

◆ ◆ ◆

Alligators, BBQs, Work and More Hunting

By the mid-1980s, the alligator population in the Big Cypress National Preserve had reached such a level that those who were still using dogs to hunt had to be very careful. Everyone knows that alligators love to eat dogs. Many lost their hunting dogs when the quarry they were chasing ran to the swamps and ponds.

Not only had the population of alligators drastically increased but also so had their size. We found very large prints of very big gators in the mud during spring gobbler season. On one spring gobbler hunt, I heard a gobbler leaving his roost. He was located on the far side of Pine Island across a marl flat. I was crawling on my hands and knees along the edge of a thick palmetto island. The bird made one good gobble after he left his perch. I returned with a hen cluck and a gobble. Just after my call had settled, I heard a loud growl and water splashing next to me. It sounded like whatever had made this loud sound was right next to me. I forgot about the gobbler for a while since I thought there might be a bear coming out of the thicket to dine on turkey. I moved away from the palmettos and remained low in the wiregrass. Then the animal growled again, and I realized it was only a big bull gator in his gator hole in the thicket. I always warned those who had never hunted during spring gobbler in the cypress about these growling gators. I told them not to worry unless they saw the gator coming and then they had a problem.

On many occasions, we heard the gator growl. This is a very special event and one that no one forgets once they have heard it. I am not talking about the University of Florida Gator Growl. I am talking about sitting in a tree stand hearing what sounds like the low roar of a small jet engine coming from the windward direction. This is the gator growl. The big and little gators for some unknown reason start growling. They give out one real loud long roar. This sound travels with the wind and the next gator downwind tries to growl louder than the one he hears.

Congressman Marlenee comparing his hand with that of a Big Cypress gator.

This awesome sound rolls through the swamps as the wind blows the sound along to the next gator. By the mid-1980s, we were regularly experiencing this fantastic display of gator communication. Each time we would think to ourselves: "We are walking in these swamps at night."

On one archery hunting trip with Stuart "Stu" Carver, we were heading toward the mother gator hole area inside the Deep Lake Strand to the southwest of camp. I had a three-notch trail made through the minor strands of this big cypress swamp. I took up the first likely ambush spot for my bow stand and explained to Stu how to follow the trail and where to go. I had been in my stand for about two hours and had seen a few does feed nearby when I heard a big animal slowly walking my way from where Stu had gone. I thought maybe he had spooked a buck and it was on the trail of the does.

The major rut is during early archery season in the Big Cypress and the bucks are most active then. I watched closely as the sound came closer. It was not long before I saw Stu. I inquired as to what happened. Since he was an avid a hunter as I and did not leave a stand early, I thought he might have deer down. Stu explained that while it was still dark, he had gone about 200 yards from me when he came across a very big gator lying in the marked trail. Stu said the gator already knew he was approaching and was lying there with his big mouth wide open hoping for a meal. Stu backed up and eased around the beast. But then he could not locate the three-notch trail so instead of beating the bush and disturbing the area he stood there for a while before returning to me. Needless to say, we left that part of the swamp to its owner—that big gator.

By the mid-1990s, while the gators in the Everglades proper were looking sicklier than ever, we were finding bigger and bigger gators in the Cypress. On one trip from camp to Monroe station, we drove up on a gator as long as my buggy. We were about two miles southeast of camp and heading home so everything was packed away, including our cameras. It was about noon when we drove on to a sand spit in the trail. This small high dry ground always had deer, hog and or raccoon tracks on it. To our surprise, we saw this very large gator resting with most of his body in the water and his head on the high ground. It was apparent he was lying in ambush for some animal to step out of the water as it traveled the cypress and to provide him with a meal. He was not afraid of us when we stopped the buggy and admired his size. All he did was open one eye, turn his head and open his big mouth to us. We left him at his ambush spot and went on again thinking that we walked in these swamps.

One of the absolute best gator experiences I had at Camp Red Bug was when I took a very special guest to my camp. I frequently used the camp and cypress experience as gifts for organizations like the FWF, North Dade Chamber of Commerce and Make a Wish Foundation. At one of these times, a banker and his wife had obtained a half-day trip to camp, with a buggy ride and lunch. I met them at the designated location, and we drove into camp in my truck. On the way in, we saw a large gator lying in the dirt road. This gator stayed put long enough for us to get close and take a picture. This made my guests extremely happy; as they had never seen a gator in the swamps, they had only seen them at Miami's Metro Zoo. Before we arrived at camp, another gator crossed our trail. Now, they were becoming a bit anxious about all these gators.

When we arrived at camp, I made them some coffee and provided a snack while I made the buggy ready for our ride. The lady would not have anything to do with leaving the screened porch because she knew a gator was waiting for her. While I was in the barn getting the buggy ready, I heard a lot of yelling from my guests. I quickly stepped out of the barn in time to see a large gator casually walking across the lawn. That was it; the lady would have nothing to do with leaving the house. After some time had elapsed, we got her on the buggy and off we went. I am sure she thought the ride would lead to her demise. We had a great ride in the cypress on the old buggy trails around camp. In a few hours, we were back, had lunch and left for town; no one was eaten by a gator. On this day, I saw more gators than I had ever seen that were not in a big lake.

In my opinion, the reason the cypress gators are doing so well while the Everglades gators are not is in the water management area. By this, I mean the Cypress has some high water as nature meant it to be. Then it has low water as nature meant it to be. It does not have the artificial water levels and durations that exist in the Everglades because of the ACoE, SFWMD and DOI/NPS/ENP. Their management of the water in the Everglades has killed off the gators' red meat food. Those gators in the Cypress have plenty of red meat, plenty of fish, and plenty of birds. Thus, they have a time to feast and time to eat less and thereby provide a strong viable population of gators in the Cypress.

Today, many will say that not only are water management practices at fault in this gator issue but also water quality. The water quality in the Cypress is far superior to that in the Everglades. This is because most of the Big Cypress receives its water from rain and not from pumps. The Everglades, on the other hand, receives both rainwater and pump water. Meaning that water is pumped, or pushed, into the Everglades from farms and urban areas. This water is not exactly as clean as rainwater. Not only does it carry phosphate (P) and nitrates (N) but it also carries all the other chemicals that come with modern living—petroleum based products, medicines, pesticides, and herbicides.

There continues to be more litigation with the potential for more far-reaching impacts of the decisions that will come from these cases. One of the largest is the S-9 litigation brought against the SFWMD/State by the Miccosukee Indian Tribe. The tribe, through Dexter Lethinen, won round one of this case; it claimed the SFWMD needed a Clean Water Act 404 Permit to move already polluted water through this pump into the Everglades and onto Indian land and ENP. The SFWMD appealed this case and organizations from all over the nation entered the case as friends of the court. These groups were on both sides of the issue, as the results would have serious impacts across the nation. For many years, western dams and other water moving facilities never needed this permit as they were not considered as polluters but only movers of polluted water. This S-9 case stands to change all of that. Yet, our Everglades gators continue to starve, no matter who wins the S-9 case.

The case I helped start while Dexter was Assistant U.S. Attorney was still going on fifteen years later. The judge who heard the case kept it open and under his authority. That is, until he made comments in the news about a new water bill that moved through the Florida Legislature in the 2003 session. This bill extended the deadline for twenty years that the P levels of the Everglades had to be met. This level was 10ppb of P. The judge's comments caused the biggest EAA folks to file a complaint and the judge was removed. Judges are to rule on law, impose penalties based on law, and declare laws illegal, but they are not to enter the political arena lest they may become considered as biased to an issue before them. It appears the judicial system considered the judge to have crossed the line. Yet, our Everglades gators continue to starve, despite judicial issues.

The lack of food in the Everglades caused the gator to adjust to new conditions. With too much water not only killing off the gator's food but also destroying the need for them to create and maintain gator holes they moved to the canals in the Everglades. There were always many gators in these canals, but there had also been gators in the Everglades away from the canals. With the big bull gators taking up territory in the canals, their social structure changed. This became evident when the big bull gators caused the population of gators to become unbalanced. You see, these big bull gators eat everything, including the other small gators. They do not care if the gator is male or female; they are hungry, so they eat. Further, scientists say the big bull gators are not the best breeders but that the mid-aged or teenaged male gator is the best breeder. With the big bulls eating the less mature males, the reproductive cycle was being thrown off. Thus, the FWC allowed the taking of these big bull gators by sportsmen. Still our gators are starving and when they disappear so does the foundation of the Everglades.

By the late 1980s, Everglade's alligators were sickly. We reported this to the experts. I did on the floor of the Sustainable Commission. No one listened and then one day, late in the 1990s, alligator researchers said so. It was obvious; we did not want to spend millions for ongoing research to tell us this. There was nothing for gators to eat in the Everglades. All the red meat animals were dead and with the gators leaving the glades for the canals, they were not keeping their gator holes open for fish to swim to when the water did drop. Everything looked fine from the road because the canals were full of gators, but they were very skinny long gators. Could we have the Everglades without gators?

Not only were the alligators in trouble but the snakes and rabbits appeared to be as well. When I was a boy, my family drove on Hollywood Blvd., U.S. 27 and U.S. 41. The game the adults and children all participated in was who could see the rabbits first and count the most. In the early morning hours and late afternoon hours, it was not possible to count all the rabbits along these roads. It is easy to understand why there are no swamp rabbits along the shoulders of Hollywood Blvd., now Pines Blvd., since the entire area has houses along the road. However, what has happened to all the rabbits on U.S. 27, on U.S. 41 on S.R. 29 and S.R. 84 (I-75)? The last time I drove this 150-mile trip, I counted four rabbits during prime rabbit observation time, early morning, or late afternoon.

I mentioned the snakes as being in trouble. When we were young and even into the early 1970s, every time there was a cold snap, the roads would become the warmest place around. This would draw the snakes out of the swamps and onto the black warm asphalt. The road would become slick with dead snakes. There were snakes of all kinds—cottonmouth water moccasins, banded water snakes, red belly water snakes, red rat snakes, black snakes and even some indigo snakes. By 2000, when we had the same environmental conditions that had pushed all these snakes onto the road, this time there would be no snakes. What happened to all the snakes?

The only common denominator that could have this kind of impact on snakes and rabbits over the entire south Florida system is water. Many think the water quality is causing this problem. It could be endocrine mimics, or it could be something else but there certainly is something wrong since there are no predatory bobcats or hawks. Even if there were predators, they could not cause all these animals to disappear from such a large area.

Not only are they not seen on the roads but also, they are not seen in the deep backcountry as they once were. This has been reported by such knowledgeable people as Tom Shirley and Franklin Adams.

Once the gator had been taken off the ESA list, the FWC started holding tightly managed gator hunts. Soon the FWC stopped managed gator hunting in the Everglades because the meat had high levels of mentholated mercury. This is the bad mercury and is extremely poisonous. It is also known as a bio-cumulating substance. That means it is consumed and increases in quantities in the meat and is passed on to the next higher predator. The gator is the top predator of the glades and had too much poison in it for human consumption. This was particularly true if the meat were to be sold and eaten in restaurants, as is much of the gator meat from Florida's management-controlled hunts. Everglade's gator hunts were resumed after many years of being closed, the FWC merely changed their

The wall of shame.

regulation and allowed sportsmen to hunt the Everglades gator under a tightly controlled process, but they could not sell the meat. In other words, it was all right for them, their family, and friends to eat this poisonous meat but do not sell it! Anyway, big gators are being removed from the canals of the Everglades hoping to stop the collapse of the alligator population before CERP is finished in thirty-five to fifty years.

While all this stuff was going on and I had some level of involvement in the issues, we were having great times at Camp Red Bug. We had our usual camp court at the end of January. Instead of cutting shirttails when someone missed their deer or hog, we held the "goods." In other words, let the story fester and grow. Then on a usually cold January weekend we would hold court. My wife, Donna K. Moller, was always the judge and found no one innocent. Thus, around a big campfire with a good meal of game under our belts, we would pour drinks and tell how each had messed up and not taken his quarry. As I said, no one was innocent despite their protests and the punishment was always the same—OFF WITH THE SHIRTTAIL, RECORD THE DASTARDLY DEED ON A PAPER PLATE, AND NAIL IT TO THE CAMP'S FRONT WALL FOR ALL TO SEE FOREVER, EVEN IF YOU DID NOT KNOW WHO WOULD VISIT. Over the years "Judge DKM" ordered the following sentences and many more to be administrated. The sentencing would always begin with GUILTY AND OFF WITH THE SHIRT TAIL. Then the sentence would be read aloud so all would know how badly the offender had done.

Even the author lost his shirt tail; cutters are Michael Dillistin and Denny.

9-8-1973; Luther Jack Moller was found guilty in Red Bug kangaroo court presided over by Dennis Wilson and Mike Carter. The before mentioned archer shot 4 times at 4 different deer, missing everyone. Each deer was closer than 20 yards. He has been sentenced to lose his shirttail.

1-2-1975: The Defendant Dennis L. Wilson is found guilty of missing 4 different hogs and deer on numerous occasions. We are tired of feeble invalid excuses from the defendant. This verdict was based on inaccurate shooting and not being overly ready for available game. The "rifle man" has been found guilty and so cut off his shirttail.

12-3-1978; Kevin Williams has pleaded guilty to squandering an opportunity to kill an 8-point buck whereas the before mentioned animal was close enough to hit with a pea shooter. The maximum penalty is being imposed by his fellow hunters: Dennis Wilson, Jack Moller, and Tommy Jarvis. The luckless hunter has been condemned to lose his shirttail!

3-24-84: Linda Dillistin, Defendant, has been tried by the "Red Bug" Hunt Court of 1983-84. The defendant has pleaded guilty and has been found guilty of missing the ONLY buck of the season. And even more incriminating, the Buck was a large 6-point, standing only 20 yards away from the buggy. The buck was standing in low grass and did not run until she pulled the trigger 2 times with no shell in the chamber. The Buck began to walk off, proving Linda clearly missed.

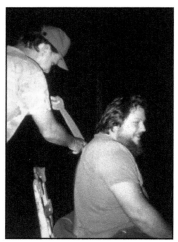

Wayne losing his shirt tail.

3-24-84, Luther Jack Moller has botched numerous opportunities at game this season. "Shooter error" in front of two witnesses. During another hunt, he discharged four rounds and the same hunter witnesses are asking "Where's the pork?" It is the finding of this kangaroo court that this unfortunate hunter be condemned to lose his shirttails.

'84 – '85: Kangaroo Court: Mrs. Linda Dillistin while sitting on a buggy waiting for two pushers working hard to bring one large buck out of the thicket. She did miss as the buck slipped out and did kill several trees. Kangaroo Court does hereby find Linda guilty of missing her only chance of the year, so cut off her shirttail.

Kangaroo Court 1984-1985: One Mr. Dennis Wilson did miss one large buck the last weekend of the hunting season. He did confess to shooting at said buck from 300 yards while said buck was standing in the open low grass. The Red Bug Kangaroo Court does hereby find him guilty! So, cut off his shirttail.

Kangaroo Count, 4-5-86: The defendant, Luther J. Moller, confessed to shooting high and shooting low, when he used to be "Dead Eye Joe." There must be a reason why he misses bucks and mistakes logs for hogs.

Could it be these lovely "Smurfette" glasses that were seen on Jack at the times of the shootings?

The Kangaroo Court finds the defendant guilty of defective equipment and sentences him to lose his shirttail. (My glasses were attached to the plate.)

Kangaroo Court, '85 - '86: One Mr. Rick Dillistin did miss one spike at 100 yards with a 58 cal. as he stood there looking. Mr. Dillistin also knocked down one of the two bucks at close range. He then allowed this buck to run off as he watched the other run. Red Bug Kangaroo Court has found Mr. Dillistin guilty! So, off with his shirttail.

2-4-89: He had a problem with his rear... That's why he missed the deer. Maybe he'll get it next year. Wayne Hoffmann was found guilty on this date and was judged by a jury of his fellow kangaroos. So, cut off his shirt.

1990: Red Bug Court has found Dennis L. Wilson guilty because he fired to assist—but he MISSED!! The hog is still on the RUN.

Feb 1990: Dennis L. Wilson was found guilty of sitting in a tree and missing a trophy buck of the year with his double over-under 50 cal. muzzle loader. He has been found guilty!

Kangaroo Court 1990: Dennis Wilson did fire two shots at close range with his 35 Rem. He later claimed to have missed because the hog was too far away from the road. Red Bug Court finds him guilty of harassing hogs.

1990: Wayne Hoffmann was found guilty of harassing large hogs with a 12-gauge mag Browning. Red Bug Court declares Wayne guilty of not putting fresh meat in the cooler.

11-20-90: Debbie Wilson. Jack appeared under her tree, made her seem nervous, we thought she would faint. Fired five times from up the tree, no deer were discovered that we could see. Her husband appeared and saved her at three and found a deer before he could flee. But she still missed the spike, so she loses her shirttail.

The offender would, with great fanfare, have his or her shirttail cut off with the sentence written on a plate and nailed to the front wall of Camp Red Bug for all to see forever.

We also had many BBQs with folks from where we worked and other places. These were some of the best times as these people by and large had never been out of sight of a streetlight. They were all amazed at what it meant to be as dark as night with no moon. They soon realized you could not see your hand in front of your face on those nights.

We had plenty of workdays. I had no partners as partners go but folks who hunted came around to help with mowing, building maintenance, and buggy work. We had a real sense of community—a Gladesman Culture. We had workdays not only at Camp Red Bug but also in other places.

We worked with the NPS, FWC and SFWMD to kill invasive exotic plants like melaleuca. Not only did we go with them to cut and squirt these trees with poison, but we also took the state's required course to receive our non-commercial applicator's license so we could be issued the NPS tree poison to kill these trees as we wandered around the Preserve. Because of this, I had no melaleuca within miles of Camp Red Bug.

Many others joined me in spending a lot of time after hunting season going back to locations where we had found exotic plants. The NPS and others were concentrating on the melaleuca, but no one addressed the Brazilian Pepper. This plant is going to be harder to get rid of than the melaleuca or the pepper tree. That is because the birds, raccoon and bear eat the berries of the Brazilian Pepper or Florida Holly. There is a real, native Florida Holly and it should not be confused with the exotic one.

This exotic is taking over a much bigger area than melaleuca, which is also known as the paper tree. We found it growing on the buttress roots of big cypress trees like an air plant. I also worked on the Brazilian Pepper (Florida Holly) around the area we hunted. The NPS herbicide issued also worked on Brazilian Pepper. By the time I left the Big Cypress, I had made a good start on controlling this plant that would destroy the habitat if it were left unchecked.

Al Bryan organized many tree plantings and workdays.

We also started finding the Old-World Climbing Fern. This plant was growing on all sorts of trees, and we found it back in big cypress strands where no man, except us, had been in years. We had been the only ones in these big cypress strands over the last few years. This plant is so bad, it has destroyed most of the islands in the Loxahatchee National Wildlife Refuge and much of the area in the Kissimmee River that was being restored. It grows like a vine and becomes so dense and heavy that it kills full-grown cypress, pines, and oaks. It then causes them to fall over on each other leaving a mass of vine and dead timber. The seeds, really spores, are spread for sure by fire and contact with animals and birds when they get near the vine. All these problems were properly reported to the NPS, but I never saw any action from them to stop the spread of these plants. Of course, I suppose their way of acting on this problem will be to stop people, and particularly hunters, even on foot, from going into these areas.

We worked with the FWC to cut fire lines in the Everglades—not by plowing but by roller chopping the tall sawgrass. We labored in the hot sun and bugs to plant trees on the uplands in the Everglades, we helped with the building of islands in the early 1970s, and we lobbied to get funds for all this work. We worked to remove Melaleuca from the Everglades.

We were successful in getting the funds for Melaleuca eradication and we were no longer needed to do the fieldwork. The NPS, FWC and SFWMD now had money and they did not need our free labor or equipment. They hired folks to do this work. It was just as well because they could apply more man-hours and get the job done in no time. By 2003, the SFWMD had all the Melaleuca out of WCA 3 north and south. They had most of them out of the East Everglades.

We had fundraisers such as raffles, truck pulls, bass tournaments and BBQs. One of the biggest and oldest BBQs was the Everglades Conservation and Sportsmen Wild Hog BBQ. This activity been had held for more than fifty years.

Up until the late 1960s, they got the hogs out of the Big Cypress. Most were taken near Austin's corrals. Nevertheless, they soon had to purchase their hogs from big ranches in Hendry County. The first year I cooked at the Wild Hog, I worked on the night crew. I liked the third shift because there were not a lot of folks coming around, it was cool, and we could sit about telling woods stories. In the 1970s, we would start cooking on Friday night and cook around the clock until Sunday noon. We cooked as fast as the charcoal grills allowed. Then we went to gas and cooked as fast as they would allow. It was all we could do to keep up with the demand for meat. We fed many people. It was a wild time with people camping all over the woods, camping at Monument Lake,

Richard Potter and his night cooking crew.

and enjoying the Big Cypress. We had buggy rides for those from the city who had never been on one. They had themselves a great time. Many of the young people would be hooked on the buggy idea and later became buggy owners and club members. The NPS soon reduced camping at the monument when we had the Wild Hog. They then closed camping within miles of the club. They accomplished their objective. They reduced our crowd down to about 1,200 people a year. We no longer had an open gate policy; all tickets were pre-sold so as not to have food left over. No longer did we cook around the clock but only early Saturday morning. No longer did we make big dollars but just about enough to cover part of the year's budget. The NPS knew what they were doing—drying up our ability to make money and to keep the doors open. Even with the much-reduced size, we still had a good time and were much more relaxed.

By 2002, politics was in my blood, and I seemed to have become well-known. During Governor J. Bush's second race, I was vice-chair of ARC

The author showing Denny's children, Cody and Amanda Wilson, how to baste ribs.

and that is why the phone call I received really surprised me. Janet Reno, now out of the DC crowd, called. She introduced herself and said she was running for Governor and Johnny C. Jones said she needed to call you. She said according to Johnny that I would not support her, but she wanted to me know that she was not antigun or anti-hunter. She wanted me to arrange a meeting with the Everglades Coordinating Council and the various clubs in South Florida. She said she intended to go across the state and talk to all the sportsmen clubs. I asked her if she knew who I was. She said she did. Then I said I was vice-chair of ARC. I also said I had sent her a letter while she was the Attorney General of America over the treatment, she, via her staff, had given me during the Florida Biodiversity ORV litigation. I told her, as I did in that letter, that I was extremely disappointed that she and her staff had not allowed us in the room to resolve the case when I was a named defendant on the side of the NPS. I told her about all the times she had spoken to my students in high school when she had preached fairness, honesty, and total involvement of the people. I said that sure did not happen when she was Attorney General. She wanted a copy of the letter. I said OK but never sent her one because I figured it was a now a waste of time (letter to Reno see appendix).

What I did was to get hold of the campaign manager for J. Bush and the Republican Party leader of Broward County. We decided not to invite her to address sportsmen groups that I had access to. I also had access to the congressional library and made a phone call to my contact there. The outcome of this call was a document establishing all of A.G. Reno's antigun actions while in DC. We then decided to not expose what we held until after the Democratic Primary, because we really wanted her to run against Bush. As it turned out, she did not make it that far. However, my document did not go to waste.

Wayne showing his card collection of South Florida to Wild hog BBQ attendees.

When she started coming out strong for the Democratic candidate, I sent out the document about her antigun actions to all those on my email list. This list was very large. It numbered well into thirty thousand.

Gone were the days when I would have to produce letters and sticky address labels in the thousands. Then, my wife, daughter, and I would sit around the dining room table, stuffing, sealing and stamping them. The clubs would purchase the stamps and supplies. Sometimes things happened so fast in those early days that I had to make a run of letters and then the Everglades Coordinating Council would hold a special meeting to hand out bundles of letters and addresses to each club leader. They would then get these out via their own club process. Technology had allowed me to get out an entire document to thousands of people in a few minutes and no postage was required.

The entire time we owned camp Red Bug, we took scouting groups, church groups and others out to visit the Cypress. I even put-up day trips for a buggy ride and lunch to charitable organizations like SCI, FWF, church auctions, and Make-a-Wish foundation. This allowed me to expose many people to the Cypress who otherwise would never have gone. These trips were always popular items and raised the organization a lot of money. I made lots of new friends.

Jamie Adams and Wayne Farnsworth at turkey camp. Jamie was a world class camp cook and turkey caller.

However, taking all these people out to enjoy the Big Cypress did cause problems. With all the people I would take Camp Red Bug, and the many articles that had been written by folks like Jamie Adams (retired Sheriff, retired game warden, Chairman of the FWC, author) and Steve Waters, it did not surprise me, but it did anger me, when I was investigated by the NPS, under Superintendent Donahue's direction, for operating a business from my camp. If I had been, this would allow them to condemn my property. I was sure then why Mr. Fagergren had connected me with the federal archeologists. It was not a mere act of goodwill on his part, but he was setting me up if I had written the wrong contract.

One day, when I was leaving Camp Red Bug at the parking lot on I-75 for the 71-milepost recreation access area, Ranger GB drove up. He and I had a special relationship since he had been in the Preserve longer than any other employee had. After we talked a bit, he reached over beside him and handed me a copy of *Florida Sportsmen*. Jamie Adams had written a very good article in that major magazine. Jamie told the truth about the NPS management direction. Well, the article GB handed me had circles all over it. Ranger GB said he was directed by someone, and I assumed that someone had to be the superintendent, to ask if I was running a guide business. I said NO and that folks who go with me split the cost. This was true and a common practice among friends who fished or hunted together. He said he thought not but this, the *Florida Sportsmen*, landed on his desk and he was directed to investigate it.

I was upset and sent a letter to Secretary Norton asking why I was being investigated for taking friends to my private property in the Big Cypress National Preserve and by what authority I was being investigated and what crime did the DOI/NPS think I had committed. She passed the letter on down the line and the Regional Director, Belson, who had been at my camp with the Barry meeting, sent me a letter saying I could continue doing what I had been doing and that I was seen taking a lot of people in and out and that prompted the investigation (see the appendix.). I let this drop but really wanted to pursue it.

The last DOI/NPS meeting at Camp Red Bug

I figured that Mr. Donahue was not pleased with me because he had attended a meeting with BJ Powell, George Dalrymple, Joe Garrott, Chief Ranger D. Sholly, Assistant Sectary Donald Barry, SE Regional Direct Larry Belson, me, and a few other folks at Camp Red Bug. I really think he and the rest of the NPS wanted to get rid of my camp and me. They figured they would do this any way possible. After a few articles were published that did not speak well of the NPS and how they treated sportsmen and refused to follow the Amended Enabling Act and the intent of these laws, they were really looking hard at how they could get rid of me. Of course, this only made me more determined than ever to work to challenge the NPS at every opportunity no matter where I lived or what I owned. After all, over the years, many elected officials, their aides, judges, and their family members had visited Camp Red Bug to enjoy their land in the Big Cypress Basin.

When I talked to the group at this meeting with the Assistant Secretary, I started, as I always did, with the history of use in the Big Cypress and then the legislative history. I was shocked when the Assistant Secretary cut me off and said he was not interested in either the history of use or the legislative history. I stopped and sat down. There was little use to continue the meeting and talk with these NPS employees about their plans to manage the unit.

Later in the meeting, the Assistant Secretary started talking about Wilderness. I asked him if that was Wilderness with an upper-case *W*. He said it was and that was in the law and the report to Congress. I pointed out that it is in the law but the report to Congress uses a little case "w" and thus they were not directed by Congress to make any of the Big Cypress a Wilderness. Of course, we did not know he would resign his position a few weeks later and go to work for the Wilderness Society as their Vice-President for Conservation. A few years later, the Wilderness Society filed suit against the DOI/NPS for not doing their required five-year report to Congress on the suitability for any of the Big Cypress National Preserve to be classified as Wilderness. In short, he was now suing himself for what he had not done while he was the Assistant Secretary.

Throughout the '70s and '80s, we used Camp Red Bug for many family outings. It seemed like we were there at least once a month as a family. There was no television, no radio, no one coming and going; it was just Donna, Kathryn, and me. These were good times and we enjoyed watching our daughter grow up at Camp Red Bug. She enjoyed going to camp as much as the rest of us.

Over the years, we harvested several great trophy bucks, see the picture to the left, and hogs like the big nine pointer on my den wall, below.

We never bragged about this and did not show them off so as not to attract many other hunters. I also encouraged those who hunted with me if they were given the opportunity to take a smaller-sized rack buck to do so and let the big boys walk. We would at least know they were still in the breeding pool. Before I left the Camp Red Bug area, there were many deer with big racks. Since it now is so difficult to get into the areas, I suspect they will die of old age or as panther food.

I sold Camp Red Bug in 2002 and a way of life was gone that had spanned generations. My dad had gone into the Big Cypress as a young man. He and his hunting partner would pay the logging train conductor fifty cents to take them in and a dollar to pick them up on a certain date. He had lived in South Florida before the Tamiami Trail was built. He had

hunted deer and turkey on the east coast where millions of people now lived. He had fished Biscayne Bay when it teemed with clean fish of all kinds and had seen the Miami Rapids blown-up. In 1987, he made his last visit to Camp Red Bug. In 2002, I made my last visit as a guest of Camp Red Bug's new owners.

Jack Wyatt Moller lived in Miami from the earliest days until the middle 1990s.

When the Big Cypress was being formulated, I tried to donate the five acres I purchased when I was a high school student. I sent the offer to the DOI Secretary. He told me to contact the Florida Department of Natural Resources (DNR). Dr. Gissendanner, who was the DNR Secretary,

Camp Red Bug was a place for family and friends to get together for many years, where rest, fun and safety were the order of the day.

25 years' work to get the public a gate to their land.

A camp family party

Mike & Kathryn

The new owners

Another Camp party with good friends.

Grand Pa King

told me that he was not interested. I put the title up and waited for them to take it. They did, I lost money, and as badly as I think the people of the United States have been treated, particularly the hunters by the NPS, I still support the Big Cypress National Preserve's intent and concepts. In my opinion, if the DOI and NPS show some real leadership, they can develop an excellent place for generations of people to hunt and explore. They will not be able to explore as my dad and I did, but they will still be able to get out of the crowded cities and attempt to get lost. They can test their swamp buggy engineering capabilities and self-reliance.

It was not long after I sold Camp Red Bug that Superintendent Donahue continued his quest to undo all the work done in the last twenty-five years. He continued to violate the NPS management plans. His first action was to change many of the items in the General Management Plan. All these items were important to sportsmen. After I sold Camp Red Bug, he started violating the approved NPS I-75 Recreational Access Plan. His first action was to close and then to remove the vault toilets at this location. He said they did not meet NPS standards. Yet, he was building the same facilities on U.S.41 for NPS visitors who came to walk on the superintendent's new boardwalks. There is nothing wrong with that but there sure is something wrong when the DOI/NPS allows a superintendent to take actions, which violate approved plans.

Chapter Seventeen

◆ ◆ ◆

Florida's Land Program from I-75 to the Acquisition and Restoration Council (ARC) of Florida Land Purchased, Legislation, Projects, Green Ways, Willing Sellers, CERP

I suppose many are wondering why the title of the book is *The Road That Changed Florida and the Nation*. After Governor J. Bush appointed me to the Acquisition and Restoration Council of Florida (ARC), I realized that if I-75 had been stopped, as it could have been in 1970, we would not have seen southwest Florida stressed by development. We would not have seen a half-million people in western Broward County, and we would not have seen western Dade County overdeveloped. However, more importantly, we would not have had CARL, P2000, and Florida Forever. These programs allowed Florida to purchase millions of acres of land for outdoors recreational activities and timberlands. Hunters all over Florida and the world will forever have millions of acres of land to hunt and enjoy in Florida. For those who do not hunt but like to bird watch or merely camp, there are millions more acres for them to also enjoy.

The legacy of the decision to allow the conversion of Alligator Alley to I-75 will live on for many years. This one decision made Florida a much different place for future generations and landowners alike. The creation of the first bill to purchase lands for conservation and recreation led to the purchase of many properties. The following lists but a few of the many public land units in Florida.

1. Picayune Strand State Forest
2. Fakahatchee Strand State Preserve
3. Allapatta Flats
4. Dupuis Wildlife and Environmental Area (WEA)
5. John J. and Marianne Jones—Hungryland Slough WEA
6. Okallacoochee Slough State Forest
7. Okallacoochee WMA
8. St. Joe Timberlands
9. Withalcoochee State Forest
10. Johnathen Dickenson State Park
11. Dagney Johnson State Park
12. Tiger Tail State Forest
13. East Coast Buffer
14. Bahia Honda State Park
15. Flagler Blueway
16. NE Florida Timber lands
17. Tate's Hell State Forest
18. Alafia River Corridor
19. Alafia River State Park
20. Allen David Broussard Catfish Creek Preserve State Park
21. Andrews Wildlife Management Area
22. Apalachee Wildlife Management Area
23. Apalachicola Bluffs and Ravines Preserve
24. Apalachicola River Water Management Area
25. Apalachicola Rive Wildlife Management Area
26. Archie Carr National Wildlife Refuge
27. Arthur R. Marshall Loxahatchee National Wildlife Refuge

28. Aucilla Conservation Area

29. Barefoot Beach Preserve

30. Big Ben Wildlife Management Area

31. Big Talbot Island State Park

32. Bull Creek Wildlife Management Area

33. Caloosahatchee Regional Park

34. Carvelle Ranch Wildlife Management Area

35. Cayo Costa State Park

36. Charlotte Harbor State Buffer Preserve

37. Chassahowitzka River and coastal Swamps

38. Chassahowitzka Wildlife Management Area

39. CREW

40. Cross Florida Greenway State Recreation and Conservation Area

41. Devil's Garden

42. Fisheating Creek Conservation Easement

43. Green Swamp Land Authority Land Protection Agreements

44. Flying Eagle Ranch

45. Panther Glades

46. Guana River Wildlife Management Area

47. Guana River State Park

48. Half Moon Wildlife Management Area

49. Joe Budd Wildlife Management Area

50. Kissimmee Prairie Preserve State Park

51. Lake Talquin State Forest

52. Big Cypress National Preserve (Save Our Everglades)

These are but a few of the many projects that were on the Florida Forever project list.

The need to create a mechanism to generate money and a law to protect land for conservation and recreation and historical purposes found its catalyst in the desire to build an interstate across South Florida. EEL, Environmentally Endangered and Recreation Lands Bill, was the product of these forces. It is true the bill was passed a few years ahead of the building of I-75, but the bill was created ahead of time as a part of the plan to make sure this road was built. The opposition was well-known and what the opposition would settle for was also well-known. The bill was actually written by Johnny C. Jones, then Executive Director of the Florida Wildlife Federation, and others.

This bill, EEL, gave way to the CARL, Conservation and Recreation Lands Act, which provided much more money and flexibility for the lands to be purchased. It was written by Johnny C. Jones at his house with the assistance of Henry Dean. Johnny told me that Governor B. Graham, who wanted this bill written, called Johnny and asked him to write it. Johnny said he was not a lawyer. Johnny told me Governor Graham told Johnny not to worry about that because he would send someone to help. Henry was a young lawyer working at the DEP and was sent to Johnny's house to write the bill. They wrote it on Johnny's kitchen table. The bill had written into it that all lands purchased by CARL would be available for hunting, camping and fishing unless the Board of Trustees (BOT-Governor and Cabinet) determined the property to be unsuitable for such activities. This use of language did not get through in the bill's final version. Again, the battles between men had weakened the FWF's ability to function as strongly as Audubon in Tallahassee. However, there was language friendly to sportsmen in the bill but it was not as strong as originally desired.

Once CARL sunsetted under Governor Martinez's administration, there was a serious legislative battle to get Preservation 2000 approved. This act provided funds to do what CARL had specified and would be sunsetted in the year 2000. It provided a tremendous amount of money and changed the process of acquiring lands. It established the Land Acquisition and Management Council (LAMAC). This council consisted of the heads of the departments of those agencies who were responsible for protecting Florida natural resources. The members consisted of the Secretary of the Department of Environmental Protection (DEP); Secretary of the

Department of Community Affairs (DCA); Director of Division of Forestry (DOF), Executive Director of the Florida Fish, Wildlife and Conservation Commission (FWC), and Director of the Division of Historical Resources. For years, these folks met in Tallahassee and had little contact with people outside their arena of Tallahassee. They not only approved the lands to purchase but also lands to sell and lease, approve easements to cross state property, and the general management plans on all these acres of conservation lands.

P2000 sunsetted under Governor J. Bush and there was another battle to create the Florida Forever Act. The Florida Forever (FF) act not only made available more funds to purchase these lands, but it had a slight language change. The law no longer stated "natural resource recreation" but outdoor recreation. The dropping of the word "natural" makes a big difference in the reason land can be purchased. The FF act had many good reasons to purchase property from willing sellers. Some of the generic reasons to purchase land were water, animals, birds, endangered species, timber, and outdoor recreation. By now, most people had come to think of these funds to purchase land as only being usable for environmental reasons and most documents that were associated with the land were written with that slant. Any recreation use was secondary to the reason to purchase and to manage these lands. This mindset created a number of growing problems.

The FF act also changed the composition of the LAMAC. The new council Acquisition and Restoration Council, ARC, would have the same heads of state but also four citizens, hence Dr. H. Swain, Paula Sessions, Sandy Walters, and me. We were the first citizens to be privileged enough to join in the process that recommended to BOT what lands to purchase, lease, sell or surplus, approve easements, and to evaluate all land management plans on the state's nearly four million acres of conservation lands. I feared that bringing four citizens into the mix of who would evaluate the work being done by these agencies and who would have the ability to criticize and impact their day-to-day work would not be accepted by the agencies. I knew ARC was in for a real struggle. However, it was pleasant to see how the agency heads and staff embraced the citizens' ideas and reacted to our ideas in a positive manner. Sure, there were many debates and discussions but in the end, I think all the agencies allowed the citizen members to truly bring about improvement in the planning and decision-making process.

The protection of these lands could either be by fee or less-than-fee (fee means to outright own the land and less-than-fee means to only own a conservation easement on the property). The latter, in many cases, made a better use of the tax dollar but it did not assure the public any use of the property as is the case when the land was actually owned by the state. The less-than-fee left the owner in charge of his property; he could continue to work the land with some restrictions. The land would generate jobs, food, lumber and taxes. If the land was outright owned by the public all this was usually gone or certainly reduced, even if the land was state forest.

The ability to purchase property for outdoor recreation and historical protection was put to the test when Cypress Gardens announced it was closing its doors. This world- famous ski and tourist center was not able to compete with Disney, Sea World and other modern tourist attractions. There was an outcry from all over the world when this announcement was made. The use of the internet was brought into play as reportedly 20,000 emails were sent to the governor's office asking him to save Cypress Gardens. It worked because in a few days a team from ARC was sent to the location to evaluate the property. Research was done by the Division of Historical and Archeological on the history of Cypress Gardens. The property certainly had the historical significance to be protected and it was certainly outdoor recreation. Thus, the ARC acted extraordinarily fast to protect this land. However, not after nearly one hundred people made their presence known at an ARC meeting. They brought the Southern Bells in their huge, beautiful dresses. They brought the city and county elected officials. They brought the employees who would be without a job when the place closed. They brought the neighbors but more importantly, they brought one businessperson who was willing to partner with the state, put up money, run the attraction, and reinvest the gate receipts back into Cypress Gardens. In the end, $11 million was taken from the Florida Forever funds and the rest came from the businessperson and local municipalities to purchase Cypress Gardens. Everyone was happy except a few of the more traditional environmental groups and land protection groups. These folks were accustomed to their money, Florida Forever money, going only to purchase land that was strictly conservation and environmental in nature. Land that had endangered species on it was considered to have a very high value for purchase under Florida Forever. But they did not raise too much of a fuss, after all there had been a land fall of support for the purchase, protection and keeping Cypress Gardens as Cypress Gardens and not turning it into high rise condos and golf courses.

These are but a few of the land units and actions that were available because those who were farsighted enough to trade the building of I-75 for the future funding of land acquisition for conservation and recreation. While some of these land units had other sources of acquisition funds, they all benefited, either politically or financially, by the actions of those leaders of the early 1970s and the funds that followed their work thirty-five years later.

Not only did ARC members spend a great deal of time evaluating new land to purchase but also, we worked on the management plans. This work seemed to draw us into every issue in Florida. This happened to me on many occasions. One day, I received a phone call from the governor's ombudsman, Benji Brumberg. Benji wanted to know what I was doing tomorrow. It seemed everything was always the last-minute emergency with Benji, but that was all right with me. He wanted me to ride to Bahia Honda State Park in the Keys. There was an issue with a butterfly—The Miami Blue. This small butterfly has very particular feeding and breeding needs. It seemed that this state park had the plants the Miami Blue needed to survive. The butterfly needs Nicker Bean to lay its eggs on and for its caterpillar to feed on. There is also some sort of symbiotic relationship between the butterfly and ants. It appears that this one type of ant protects the eggs of the butterfly. Anyway, Benji arrived at my house early in the morning and we drove to the park some three hours away. On the way, I was briefed on the issue and needs of this critter. I placed a call to Mark Glisson, our chief of staff in Tallahassee, and asked him to get the Bahia Honda Park management plan and see what it said about butterflies. Mark called back in a few minutes and as we sped along the interstate toward the park to meet with a very upset and concerned Audubon person, Mark told me all the management plan said about butterflies was that they were a major attraction for tourist and that a butterfly walk was established.

This was not the first time that Benji and I had met. The very first time was at an Everglades Coordinating Council special meeting. Barbara Jean Powell had contacted Governor Bush's office about the abusive attitude of the National Park Service's new superintendent that had been handpicked by Assistant Secretary Donald Berry. She did this after we held our meeting at Camp Red Bug on the impending ORV management plan. The governor's staff referred Mrs. Powell's call to their ombudsman, Benji Brumberg. He came to this special Everglades Coordinating Council meeting and listened to all the concerns, asked a lot of questions, and said he would contact the other parties involved in this issue. We went on to meet with him even though he was known as a big time Sierra person in Broward County. Benji was very open-minded and concerned about what he heard. He met with the Florida Fish, Wildlife and Conservation Commission, Florida Biodiversity, and the National Park Service people in the Big Cypress National Preserve. He had everyone ready to sit down at the same table and work out a solution. He told me he tried to talk with Mr. J. J. Donahue, Superintendent Big Cypress National Preserve, but Mr. Donahue would not take his call. He left a message with his staff member that he, Benji, did not want the Record of Decision (ROD) signed until we all met. Well, you know what happened. The superintendent, like all others, had no respect for Florida leadership nor the intent and words of the Amended Big Cypress National Preserve enabling act. He signed the ROD and several years of costly litigation occurred. But more importantly, the sportsmen no longer believed in or would work with the major environmental groups on Florida that were involved in this newest action to remove hunters and fisherman from these public lands.

On another occasion after the Miami Blue trip, Benji called me and wanted to know if I would go to Highlands County with him. Well, I had spent the full day traveling to Bahia Honda State Park and was not eager to drive to Highlands County. This was so far from where I lived that it would require an overnight trip. Before I could say a word, he said we would fly in the SFWMD helicopter. There was no problem with me doing this because of my ARC chair and my Water Resource Advisory Commission Chair. We had to go and meet with leaders of Highlands County, elected officials of Highlands County, ACoE, FWC and SFWMD over another access issue.

The ACoE and SFWMD in their haste to restore the Kissimmee River had failed to properly notify and work with Highlands County leaders and elected officials. The restoration work was removing the only boat ramp to the Kissimmee River for sixty miles. Needless to say, folks were not happy.

We had a great helicopter ride from Ft Lauderdale Executive Airport to the center of Florida. We were able to ride over Lake Okeechobee and the restored portion of the Kissimmee River. We had a real exciting ride because the clouds dropped down, and we had to almost fly on the water of the lake to find a way out of the "soup." Then, as we approached the Highlands County airport, we received a call from Park Air force Base. They informed us they had a gunship in the air, and we could not go beyond a certain point north of Highlands County. There was an aircraft accident of some type, and their gunship was standing guard. Needless to say, we did not fly to the next boat ramp north and challenge the military gunship.

We spent most of the day listening to what folks had to say. We heard why this boat ramp had to be rebuilt and how it could be done without harming the restoration efforts. We heard from the SFWMD and ACoE why it could not be rebuilt and why it would harm restoration efforts. Benji and I made several recommendations and not one was done or followed up on. In the end, the FWC, SFWMD improved another small backwoods boat ramp that would require a boat trip of several miles to the river via a narrow canal that was going to remain after restoration work was completed. I suppose all went well because we did not hear from Highlands County again.

The outcome of this Highlands County meeting led to a new committee being formed. At the next WRAC meeting, I jumped all over the involved agency heads for this failure in communications and that they were indeed driving the sportsmen out of restoration. We also had problems developing access to the Everglades and other locations in the restoration areas. We beat up the issue a good bit and the ACoE decided to create a recreation committee to address this issue during restoration.

This ACoE recreation committee sounded like a good idea but after a few meetings it was apparent that it would not work. It would not allow citizens to sit on the decision side of the table and all they could do was talk to the agency heads for a few minutes at each meeting. They could already do this. We did not need another committee to allow this communication to happen. I explained the problem at the WRAC meeting and Rock Salt started talking about violations of Federal Law. I suggested that WRAC start a recreation (WRAC-REC) subcommittee like the lands subcommittee I chaired. This would allow all the agencies and interested citizens to sit on the same side of the table to develop a good recreation plan. Rob Barton took up this task when he replaced me on WRAC and did a great job. The WRAC-REC report was so well-received by the state that the Secretary of DEP, Colleen Castille, contacted Mike Collins, Chair of the SFWMD Board of Directors, and thanked him. According to Mike, Colleen thought all the Water Management Districts should do the same. Through Rob's work, all the STA have been opened to the public, not only for birding but also for duck hunting and fishing.

In 2005, Secretary Colleen Castille created the Keys initiative. This was an aggressive plan to protect as much of the remaining undeveloped property in the Keys as possible. It was not long before ARC reviewed and approved a boundary amendment to our current small Keys projects. This boundary amendment totaled nearly 4,000 acres. Now, this does not sound like a lot of land but in the Keys of Florida, this is a lot of land. It was all too clear that if clear water and health reefs were to survive, the upland areas had to be protected. If not, the polluted runoff from urban development and the additional pressures by all the people who would live on these 4,000 acres would most assuredly harm the natural resources of the Keys. This harm would create an unimaginable negative impact on the Keys and Florida economy. The Keys only has one resource driving their economic engine—the clear ocean waters, healthy reefs and the fishing that goes along with these attributes. ARC put into action a process to purchase these properties.

I was surprised to hear that not one mention of the needs of this endangered species was in the management plan. After all, with this small chunk of land being the only known place this species lived, it would only take one hurricane or an accidental overspray by the mosquito control district and the Miami Blue would be gone forever.

When Benji and I arrived at the park we were met by a concerned citizen who explained the situation. The gentleman was really rational and made good sense in what he was asking for—proper management of the Nicker Bean plan and for this butterfly's needs to appear in the unit's management plan. We spent way more time than was needed to realize that his request was valid and should be done.

Once again, the issues of the Federal Endangered Species classification were about to get in the way of good wildlife management practices. I was involved with Benji in several phone conferences with the FWC and university experts. We wanted to make sure that the butterfly could breed in captivity, it could. Then we had to make sure that the Federal USFWS did not list this insect before the FWC could issue a collection permit, that there was money to collect and breed the insect, a place to breed it, and then places to release it. All this was accomplished in a few months. Benji had talked with Governor Bush and obtained $60,000, which in itself was no easy accomplishment.

The University of Florida people collected the minimum number of butterflies they needed and started their captive breeding program. Then, Monroe County raised its head. They were concerned that if the Miami Blue was classified by the USFWS as endangered and then re-established in many parts of the Keys then it would stop them from spraying for mosquitoes. The issue of Nile Virus was just getting started and the public was afraid that with an endangered species bug they would have to live with hordes of mosquitoes and be exposed to Nile Virus. One butterfly expert told me, "Never mind that the changes of catching Nile Virus are far less likely than getting cancer from the bug spray." I had dinner with the Executive Director of the FWC, Mr. Ken Haddad, and Mr. John Rood, Chairman of the FWC, Ken's boss, and we talked about the Miami Blue. I assured both this action of the FWC to classify the Miami Blue Butterfly as a Florida endangered species was the correct action to take and why. Well, the Florida Fish, Wildlife and Conservation Commission listed the Miami Blue Butterfly as an endangered species on the Florida list. I do not think the USFWS ever listed it. In my last contact with the U of F people, we had many generations of Miami Blue Butterflies in captivity, and many being released. There was an agreement reached between the County and the FWC that captive butterflies would only be released on National Park land. This solution seemed to be working and more colonies of Miami Blue were being established in the National Park properties of South Florida.

Benji, and rightly so, received recognition by National Sierra for his work in saving the Miami Blue Butterfly. The next management plan submitted to ARC by the Department of Parks and Recreation for the Bahia Honda State Park had language in it that was suitable for a natural resource as important as the butterflies in the park and the Miami Blue Butterfly. Department of Environmental Protection Deputy Secretary Ballard told me that Benji should be credited with saving this species of butterfly from extinction.

Benji drew me into all kinds of land management related issues. He seemed good at this. One of the stickiest and yet unresolved issues was noise. That is right—noise. The noise an airboat makes as it runs the waters and marshes of Florida. It seems that as people retired from other states or the cities of Florida they were moving into the hinder lands of Florida and for the first time learning that their quiet, secluded, retirement home was in the playground of ol' Florida. They did not like hearing the noise of an airboat engine or prop no matter if it was day or night. Thus, Benji would have folks contact me and expect me to resolve the problems or give him potential solutions. The only solution I had was for him to bring together all the concerned and interested parties to see if they could work out a way to solve the problem amongst themselves. With the complexity of airboat operation, the different reasons to operate them, the industry that was dependent on the airboat (tourist rides to manufactures) this problem is not going to be solved any time soon. In my opinion, ol' Florida will be pushed out as new Florida retires from other places.

If Benji was not drawing me into human natural resource problems, then others were. A friend of mine, Bill Losner, called me one day and asked me to drive to Homestead for lunch to meet with a few folks and Rodney Barreto. Rodney was a Commissioner of the FWC. I said sure; after all, I had nothing better to do other than drive eighty miles to Homestead that day and I wanted to talk with Rodney about the Big Cypress.

Well, when I arrived, we had a good lunch and then the real reason for my visit came out. The other folks lived in rural South Dade. The area was still zoned agriculture as there were many ranchetts there. These good men had lived in the area several generations. Recently a new person moved in. He had been displaced by CERP and the ACoE/DOI/Environmentalist destruction of the rural agriculture community referred to as the 8.5 SMA. This land as already mentioned was being taken for CERP and ENP needs. The new neighbor was running an exotic bird farm.

They did have a problem, noise. If you have been near a large group of parrots and other exotic birds, you know they are loud and do not know the difference between day or night. The gentlemen laid out the problem in a very professional way and all they had done to that time, and that no one had been able to do anything. Rodney called his regional director and shared the problem. Of course, the FWC regional director already knew of the problem.

I realized the FWC did not have authority over this issue because the gentleman was running an agriculture operation and other than the permit issued by the FWC to own and raise these birds, the real oversight was with the Florida Department of Agriculture. The oversight was not with the ARC or FWC. This is but one example of how CERP was destroying or harming the rural culture of Florida. Implementation of CERP was not following one of the major goals of the Sustainable Commission—to protect the diverse culture of the South Florida greater ecosystem. Instead, it was destroying the rural family lifestyle along with the outdoorsmen culture established in the Big Cypress National Preserve research document on ORVs.

I was asked to go with hunters to tour the Black Water State Forest to hear their concerns, to other land units to hear their concerns, and to help them obtain new regulations to better protect the deer and other wildlife. I was asked to tour the karsts lake area north of Panama city to better understand why Audubon and state parks thought this area should become publicly owned. Ol' Florida folks were concerned about protecting the natural resources as well as the activities they had enjoyed for generations. People were looking for solutions and seeking help. In my opinion, it is the responsibility of government and the agencies to reach out and facilitate these folks in their effort to make sure their natural resources and activities are around another 200 years.

The above were but a few examples of the many different issues citizen members of ARC were drawn into. After all, with a state that has 27% of its total land mass in public ownership, there will be ample issues to address.

As of 2001, Floridians owned more than 8,662,629 acres of non-submerged land for conservation, water resources, timber resources and natural resource recreation activities, including all public lands in Florida—state, county, and federal properties—even the nationally held lands benefited by the Florida's land fund. In many cases, these national units would not have been created if the state had not put money up first. In almost all cases of the nationally owned lands, their lands have been enhanced by the purchase of property around them by the State of Florida. This enhancement includes the military bases in Florida. At many ARC meetings, military commanders had representatives attending who were seeking funds from ARC to purchase adjoining property to their bases. In one case, an entirely new project was developed called the NW Greenway. This was really a method to protect the flyways for Eglin Air Force base and other bases in the region from urban development. Urban development, which by 2003 had exploded in northwest Florida, would soon harm the military's ability to perform their task. Air bases do not operate well when housing developments are in their flyways and on their fence lines. Of course, it was hoped that the federal government's Military Base Reduction Committee would look upon such actions favorably and Florida would have none of its bases closed. The thought was—what other state would purchase land to protect the integrity of a military installation? This action would also make the environmentalists happy because it would remove land from potential urban development. This action would make hunters happy, as the action would keep large blocks of land open to hunting, maybe. This action would make the hikers happy because they could establish more hiking trails in the woods under the banner of the Florida Hiking Association (FHA). This action would help the economy of many rural counties in Florida whose major industry was a military base. In short, once again, land protection would be a win-win situation for all except the landowners who wanted to build housing projects on their property. Of course, as it was conceived, this greenway, like all others, would be created from willing sellers only.

This was not the only greenway. As of 2003, we were really close to having a greenway that in southwest Florida extended from the Ten Thousand Islands, ENP, and Big Cypress National Preserve all the way north of Lake Okeechobee. Another part of this greenway went from Charlotte Harbor to Lake Okeechobee. This massive block of land would be protected from urban development via fee purchase or less-than-fee (conservation easement); outside the federal lands, all property purchased would be from willing sellers.

At the same time, massive New Towns or Chapter 189 districts were being sought and planned around Immokalee, Florida, and other areas of southwest Florida. Under Governor Chiles, the concept of New Town had been supported by the Sustainable and it was now coming about. These big New Towns were being planned by major landowners and usually in conjunction with some project that no one would really oppose. Such a project might be a new university that would compete with Notre Dame.

There were not only Greenways but Blueways. Blueways were mainly in northeast Florida and along the St. John's River. These projects would protect this river from the same type of development that occurred along the Intercostal waterway and other river bodies in southeast Florida. It seemed that the rest of Florida did not want to look like or be like southeast Florida, with its intensive development and dense populations. They did not want to be another "Little New York." Mayor Delaney wanted money from ARC to protect parts of Duval County. The mayor pledged to split the cost of land 55/45 with them paying the larger part. He also stated that the state would hold the title and the land would manage as ARC said. This agreement made sure land projects in Duval stayed on the 'A' list.

The listing for acquisition was a major revision of the way land was purchased under ARC's implementation of Florida Forever. Since the State of Florida had started purchasing land, the process to decide what land would be bought was revisited once a year. During the annual re-ranking meeting, all interested parties would do what they could to convince the LAMAC or ARC members that their project should be number one. At this time, land was purchased in the order it was ranked on this list. Such a process gave the landowners no incentive to negotiate with the state. They knew their land was at the top and thus would be worked on in the order of the list. Further, only the ten top properties would be worked on. ARC decided to change the ranking system to a grouping system. This grouping system would allow ARC to establish, 'A' list, and a 'B' list. Only the projects on the 'A' list would be actively worked on. The projects on the 'B' list could be purchased but staff would not work on them. If a 'B' list property owner or other government entity wanted their land purchased, they would have to approach the state and provide a "good deal." Good deal is in quotes because there was never any real definition of "good deal." As with any change in the process, there was a lot of opposition to this new idea. In the end, it worked, and it did not work. It worked because landowners who wanted to sell their land had to aggressively work with the state or the money would go to the owners who did work with the state. It did not work because in the operational change, ARC had dropped the 'impasse' list. This list had been used when landowners and the state could not come to agreement. Thus, in the new process, once a landowner reached an impasse the property had to stay on 'A' or move to 'B' or be removed from all listing. The result was that the 'A' list continued to grow and soon was too large for the number of resources available to work on all the projects at the same time.

All five Water Management Districts benefited from the decision to parlay a road for future laws to fund land acquisition because the fund from each authorization act gave the districts money they controlled. This money had to be used to purchase land. Not only did these agencies get funds but so did all the other state agencies that were designed to manage land, natural resources, and people. Agencies used these funds to purchase in-holdings and additions to their existing units thereby improving management and public use of the unit.

By 2003, water had become a major issue all over Florida. Everyone finally realized that water was not an endless resource. Like the buffalo in the west or other natural resources of massive size, cheap, potable, fresh water, too, was limited. By 2003, Florida had already lost more than ten percent of its First Magnitude Springs. This led Governor Bush to create the Spring Initiative. This state initiative was considered in the decision process ARC used to determine what property to approve for purchase and not approve. Land that a few years earlier would not have been even looked at now became desirable to satisfy this much-needed initiative and protect the major springs of Florida from pollution and drainage. The goal was to not only protect the spring and the spring run but also the trace where the water came from that fed the spring.

As of 2003, the State of Florida had the largest land acquisition program in the nation. It was even bigger than the federal government's program and it was designed for willing sellers only. In a few cases, the willing seller idea was lost, and condemnation took over. In most of these cases, it was because Department of Interior money was given to the state as a grant. This money brought a different attitude to the table and caused violations of the intent to all the authorization acts Florida had used to purchase land—EEL, CARL, P2000 and Florida Forever. One of the most continuous drawn-out purchases was Southern Golden Gate Estate (SGGE), or South Blocks as the land was called (which became the Picayune Strand State Forest).

In 2003, the Florida Fish, Wildlife and Conservation Commission managed hunting on more than 5.5 million acres of land. This is not bad; particularly, when you consider Florida was among the top four most populated states in the nation in population with a land size of thirty-six million acres. If you consider the size of Florida when compared to the size of Texas, the sportsmen and outdoor lovers of Florida had a virtual public playground.

The action of taking people's land for an Everglades Restoration Project—Southern Golden Gates Estate—brought the land rights people from out west to south Florida. In 2002, they held a drive-in from all parts of the nation to Florida. There was extensive press coverage from their quarter, but little resulted from their efforts. The Comprehensive Everglades Restoration Plan (CERP) had too much steam to be slowed down.

With all this money and land changing hands, there had to be problems and there were. To put it politely, in the late 1980s, one of the top people involved in these issues went to prison for improperly handling these funds. This resulted in a very complicated process for land purchases;

but such a process was needed and helped to assure that land purchased by the state was land that was really needed, would benefit the objectives of the land project, protect the rights of landowners, and assure the public their money was going to the proper places.

This process worked as is evident for easement purchased. Many projects started out small. One was originally submitted as two hundred acres but in time it grew to more than 8,000 acres. This happened because landowners were treated right. Sure, they often did not agree with the value state appraisers set or the appraisal process, but the process was working because landowners wanted to sell their land to the state. There was also an attitude expressed by many landowners of—*I like my land as it is and do not want houses on it. I do not want my children to sell the land to developers or develop it themselves.* Thus, many landowners saw state acquisition as a way to have their cake and eat it too. The state had money, the state had rules about conservation, restoration, and uses and many landowners liked this. They could give their money to their children to fight over while the land would remain intact. The federal government should take a look at the way Florida purchases land. They just might learn something. What difference does it make to the environment to have a few in-holders on a large chunk of land? It makes no difference. Sure, there are management issues with in-holders and neighbors but when these issues are addressed properly, most of these owners will be the government's best supporters.

A part of the process of evaluating what lands to recommend for purchase to the Board of Trustees to purchase included endangered species. The property was either known to have endangered species on it, or the habitat could support endangered species, or the property could allow endangered species to migrate to other public lands. The issue of endangered species in Florida became a very contentious matter. Big landowners did not want anyone knowing, surveying, or seeing ESA animals on their property for fear that they could not do what they wanted with their land. But whenever they wanted the state to purchase their land, they were pleased to share all types of evidence that these plants and animals lived on their land.

Not only did the work of ARC help protect some of Florida's natural resources and recreation lands but it also became a part of national security. At one of our early ARC meetings, the Navy came to ARC seeking permission to have an easement on about five acres of a state park. They needed the land to move one of their radar installations on to this land. When we asked what happened to the radar facility nearby, the Navy's spokesperson said that a new high-rise building was blocking a good portion of the radar's view of the horizon. We asked the Navy if they had known of the building changes and participated in the zoning process. They said they knew but that at that time they were not supposed to become involved in civilian matters off their base. Thus, the high-rise went up. We passed a motion on our public hearing day to approve the request, but with an attachment, stating there would not be any more, because we thought the military should have been paying attention to what was going on beyond their base boundary and act on what would harm their mission. I did not expect this type of motion to survive the next day's ARC meeting and was prepared to amend it myself to remove the restrictive second part if no other ARC member did. At the meeting, the restrictive part was removed. We had made our point and military bases started looking beyond their base boundaries to see what land use changes would harm their bases' integrity and mission.

A few meetings later, we had a land project come to us that would be good for the natural resources and recreational needs of Floridians. It would also be a good project to help protect the flight pattern around this base. The base spokesman asked for our support for all the previous reasons. I do not think this individual was really prepared for what came next—was the military willing to help with purchase of the land via partnering with the state and bringing some money to the table. Everyone on ARC knew the military was not prepared for this but the question was asked anyway. The spokesmen said he did not think any money was available but that they would support our efforts to get Florida's Congressional Delegation to obtain some. All this was before the attack on the World Trade Center. After 9/11, the military found money to help with purchase of property for fee or less-than-fee. Additionally, the protection of the mission of a military base became so important that President Bush included money in his budget to purchase land in the NW Florida Greenway, which was a way to protect the flight zones for a number of military bases in that part of Florida. Also, in the same budget was money for protecting land around some Texas military bases. This type of land protection was certainly needed. One military spokesman explained how his base was a parachute-training base to train military people how to resupply people in the combat field. We were told after one recent training mission on this base, the officer in charge received a phone call from a very upset off-base civilian neighbor. This person had a Humvee in his pool. It seems that the parachuted Humvee had drifted off the base's land and landed in a neighbor's pool.

Florida is a state that ranges from sub-tropical to a more northern habitat and a variety of animals and plants living in it. There also are a large number of endangered species living there. The attached map made by the Florida Natural Areas Inventory group (FNAI) is a good indicator of the amount of land that holds ESA species. These species became a thorn in the side of the sportsman. Because of them, hunters were almost run out of the 750,000-acre Big Cypress National Preserve. They were running fisherman out of the bays and shallow protected areas all over Florida because this was prime Manatee habitat. Sure, there were some conservation hunting group leaders who thought this was a good thing because they could access these places in the most primitive of manners. However, for the average person who was not paid to play in these Wildland natural resource areas and had limited time to enjoy what their tax money had purchased and protected them could no longer enjoy these resources. There was no way of knowing what the ESA law was going to cost. Developers would either pay to have these animals relocated to protected areas, pay by donating land to the state, or pay into one of the state agencies' mitigation banks. This action alone added greatly to the cost of housing in Florida, and it led to other demographic and social problems. The "haves and have nots" were growing apart. The cost of housing continued to rise as developers had to create affordable housing units as a part of their development plan. Now those who could afford to purchase very expensive houses were paying to protect the ESA species and subsidizing housing cost for others. Well-educated families were now working two and three jobs to pay for their house. This, in turn, led to youth gangs and other such problems in these upscale neighborhoods. The very problems many had moved out of the cities to get away from were now in the new, expensive, New Town projects.

ARC's work and previous land protection actions were important to the uplands and wetlands of Florida's reefs and fisheries in the Keys. Fishing in the Keys, as you read about earlier, allowed me to understand the importance of upland management and habitat protection to the well-being of Florida's reefs and fisheries in the Keys and other marine places. One has to remember that all systems are connected—the land is indeed connected to the water. Some areas are more directly connected than others, but they all have an impact, good or bad, on each other in some way.

We saw that the Florida program was working as private citizens who lived in the woods of Florida often would bring a new project or boundary addition to an existing project. They would not do this because they were conservationists, after all they already lived there, but because they did not want a lot of people living around them. With population growth in Florida at an adjusted 800 people a day, the pressure to build in the rural wooded areas was great. This pressure was enhanced by existing laws.

I made one of the older leaders on the Sustainable Commission angry when I attacked his pet law—Concurrency. In short, this law was passed with good intentions but without foresight into what it would really do. The law requires that a developer include in his project all the roads, storm drainage and other needs for all of the local society before he can build his own project. I once had the Vice-Mayor of North Miami Beach explain what this law meant to folks along a major road in his city. I was told that if a landowner wanted to place another driveway to the road, he would have to build an additional lane on both sides of the road for nearly fifteen miles. This cost stopped any such improvements even if they were needed.

What the Concurrency law also did was to make development in the hinterlands of Florida cheaper. Thus, developers started to leapfrog out from towns and cities. They would build a new place a few miles out of town because it would be cheaper than building in town. Then the next developer would leap again for the same reason and so on until there were no open spaces between these new towns. Yet, because of the Concurrency law making it cheaper to build in the woods, the traffic on the road to the existing towns was ever increasing and no one corrected this problem. Gridlock was the result.

This and similar discussions were held by the Sustainable Commission leading to the creation of the concept—Eastward HO. This concept was simple. The recommendation would lead to changes in laws that controlled development such as Concurrency, brown field laws, education and more. Such actions would encourage instead of discouraging development along the eastern ridge on the Gold Coast. It was the hope of the Sustainable that such incentives would discourage developers from continuing to press on to the west and deeper into the historic Everglades. Of course, there were many, many problems that Eastward HO would create. Further, the idea was about twenty-five years late, since most of these now drained and once historic Everglades already had urban development on them or serious plans for development already existed.

Further debate and discussion led to full support for the idea of "New Towns" presented by DCA Secretary Jim Murly. The idea again was simple. A developer could develop a complete town in the middle of nowhere. He would not only build the houses, streets, water, and sewer facilities but also the schools, shops, jails, courthouse, town hall etc. If the developer did this, he would get fast track permitting. This entire idea seemed to be contrary to what the Sustainable was trying to accomplish but it too was approved. It was not long before legislation made the idea a reality and New Towns were on the planning board in other parts of Florida. During development of this new idea, I tried to get it required in a New Town development that the developer would have to purchase and donate in fee or an easement on land that extended several miles deep around the New Town to the state. Without doing this, each New Town would eventually grow together like all the small towns in southeast Florida had already done. But this idea was not approved either.

I tried to encourage the same concept for the West Coast by calling it WestwardHO for the small cities on the west side of the state. We should have created InwardHO for the still small cities in the interior of south Florida. These western and interior urban growth boundaries would prevent the two coasts from being joined as one big housing project like Miami to Palm Beach were already joined, but no one was willing to take up this cause and my ideas died.

New Towns would become another tool to drive the price of land up when they were offered to the state for purchase as conservation lands. The Babcock Ranch at 92,000 acres was one of the largest family ranches in the state. They decided it was time to get out of the business of ranching. Not only did they want the public to purchase their land, but they also wanted the business stock purchased, too. In short, the public would own the mine, the farms, the cattle, the tractors, the hotels—the entire business. Their attorneys had figured out that if they pressed the idea of turning the southwest part of the ranch into New Towns, these 19,000 acres of cities would scare the locals, conservationist, sportsmen, and state and national leaders into acting hastily and purchasing with tax dollars the company and not just the land. This issue became very contentious, and it encouraged other big landowners to do the same. Folks were scared so bad the idea was even given a review by the Center for Environmental Quality (CEQ) in President George W. Bush's 2004 White House.

It was not long after the Babcock folks started talking about dividing and developing their land that the bigger landowners with property on the Florida Forever project list started doing the same. St. Joe Paper Company announced that they were going to subdivide and sell land in one of our important and big projects. They would sell ten-acre and up ranchetts for $20,000 an acre. The McDanial Ranch was applying for the required documents to sell their property and make it New Towns and ranchetts. Devil's Garden, ALICO property, announced they were selling ranchetts at $1,500 an acre. There is no doubt in my mind the actions of the Babcock Ranch people and the reactions to this by the public and politicians played a major role in the decisions of other big landowners to follow the Babcock Ranch example. The Lykes Brother's ranch, Fisheating Creek, decided to hold off on selling another easement on their property. They, too, wanted to see how the water issue played out on the Babcock Ranch. Big landowners already understood the value of the water under their property and the Babcock Ranch deal just made them more set in their minds.

The idea of purchasing the company stocks was taken seriously by all. The Division of State Lands (DSL) had approached a good number of companies with the idea that they would act as the third party in this deal, see the appendix for more information on this. The idea would go something like this. The third-party company would purchase the stocks and sell the land to the state to do whatever they wanted with the stocks, hotels, equipment and other assets of the company. The issue of taxes came in to play and, in the end, no third party was willing to accept these tax liabilities so the "marker bill" in the 2005 Florida legislative session that held the money ready to come from a special appropriations, along with the Florida Forever funds, died. The deal to purchase the Babcock Ranch finished when the family turned down the final offer made by the state and the timeline to pass this special bill also passed. The story on the Babcock Ranch land is still out but one thing is for sure, if the land is sold to the State of Florida, it will not be by the Babcock family. In mid-July 2005, the ranch was sold to a developer in Palm Beach County Florida. The actual sale price was not published but it had to be more than $500 million, which was the price the family had reportedly wanted. The new owners, Kitson & Partners, with their financial partner, Morgan Stanley Real Estate Fund, said in their press release they were willing to work with the State of Florida and counties to protect some of the property from development. This was an interesting turn of events, particularly since Kitson & Partners had been involved with the parties who wanted to purchase the entire 91,000-acre ranch and to preserve it as an undeveloped area.

Finally, in November 2005, DSL was able to develop an agreement to purchase the Babcock Ranch with the new owners. This was a very complex agreement that involved four different governmental entities to manage parts of the ranch, a private holding company to manage all of it for ten years while the owners were bought out, then a non-profit organization to run the ranch operations once the public owned all the land. The water issues were resolved after two Board of Trustee meetings. The resulting agreement allowed the new owners to keep their commercial well locations and permits but before development of these assets occurred in the future, they would have to go through all the regulatory permitting processes. This seemed to appease most people. The land purchase was moving forth in fine order except for one issue.

This issue that had not been addressed as of yet had to do with the Florida Panther. The ranch owners approached ARC and the public with how important this huge ranch was to the public, environment, and animals like the Florida Panther. They did a good job of selling this importance. The question asked by a longtime Florida Wildlife Federation board member was, "how can they develop the ranch when it has panthers living on it." This is a very important concept because the FWF had recently won litigation concerning the destruction of category two panther habitat by rock miners who were trying to dig up Southwest Florida. The question remains open and valid. How can they develop Florida Panther habitat that is so important that the Florida legislators are willing to pass a law that would pay for the entire property and no Florida Forever funds needed. Further, the issue had risen to a level of importance that Senator Mel Martinez, FL, had already established three million dollars in Federal appropriations to help with the purchase.

These Federal monies raised another nagging issue: the Federal takeover of all of Florida's natural resources either by direct actions, as in passage of legislation to create Federal lands, or indirectly via the funding process. This funding process always carried strings attached that the public did not see until it was too late. Governor Bush had stated that these federal funds were to have no strings attached. The subject was broached at the December 2005 ARC meeting. The director of state lands explained what the governor had stated and at that time the only strings attached the property this Federal money helped purchase on a 50/50 cost share was that the land could not be used for agriculture or aquaculture activities. Further, the fund's restrictions would only apply to the land purchased and unlike the Picayune Strand State Forest would not apply to all the property in that unit.

Not only was water an issue but the ability to develop a New Town was important too. The new owners were able to work into the sale's agreement that they could remove development rights from the developable land being purchased and apply this density to the 17,000 acres in the southwest corner of the ranch where they would build a New Town.

It certainly would have been nice to purchase the entire ranch in a different manner but there was not enough money in the state to accomplish this without all the complexities and retained rights. However, this 80,000 plus acres of public land would certainly be nice when added to the 3,300,000 acres of public property we purchased in my six years on

ARC. The Director of state lands, Eva Armstrong, had certainly been able to light a fire under the acquisition process and we had certainly expressed high expectations for closing deals by continuing to press the agency to close on land deals or we would move property to the "B" list or off all lists. At every ARC meeting we pressed to move projects that to our knowledge were just sitting there and not moving quickly to closure.

While more than three million acres were protected via fee simple or less-than-fee purchases there could have been many more acres protected if the money had not become a means to drive other issues in Florida. For example, the Harris School House on Key West was brought to ARC as a project. The folks presenting the project came with a letter committing twelve million dollars to restore and manage the property if the state purchased the property from the Monroe County School Board and assigned it to this group. They would set up the property as a museum and art training studio. ARC recommended the project, and the BOT approved it. However, once the evaluations and negotiations were done, the state told the School Board they had to use five million dollars of the money they would receive to pay for affordable housing for middle income families. You see, the cost of housing in Monroe County had become so expensive that moderate income people could no longer afford to purchase a house in the Keys. This meant that people who were teachers, nurses, police and fireman or similar type professions could not live in the Keys. The Monroe County commission had raised this issue a number of times in Tallahassee and wanted the state to subsidize this affordable middle income housing issue. This was not a popular idea. Thus, the sale of the Harris House became wrapped up in this housing issue. Of course, the school board did not accept the strings or the deal. They needed the money to support their building needs and other costs.

Another way to kill a land purchase or Florida Forever Project was for staff to decide to not purchase a portion of the property. This decision-making process was a constant source of policy debate between members of ARC and staff. One example of this happening occurred with the Devil's Garden property. The eastern portion of the ranch had a good number of sections in row crop. Staff had been beaten up badly by the Attorney General over their attempts to purchase a conservation easement on the Fisheating Creek project. Thus, staff decided to cut out the row crop land in the fee purchase project of Devil's Garden. The new leadership of ALICO did not want to sell a part of the ranch and did not want to keep the row crop portion. Thus, the project died before it really had a chance to move forward. In the opinion of many at ARC, staff should have brought this project and new problems back to ARC. At this time, ARC could have evaluated the conditions and most likely would have recommended them to the BOT and hopefully they would have agreed to purchase the row crop portion of the ranch but not to consider the row crop area as conservation lands. Further, with these lands so classified and with directions to remove the development rights and to sell or trade the row crop properties, all would have been happy, and Florida would have had another huge area protected from development while preserving working lands for food production. But sadly this did not happen and most likely Devil's Garden will move onto ranchetts or houses and golf courses.

My association with Devil's Garden, owned by ALICO or the Ben Hill Griffin family, which was 82,000 acres in Hendry County and north of the Big Cypress National Preserve went back many years before ARC. The family decided they would like to sell this land. No one really knows why they wanted to sell, but the rumor was that there was a family estate battle going on. Some interesting history about this land and the region was how I was involved in actions to try to protect the habitat on this property. In the mid-1980s, after a severe freeze in central Florida that killed most of the citrus groves in that part of Florida, the citrus industry moved to Southwest Florida. Farmers had developed a rootstock that could tolerate the higher water levels of south Florida. Grove owners started with an aggressive plan.

Franklin Adams, Manley Fuller and I tried to get the ACoE to require a dredge and fill permit for the work of converting what ended up being 250,000 acres of groves, raw land, and unimproved pasture into groves. We also were seeking involvement by the USFWS under the Endangered Species Act. We knew that while the public was being told by the agencies that the only place the Florida Panther lived was in the

Big Cypress National Preserve region, there were more living on the private lands north of the Preserve. Remember, panthers do not have webbed feet and prefer uplands as do their primary prey—deer and hogs. We had hoped to protect as much of the panther's home range north of the Preserve as we could, but the USFWS would not become engaged in the matter because the ACoE would not require a 404 Permit. They chose to do this because they had determined that less than ten percent of the land was wetlands. Thus, the citrus industry cleared 250,000 acres to bare soil.

Although the USFWS position on panthers in the orange grove area was the panther would live and do well in these groves because there would be spillways, reservoirs and prey to take, they did not consider the fact that there would be people, motors, farm equipment and related activity in the area on a daily basis. This was their position while at the same time they had a position in the Fakahatchee Strand State Preserve, Big Cypress National Preserve, Picayune Strand State Forest, and the Florida Panther National Wildlife Refuge that the use of swamp buggies which are nothing more than homemade lightweight farm tractors, and the use of this farm equipment would harm the very existence of the Florida Panther. Also, at the same time they knew more than fifty-five percent of the Florida Panther population lived on lands north of these public properties and that on this northern range of the panther there were swamp buggies, dog hunting for deer and hogs (hogs are hunted year around), and hunters. Their position was used by other Federal agencies as it satisfied their real agenda to stop hunting on public lands—property that the people of Florida had given them management control over. Control was needed to save some of old Florida while unknowingly allowing an illegal road to be built that benefited the major landowners along the route.

Word of citrus moving into southwest Florida came to me from leaseholders on Devils Garden that the company was removing all the pines from their 82,000-acre ranch. These large mature pines were being cut without a survey for the ESA bird—the Red-cockaded Woodpecker. We tried to get the USFWS to require this survey; they would not. Years later, I was fortunate enough to tour this ranch when it was offered to the state for purchase. While all the pines were not gone, most of the land had been clearcut and converted to Bahia grass pasture. I asked how so much land was turned into Bahia grass pasture. I was told by the ranch manager that they planted seeds after cutting the pines, burning and chopping the palmettos, and then the cattle spread the seed as they grazed.

Many have also expressed their opinion as to why the USFWS did not want to cross ALICO on the issue of an ESA bird impacting their operation. The company was well-connected with many people in influential positions. Some years later, Kathryn Harris, who is the granddaughter of Ben Hill Griffin, was elected secretary of state and we all recall her part in the election of President G. W. Bush. She later became Congresswoman Harris for the State of Florida. Certainly, the USFWS would think very hard before crossing such a well-connected family business even if there was an endangered woodpecker living on the land. There is no proof of any undue influence, but one certainly can wonder about this issue. After all, the same agency turned their head for the building of an illegal road as it would help important people open their land and develop it.

As a part of CERP, the Sustainable Commission of South Florida was able to get the ACoE to do a region-wide Environmental Impact Statement (EIS) for southwest Florida. This was one of the items Franklin Adams, Manley Fuller, and I had attempted to get during the battle to provide better oversight of the citrus invasion in the late 1980s. After hearing the public which addressed the Sustainable Commission in Naples and other cities of southwest Florida as a Sustainable member, I was able to once again able to push the idea of an area wide EIS. I placed a motion on the floor that we recommend an EIS be done that covered all southwest Florida. This was finally approved with the idea that the EIS would tell developers where they could develop easily, where development would be more costly and difficult, and where not to even think about developing. By 1999, this document was finished and as usual, there were those who did not think the EIS was done properly or well and then there were those who thought it too stringent. I am not sure what position to take on this document and only time will tell if it has any value at all in protecting the natural resource values sportsmen treasure in southwest Florida, but one thing is for sure—it is better than what we had.

There were many concerns about how the Water Management Districts spent their portions of the Florida Forever funds. The greatest concern was how the South Florida Water Management District spent their money to purchase land for CERP needs. Considering the explosive cost of land in southeast Florida and the pressing need to acquire property for Restoration needs, I do not think this District had much choice but to purchase land at a high price. If they had not, then they would not have been able to purchase the land or if they delayed, they would pay more. Frequently, I had landowners contact me and explain that if the District took their property, the price would be more after all the legal expenses were paid. In Florida, the state pays the legal expenses of the landowner when property is condemned. Additionally, land being taken has to be considered for its highest and best use thus the prices are forever going up. Under the federal policies, this is not the case. The expense of a lawyer and court are paid by the landowner.

The difference between the federal and state process to condemn land became a major issue for the Sustainable. The Everglades Expansion Act of 1988 allowed the Governor of Florida to request the Secretary of DOI to use federal employees, processes and policies to take land in the Kissimmee River Valley, Lake Okeechobee basin, Everglades Basin and Big Cypress Basin. There was an action on property in the upper Kissimmee River Basin by the SFWMD. The District took property and the Florida legislators let the Sustainable Commission know that if such actions continued, there would be no funds for restoration. Legislators let us know that Florida policy and its constitution must be applied. Thus, the Sustainable Commission had to reconsider their position on such matters. Again, a trade-off was made and to obtain the major objective the Florida process rather than the federal process was recommended.

However, state processes were not used with 8.5 SMA as there was a federal act that allowed them to take this land and add it to ENP. This is another example of how the DOI/NPS work. In 1990, they agreed to leave the 8.5 Square Mile Area (8.5 SMA) alone so they could get the rest of the East Everglades. However, within a few years, they and their supporters were right back at the trough in Congress wanting more land.

It was a well-known fact that Florida is the highest paying entity for condemnation of land while the federal government is the lowest. Further, with the highest and best use of land in the Florida Constitution, condemnation prices of land for CERP were very high. But as Will Rogers once said . . ."they ain't making no more land." Even though Florida was not printing money, it had a tax program that was almost as good. The funds for these land purchasing activities came from a DOC stamp tax on all land purchases and mortgages. Even when interest rates went down, Florida land coffers would grow. Additionally, since the value of land and property in Florida goes up, the amount of money gained to purchase property in the undeveloped areas of Florida only grows exponentially. The expected amount of money to be generated with this tax program was bonded so it thereby provided the funds needed to purchase land. These bonds were guaranteed by the fact that Florida had a full year's bond debit in the bank. Thus, the state's rating was good, and its interest rate was low.

Considering all the good and bad that came from allowing an illegal road to be built, in my opinion, this was a good trade off because I liked to go to the woods and enjoyed big open spaces just like the Florida Panther or Florida Black Bear.

I have been reminded by some of my more business-minded friends that the work I am doing is good and the state is merely placing its best assets into reserve. Many years ago, the state was in the red and the State Constitution required the state to operate only in the black. When the state needed money, it sold four million acres to Hamilton Dissten for a quarter ($.25) an acre. Hamilton made one payment of a million dollars, started digging the contractually required canals to drain the Everglades and control Lake Okeechobee, and then folded. He started the real drainage work that we are paying more than $8.5 billion to correct today. My rich friends like to tease me by saying one day the state will need money and they will sell the lands we are purchasing today to keep the state in the black. I hope this is not true and only time will tell. I did not let them know they most likely were correct. *(When President George W. Bush Sr. was in office, the Big Cypress National Preserve was, I was told by DOI people, the hottest DOI land unit in the nation. By this, they meant that it was very controversial and that politicians were concerned about the unit's viability. One night, I received a phone call from a western congressional aid. This person asked me what I thought of the idea of selling the Big Cypress to a major land company with deed restrictions placed on the deed at the time of sale. I quickly, without hesitation, told the gentlemen no way, as much as I do not like what the NPS was trying to do, I would not support the sale of this land and thought we could work out the problems if enough pressure was applied to the NPS to make them recognize what the Big Cypress National Preserve was supposed to be. I never heard from this gentleman again nor of the idea of selling the Big Cypress National Preserve to a major land company.

The following appendix only has a few of the documents that have caused the author to truly believe the DOI/NPS has no intentions of managing the Big Cypress National Preserve as Congress directed and will only manage it a manner that will continue moving the Big Cypress toward being a Park. As one Big Cypress National Preserve ranger told a young hunting friend of mine, "We are not concerned about you as we have all the time in the world to convert this to a PARK!"

The appendix will allow you see one section of a series of maps that the NPS made in 1986. This section of map demonstrates the extent of the ORV trails and the number of camps in only a small part of the Big Cypress National Preserve. This map shows most of the Bear Island Unit, most to the western part of the Addition lands north of I-75 and the Turner River Unit with a small part of the Corn Dance Unit and the western part of the Stair-Step Unit. The ORV trails shown were the major travel routes used by people who used the Cypress long before the NPS was given control of the land. The Loop Road Unit once looked like the rest of the area but in the early days of the Preserve's history, the NPS took all the ORVs out of this unit. Within five years, these trails were no longer visible from the air. Therefore, there are no trails shown in the Loop Road Unit on the map. The same conditions existed in the Deep Lake Unit. All these trails, uses and impacts were seen firsthand by folks like Assistant Secretary Nat Reed, state leaders, and congressional leaders before they acted to take property from private landowners. They all knew the area was not pristine and had been well-used by 1970. Yet, they went to Congress and told them it was a pristine area and as such had to be saved.

In the appendix, you will see a map showing the extent of the 750,000 acres with most of it essentially closed to the public because people no longer have reasonable access. The NPS has made most of the Big Cypress

National Preserve a roadless area. They have gone against their word to Congress and the people of the nation. They have learned how to attack and stop hunting, not by regulating hunting because this is what the FWC is supposed to do but by stopping the use of the ORV and thereby stopping access to the interior of the Preserve. In 2004, they discovered they could further stop hunting by limiting the number of cumulative days of camping to fourteen days per year. They stopped people from being able to enjoy the land when hunting season was closed and for the entire hunting season. One could no longer go to the area to camp to enjoy the Cypress, and then be able to hunt because they would run out of days to hunt due to such limits on camping.

Buggy trail across a pine prairie during the dry season.

Epilogue

The trip through time and the outdoor experiences of the author have been shared. The fight to protect habitat and the Gladesman culture will be one that is ongoing. The habitat is public ownership but the big battle to protect a way of life and continued human use of these lands will continue. This is because there are some well-funded groups who do not support the Gladesman culture and would like to see the big cypress national preserve turned converted into a national park. Their tactics are litigations via the endangered species act, and failure of federal agencies to follow the required development of regulations. (Since the initial writing of *The Road that Changed Florida,* there has been litigation brought forth by these groups to stop hunting and the use of off-road vehicles in the addition lands and to stop the backcountry management plan which covers the addition lands and the original 570,000 acres of the Wildlife Federation) joined this litigation to protect the amended Big Cypress National Preserve Act which included language protection for traditional uses and cooperation with the Florida fish, wildlife conservation. The plaintiffs lost. This has led them to use a different tactic to stop the uses they no longer support. This strategy is to apply political pressure to delay the finalization of the backcountry plan. They know that without this plan the goal sought via litigation can be obtained because with no plan there is no or very limited use of the backcountry. Sadly, I predict in the end these groups will achieve their goal. What their actions have done is to prevent similar actions across America from protecting large habitat areas. Since the passage of the addition law, there have been other legislative acts to protect more areas. As to the future of CERP and the impacts it will have on the Big Cypress National Preserve I am not sure it will help the cypress. The sub-project, called Western Everglades Restoration Project (WERP) is being designed to bring more water into the cypress via the Kissimmee Billy strand. The biggest problem is the quality of this water. The first draft released by the Army Corps of Engineers (ACOE) and South Florida Water Management District required a huge storm water treatment pond. They said this was needed to enable the incoming water to be properly cleaned so it could move south in the water conservation area and Big Cypress National Preserve. They had not done their homework and placed this pond on the Kissimmee Billy Strand and in the Florida wildlife corridor. This corridor had been in the books since Johnny Jones helped start it in the mid-1970s. The corridor is intended to allow the Florida panther and other animals to move from SW Florida to North Florida and beyond. The ACOE brought forth a changed plan without the storm water treatment pond. Thus, the unacceptable water was not cleaned and would be sent directly into the water conservation areas and the Big Cypress National Preserve, which is classified as Florida outstanding water (FOW). In my opinion and experience, this dirty water will convert much of these two areas into a cattail habitat as has happened on water conservation area 2b's northeastern area and is happening in the other storm water treatment areas. The battle to undo the drainage of the everglades and to protect the Gladesmen culture is not over.

There is an even bigger battle and that is the issue of invasive exotic species. The newest and biggest species is the Burmese python. This snake first appeared in the late 1990s. Today, February 2023, this snake has nearly eaten all the protein in SW Florida. Couple that with the protein needs of the Florida panther, black bear and alligator and there are not many other animals left. Then there is the problem of invasive exotic plants. Plants like the melaleuca tree (common name paper tree), the Brazilian pepper tree (Florida holly not the real Florida holly) and many weedy plants. Not only is the land under attack by plants but there are many invasive exotic aquatic species, walking catfish, cichlid, Oscar, and more. All these new fauna and flora invasive species will most assuredly bring unknown changes.

Appendix

Documents and Correspondence regarding the Big Cypress National Preserve, Florida Land Protection Actions and Plans

```
*******************************************************************
Subj: Re: BNCP Issues
Date: 8/13/99 6:10:51 PM Eastern Daylight Time
From: dandb@intr.net (Joe Browder
To:   LJMoller@aol.com
```

I like the way you do business. And of course, if you're naming me after a county now, if we win this one maybe I'll start calling you Jack Florida!

So you will know the history: After all the other pieces had been put in place, that is, after years of pushing with help from everyone, the one person who had to agree was Spenssard Holland. It had been Holland, during the Eisenhower administration, who introduced the legislation removing Big Cypress from ENP's boundaries.

Lawton Chiles took me to a long, informal meeting with Sen. Holland. We went through everything, with particular focus on why we were creating a National Preserve instead of simply adding Big Cypress to ENP. We talked about my negotiations with the Colliers, and the resulting boundary agreement (I made a last-minute plea with Holland and Chiles to include the O. Slough above Alligator Alley, but as expected got turned down, so it didn't get protected until the State finally did so a couple of years ago), about the rights of people who actually owned camps, homes, and business buildings, the rights of hunters (including access by orv), and the rights being established for the Miccosukee and Seminole people. Bobo

Dean, who was the Washington lawyer for both tribes, had worked with me on that.

We explained to Sen. Holland how many of the conservation groups opposed the rights we proposed be granted to the Miccosukee and Seminole, opposed the unprecedented rights for homeowners and camp owners, and opposed continued hunting and orv access—but we (and Lawton Chiles personally expressed himself very strongly on this) talked about the value of people of the Big Cypress. Not the people who would come and go to appreciate it, but the people who actually lived there, or spent so much time in the cypress country that they had bought land and put up hunting or fishing camps. And we talked about hunting and the people who hunted, as a way of experiencing and coming to know and love nature that reaches some people in ways that are important to our country.

I think what we are engaged in now, as then, is more of a cultural conflict than a resource management issue. Of course this gets to the point I discussed with you earlier, about what a mistake NWF/FWF will make if they focus largely on Big Cypress and defer to other groups on overall Everglades leadership. That will inevitably lead to NWF/FWF being seen as "user" groups, and make them second-class citizens in the fundamental debates about how Big Cypress, too, should be managed.

Back to the point of this discussion: BCNP was established as a different kind of federal protected area, one that would prove that continuing to recognize (in perpetuity) the ownership and access rights of the relative handful of people who lived and worked in and loved the country could be compatible with protecting the land's environmental values.

We can have another discussion about the present situation. But I think that over the past twenty-five years the only significant instance of environmental damage coming from this experiment has been the result of Congressional (Senatorial, really) indulgence for a handful of commercial airboat operators who, in violation of the Big Cypress legislation, haul tourists around in limited areas. Dealing appropriately with that or other genuine resource protection issues is no excuse for the National Park Service to revert to its historic hostility toward people, and uses, not part of the traditional NPS constituency.

Your note, as usual, is so interesting. Years ago I told Manley that the top priority for hunters in Florida should be securing the big Panhandle tracts—that from a statewide perspective, putting lots of energy into issues like Everglades expansion might be ok as a matter of principle, but what will really influence the ability to keep hunting in Florida will be the fate of the big timber tracts—and unless they become public land, they will be lost to hunters (and everyone else).

Your point about the dog hunters and lawbreakers is right on target. In the Big Cypress, the first people I spent time with were the Loop Road folks—and truth be told, when people such as Gator Bill Schoelerman became active opponents of the jetport and proponents of saving the land, that helped more than a little with the lawful hunting folks. And the gator hunters helped us in many other ways—giving us inside info when they were hired to run survey crews for real estate developers, and, most important personally, being very persuasive in getting one of the real estate speculators to tear down the wanted posters he had plastered in every gas station and bar along the Trail ("God Will Reward Any Man Who Accidentally Shoots Joe Browder"). Gator Bill told the guy that if anything accidentally happened to me (or two others named in the poster, Bob Graham and Nat Reed), the guy would end up as chunks on a gator hook. That, more than the FBI agents Nat called, convinced the guy (chairman of the East Collier Landowners Protective Association) to pull his posters down.

And when working with Buffalo Tiger to see if the Miccosukee would drop their support for the jetport and join us in a campaign to turn Big Cypress into public land (they did), one of the issues he raised was the ability of some Miccosukee people to continue enjoying "curlew" once in a while. I told him that if he helped us and we one, I would shoot and cook the ibises myself. He never tried to collect on that promise. But if he were to ask now, you can bet there would be birds in the pot.

As you know, the politics of saving great pieces of nature (particularly when the land is privately owned) is a little different from what's described in the civics books. We need to work with the folks who are there. Wish I had the time to help—but I hope that you and Manley and Barbara Jean, and some good people in north Florida, can put on a real campaign.

I will call you this afternoon or this evening. . . . Joe

Buggy trail through a Big Cypress strand.

J. HERBERT BURKE
10TH DISTRICT, FLORIDA

COMMITTEE:
FOREIGN AFFAIRS

SUBCOMMITTEES:
ASIAN AND PACIFIC AFFAIRS
EUROPE (EUROPEAN AFFAIRS)
FOREIGN ECONOMIC POLICY

Congress of the United States
House of Representatives
Washington, D.C. 20515

WASHINGTON OFFICE:
1127 LONGWORTH BUILDING
202-225-3026

DISTRICT OFFICE:
325 S.E. 6TH STREET
FT. LAUDERDALE, FLORIDA 33301
305-522-3739

August 13, 1971

Mr. L. Jack Moller
7310 Pembroke Road
Hollywood, Florida 33023

Dear Mr. Moller:

This will acknowledge with thanks your letter of July 25th, received in my office on August 13th, expressing your ideas regarding development of the Big Cypress Swamp.

Two months ago Rogers Morton, Secretary of the Department of the Interior, held a briefing for members of the Florida delegation on land use for the Big Cypress Swamp. At that time he released a report by the Everglades-Jetport Advisory Board which recommended that 587,000 acres of the Big Cypress Watershed be protected by Federal land use regulations.

Secretary Morton stressed, however, that several alternative programs to preserve the area were being considered, including full Federal acquisition of sufficient acreage necessary for the protection of the Big Cypress Watershed.

To date no decision has been made by the Department of the Interior regarding this acquisition as responses from private citizens, community organizations, political subdivisions, etc., concerning the proposals are still being received. I have taken the liberty of forwarding a copy of your letter to Secretary Morton for consideration of your suggestions.

With best wishes,

Sincerely,

J. HERBERT BURKE
Member of Congress

JHB:mwg

United States Department of the Interi

NATIONAL PARK SERVICE
WASHINGTON, D.C. 20240

IN REPLY REFER TO:

A3615-IS

AUG 27 1971

Hon. J. Herbert Burke
House of Representatives
Washington, D.C.

Dear Mr. Burke:

Secretary of the Interior Morton has asked us to thank you for your
recent letter in behalf of Mr. L. Jack Moller concerning the Big
Cypress Swamp.

Important decisions are involved in selecting the most desirable land
use alternative in Big Cypress, and the Secretary has asked that no
action be taken on the Big Cypress report until the comments of
interested individuals, like Mr. Moller, are solicited and reviewed.
The project is only in the planning stage, and Mr. Moller's
suggestions are appreciated and will be carefully considered.

Your continuing interest and that of Mr. Moller in our efforts to
preserve and protect the environment of south Florida are greatly
appreciated.

Sincerely yours,

Associate Director

ROBERT L. SHEVIN
ATTORNEY GENERAL

STATE OF FLORIDA
DEPARTMENT OF LEGAL AFFAIRS
THE CAPITOL
TALLAHASSEE, FLORIDA 32304

August 3, 1971

Mr. L. Jack Moller
7310 Pembroke Road
Hollywood, Florida 33023

Dear Mr. Moller:

Thank you for your recent communication.

As you know, the state of Florida is asking the federal government to purchase land in Big Cypress Swamp. As Florida's Attorney General, I feel that it is my duty as an elected public official to prevent the destruction of Florida's natural resources.

In your letter you proposed a three-fold plan for Big Cypress Swamp. Your plan does bear some merit and I will keep it in mind when making my decision on this matter.

As a native Floridian, I must wholeheartedly agree that we must keep Big Cypress in a state of ecological balance with its surroundings, without restricting the average citizen.

Again, thank you for your suggestions.

Sincerely,

Robert L. Shevin
Attorney General

RLS/GClw

State of Florida

REUBIN O'D. ASKEW
Governor
RICHARD (DICK) STONE
Secretary of State
ROBERT L. SHEVIN
Attorney General
FRED O. DICKINSON, JR.
Comptroller
THOMAS D. O'MALLEY
Treasurer
DOYLE CONNER
Commissioner of Agriculture
FLOYD T. CHRISTIAN
Commissioner of Education

DEPARTMENT OF NATURAL RESOURCES

RANDOLPH HODGES   LARSON BUILDING / TALLAHASSEE 32304 / TELEPHONE 224-7141
Executive Director

PLEASE ADDRESS REPLY TO:

August 1, 1973

Mr. Jack Moller
610 Northwest 93 Avenue
Hollywood, Florida   33023

Dear Mr. Moller:

Thank you very much for your letter of July 26, and the generous offer to donate to the State, with certain reservations, your property in the Big Cypress area.

We greatly appreciate this gesture on your part, but feel we cannot act in the matter until certain land acquisition policies have been worked out with the U. S. Department of the Interior. As you know, the Big Cypress is proposed as a federal project, and our land acquisition efforts at this time are designed primarily to facilitate that project.

With your permission, we will hold your offer in abeyance for a few months while we work with the federal people on the acquisition policies. I am inclined to recommend that, if at all feasible, your offer of a restricted donation be accepted.

We will be back in touch with you in this matter as soon as possible.

Sincerely,

Ney C. Landrum
Director
Division of Recreation and Parks

NCL/jap

DIVISIONS / ADMINISTRATIVE SERVICES · ENVIRONMENTAL RESEARCH AND PROTECTION · INTERIOR RESOURCES
MARINE RESOURCES · RECREATION AND PARKS

37

National Wildlife Federation

1412 SIXTEENTH STREET, N.W.
'ASHINGTON, D.C. 20036
—ione: 202-483-1550

December 11, 1973

38th ANNUAL MEETING
March 29-31, 1974
Denver Hilton Hotel
Denver, Colorado

Mr. Jack Mailer
610 N. W. 93rd Avenue
Hollywood, Florida 33024

Dear Mr. Mailer:

Enclosed is copy of the Big Cypress bill.

It would be my recommendation that you wait until the bill
is passed before attempting to work out your donation of land.
The Federal government will not be able to determine provisions
until the bill passes Congress and details are worked out.

In the interim, you can work through the State of Florida.

Sincerely,

THOMAS L. KIMBALL
Executive Vice President

Enclosure
cc: Mr. John C. Jones

1 3

United States Department of the Interior

OFFICE OF THE SECRETARY
WASHINGTON, D.C. 20240

MAY 2 3 1972

Mr. L. Jack Moller
7310 Pembroke Road, No. 3
Hollywood, Florida 33023

Dear Mr. Moller:

Thank you for your letter on the use of swamp buggies in the
proposed Big Cypress National Fresh Water Reserve.

We delayed a reply while we thought through the many questions
your letter stimulated. Your letter was very timely, and we
feel that it contributed greatly to what will likely be our
management policy toward swamp buggies and other vehicles in
Big Cypress. Travel through the swamp by air boats and swamp
buggies will be permitted to continue, but in certain sensitive
areas they may have to be controlled to insure against rutting
and other impairment of the area.

Thank you very much for writing.

Sincerely yours,

Assistant Secretary of the Interior

50

United States Department of the Interior

OFFICE OF THE SECRETARY
WASHINGTON, D.C. 20240

In Reply Refer To:
L58-LL

FEB 27 1974

Dear Mr. Moller:

Thank you for your recent letter regarding legislation for the proposed Big Cypress National Preserve and inquiring about aerial photographs of the area.

We appreciate your suggestion that the date used for defining "improved property" in the legislation be changed from November 23, 1971, to July 1, 1973. The date now used in the legislation, November 23, 1971, was the date on which President Nixon announced that "it is now essential for the Federal Government to acquire this unique and vital watershed," and proposed legislation to authorize the area. This date provides a base for the established policy of this Administration to acquire the requisite legal interest in the Big Cypress swamp. Therefore, we believe the date should not be changed.

The aerial photographs you inquired about may be obtained from the United States Geological Survey, Federal Building, Miami, Florida 33130. You may wish to write that Agency concerning the price of the photographs.

Sincerely yours,

Assistant Secretary of the Interior

Mr. L. Jack Moller
610 NW 93 Avenue
Hollywood, Florida 33024

CONGRESSIONAL TESTIMONY GIVEN ON THE BIG CYPRESS ENABLING ACT

Written Statement of Senator Lawton Chiles

September 21, 1986
S.2029, Big Cypress Expansion Legislation

Page 49 of the record 346

Today I want, first, to outline reasons why these particular lands should be in Federal ownership. Then, I want to explain why we should move on this land acquisition program as soon as possible. And, finally, I want to make a few comments on the management of the Big Cypress.

Page 527
Management of These Lands

The legislation I have sponsored contemplates that the lands added to the existing Big Cypress National Preserve will be managed consistently with those within the already established boundaries. The legislation amends the original act, however, by including a mandate in Section 10(b) (which became Section 5 in S.90 as passed) for the Park Service to promote and encourage recreational use. I appreciate having this opportunity to comment on the Park Service roll in allowing and regulating various activities allowed for under the original Big Cypress National Preserve Act.

water that is so essential t the livelihood of Everglades National Park. The important investment of Everglades National Park needed further protection and, for this reason, we worked to purchase the Big Cypress to act as a buffer to the Park. Those of us who worked to provide for the public ownership of the lands now included in the Big Cypress did so with the understanding that the area would not be another National Park. Public ownership of thee lands which would, in turn, further disrupt the sheet flow of water.

Recognizing the "recreational values of the Big Cypress Watershed," the Preserve concept was developed so as to permit the continuation of the traditional activities associated with this area—activities which may have not been compatible wit the more stringent management requirements of a National Park. The Public Law establishing the Preserve charges the Park Service to provide for "the enhancement and public enjoyment thereof." While I did not envision that the allowable activities would be unregulated, I certainly did envision that these activities would be permitted and encouraged. My overriding concern, however, is that over the years the Park Service has moved toward employing managing objectives for this area as if it were a Park as opposed to embracing a more flexible management structure as I believe was envisioned in the creation of the Preserve concept.

I understand and appreciate the difficulties in achieving a balance between providing for the public enjoyment of the recreational values of the Big Cypress and assuring the ecological integrity of the preserve. While it is not an easy task, it is certainly one which was full contemplated when the Preserve was established. Resource problems other than the original hydrological concerns, such as the endangered Florida Panther, have surfaced since the creation of the Preserve, which need attention and action on the part of the various affected agencies. Public use and enjoyment of the area should be encouraged. What I don't want to see is the resource problems being a means by which to reduce and/or eliminate the public use and enjoyment of areas where public funds have been used to acquire the land. I believe we can reach a balance and have expressed my concerns to the Regional Director of the National Park Service. I stand ready to work with the Committee as well as we strive to solve the diverse and complex problems associated with the unique area.

(While S.2029 did not pass that year the next year, January 6, 1987, S.90 was introduced and Senator Chiles made the same written statement. See pages 49 through 53 of the record.)

It is my opinion, after many conversations, meetings and exchanges of communications; with Senator Chiles that he was not happy with the way the National Park Service was moving to manage the Big Cypress National Preserve, neither were many other Congressional members. The National Park Service and there 'booster clubs' were attempting to manage this unit of the National Park Service as a park and not as a Preserve as intended by Congress when they created this new classification of property within the Department of Interior's jurisdiction. Thus the new section 10(b) (which became Sec. 5 in S.90) Senator Chiles addressed were added. This section states and applies to the entire Preserve:

Senate bill 90 "Section 5; Cooperation among agencies; The Act of October 11, 1974, is further amended by adding at the end thereof the following new section: "Section 10. The Secretary and other involved Federal agencies shall cooperate with the State of Florida to establish recreational access points and roads, rest and recreation areas, wildlife protection, hunting, fishing, frogging, and other traditional recreational opportunities in conjunction with the creation of the Addition and in the construction of Interstate Highway 75. Three of such access points shall be located within the preserve (including the Addition)."

In addition to the NPS not complying with the intent of Congress and the spirit of the enabling act as amended and approved, they have not made their required reports to Congress.

Senate Bill 90; Section 7. Report to Congress. The Act of October 11, 1974, is further amended by adding at the end the thereof following new section: Section 6. Not later than two years after the date of the enactment of this section, the Secretary shall submit to the Congress a detailed report on, and further plan for the preserve and Addition including—"(1) the status of the existing preserve, the effectiveness of passed regulation and management of the preserve, and recommendations for future management of the preserve and the Addition; "(2) a summary of the public's use of the preserve and the status of the access points developed pursuant to section 10; "(3) the need for involvement of other State and Federal agencies in the management of the expansion of the preserve and Addition; "(4) the status of land acquisition and "(5) a determination, made in conjunction with the State of Florida, of the

adequacy of the number, location, and design of the recreational access points on I-75/Alligator Alley for access to the Big Cypress National Preserve, including the Addition.

None of these reports have been done.

It is our suspicion that the reason these reports have not been done within the time established by Congress is the NPS does not want to admit or show the level of use that occurred in the Addition lands at this time. By dealing with these reports in this manner, the NPS would be able to justify, in their minds and the minds of those who do not know the history of the area, the creation of a Wilderness Area. This is what the current superintendent is doing at this time. It is said the NPS cannot document any uses in the Addition lands, thus there is cause to make it a Wilderness Area. While those outside of South Florida and new people to the area do not know the uses and levels of uses at the time these reports were supposed to be done they can accept this classification. They do not want to realize the creation of I-75 with the tall limited access fence has, along with the NPS no entry policy, except for hikers and mountain bike-riders (which is a new recreational activity for the Big Cypress), changed the uses of the area from what was there at the creation and passage of S.90. One can certainly understand how and why the NPS administration under President Clinton has decided to manage the Addition in a manner different than intended by Congress, the sponsors of the act and the public who supported the taking of these private lands. After all, the 'traditional' activities in the Big Cypress area are not really acceptable to the management philosophy of the National Park Service and their supporters.

Leadership in the NPS said they had not done these reports, just as they had not done their ORV management plan, because they do not/did not have the funds. I have to disagree with this tactic. They have the funds; they have not spent the funds in the proper manner. That is they have spent money on a Scenic Highway plan and other activities within the Preserve. Why is this? In our opinion, this strategy has been used because the NPS does not support the intent of the Preserve nor the uses in the manner Congress directed. What the NPS does support is those activities that they have, over the years, considered being standard activities and acceptable activities for units of the NPS. Thus, they have not spent their funds in a manner that would not support their real desires and that is to make the Preserve a Park. As evidence to this though I submit the following: At Superintendent Fred Fagergren's departing party in the late 1980s he stated, according to our representative (City Commissioner Fisikelli: "In short, we believe the lands to be added to the Big Cypress should be managed under the same terms and conditions as have guided management of the Preserve for the last 12 years. The NPS should not be asked to manage one portion of the Preserve with one set of rules and the remainder with another. For this reason it is critical that the Subcommittee amend Section 4 of S. 90 to ensure that language regarding administration of the addition conforms to the language in the original legislation on this subject."

They asked that the Subcommittee delete "promote and encourage" hunting, fishing and trapping within the Addition. They also stated: "We do not oppose hunting and fishing in the Big Cypress."

We know from the bill that was finally approved addressed the issue of hunting, fishing and trapping and was changed by including *"frogging and other traditional opportunities."* This new language further amended the enabling act thus it applies to the entire Preserve and not merely the Addition lands. If Senator Chiles and Congress meant for this language to apply only to the Addition lands it would have been so stated. The reason for the change, to include frogging, was after P.L. 93-440 passed; the NPS created a regulation to stop the taking of amphibians on all their land units. Thus, the NPS was starting to talk about stopping frogging. Thus trapping was dropped; in 1986, there was no trapping in Florida, and frogging inserted. This way, we continue having frogging on the Preserve, including both the Addition and the original portion.

The companion to S.90 in the House had similar discussions and presentations but the House Subcommittee consisted of Congressman Vento of Minnesota who was known to be not particularly friendly to sportsmen and very friendly to "pure" park. Thus, the following exchange between the Subcommittee and Senator Chiles and Congressman Lewis is very important to consider and to understand how the final Addition Act was adjusted to move get it through this Subcommittee.

Mr. Vento. Why should the addition be managed different and in what manner do you intend it to be managed? I guess I would like you to both (Senator Chiles and Congressman Lewis) address that generally and maybe we will be working on it specifically. But administratively, this may cause some difficulty. In other words, there is no natural boundary really between the proposed addition.

Mr. Chiles. If I may speak to that. You did not mention, and I appreciate your kind mention that I was the original co-sponsor of the Big Cypress National Preserve legislation. I remember when we were first discussing the need for Big Cypress National Preserve—Congressman Haley from Florida was the chairman of this committee at that time, and of course he had a world to do with the legislation as well. But what we were talking about, when they said we need to establish a Big Cypress National Preserve, was the fact that the park did need this sheet flow, and there was a real danger that what was happening in the Big Cypress National Preserve at that time, a lot of development was going on there, canals were being dug, a lot of drainage was taking place, and the fear was that that was going to disturb the sheet flow.

At that time we were talking about creating the Big Cypress National Preserve, though, it was clear that we were not looking to create additional parkland as such.

As you know, the Everglades Park is a tremendous area, a tremendous habitat. You have already spoken about that. We were looking to protect the sheet flow and to protect the park itself, but there was no reason to sort of hold the land in exactly the same status. It was our intent in the Big Cypress National Preserve, if you look into the legislation, and we tried to spell out there, that we wanted it used for recreational use, as long as it did not conflict with the purpose of trying to protect the park. The feeling was that you got the park in one area, you limit the use there, you can't hunt or fish or camp in the park as such, and that is necessary.

What I have found over the years is that there is park mentality that goes with the Park Service having jurisdiction of the Big Cypress. Over the years we would find that in many instances in Big Cypress, they were attempting to close access attempting to limit what uses could be made in Big Cypress. So, in effect, we don't see the legislation as a change, we see this as a means of trying to spell out what was our original intent in creating the Big Cypress.

Later on in that meeting Congressman Lewis states: "Mr. Chairman, the recreational access is what we are looking for. We feel that with the length of this road (I-75) in cutting off all access completely, it is necessary to point out there should be access with the legal and recreational access together."

Mr. Lewis was explaining the need for three recreational access sites in the Big Cypress National Preserve including the original property and the addition. Thus, again Section 5 applies to the entire Preserve. If not, then the current recreational access site within the original boundary would not have been built. The other two are waiting to be built in the Addition (lands commissioner Freddy Fisikelli) that he, Fred Fagergren, did his best to make the Preserve a Park. Today we have an NPS that is attempting to do the same.

The issue of management was addressed by The Wilderness Society; speaking for the National Audubon Society, Sierra Club, Defenders of Wildlife, Florida Audubon Society, American Rivers Conservation Council, Friends of the Everglades, Florida Defenders of the Environment and the Environmental Policy Institute, Mr. Steven C. Whitney testified on the topic of management by saying the following:

All of the preceding information is very important so you will understand what led up to such dialog and the position taken by Florida Congressmen. You must review the history of the original enabling act and the section concerning State and Federal working relationships. The original enabling act states:

Original enabling act Public law 93-440: Section 3. (b) In administering the preserve, the Secretary shall develop and publish in the Federal Register such rules and regulations as he deems necessary and appropriate to limit or control the use of Federal lands and waters with respect to: 1. motorized vehicles, 2. exploration for and extraction of oil, gas and other minerals, 3. grazing, 4. draining or construction of works or structures which alter the natural water courses, 5. agriculture, 6. hunting, fishing and trapping, 7. new construction of any kind, and 8. such other uses as the Secretary determines must be limited or controlled in order to carry out the purposes of this act: Provided, That the Secretary shall consult and cooperate with the Secretary of Transportation to assure that necessary transportation facilities shall be located within the existing or reasonably expanded rights-of-way and construction within the reserve in a manner consistent with the purposes of this Act. Section 5. The Secretary shall permit hunting, fishing, and trapping on lands and waters under his jurisdiction within the preserve in accordance with the applicable laws of the United States and the State of Florida, except that he may designate zones where and periods when no hunting, fishing, trapping, or entry may be permitted for reasons of public safety, administration, floral and faunal protection and management, or public use and enjoyment. Except in emergencies, any regulations prescribing such restrictions relating to hunting, fishing, or trapping shall be put into effect only after consultation with the appropriate state agency having jurisdiction over hunting, fishing, and tapping activities.

Big Cypress Hearings before the Subcommittee on Parks and Recreation of the Committee on Interior and Insular Affairs United States of America, 93rd Congress, second session page 81:

Senator McClure. One final question. On a police matter, as I think the Department has settled upon the division between responsibility for hunting and fishing in the light that I stated it earlier.

Mr. Reed (Assistant Secretary Nat Reed). Yes, no problems with that. That is our standard language. The State of Florida is doing an expert job managing the deer herd and the turkey flock down in this part of the world. It has state wardens down there. We don't have. This is a natural area for the state to continue to manage.

Senator McClure. Again, briefly stated, the State of Florida would continue to control hunting and fishing regulations?

Mr. Reed (Assistant Secretary). Yes, sir all the bills direct the Secretary to permit hunting and fishing in the area in accordance with applicable Federal and State laws.

As one can see there is not clear language in the enabling act telling the NPS that they must allow the state to manage wildlife and related activities. Yet, the following statements and positions from significant individuals who testified before Congress as to how the Preserve would be managed and this relationship should have told the NPS how they were to deal with this matter.

Considering the position taken by the author regarding these acts and that of Congressional committee members, whose actions were supported by an approving vote of the entire Congress, the NPS should know that they are to treat the entire Preserve as one unit with the same management actions. Mr. Reed pointed this out when testifying before Congress about the Addition Act. It was also stressed by all presenters and members of Congress that the entire Preserve is to be managed under the same policies.

However, today this does not appear to be the case. It is strongly rumored that the current NPS administration is considering making a portion of the Preserve a Wilderness Area. The subject of Wilderness designation continues to arise in part because of the language in the original enabling act. Assistant Secretary Reed when testifying before Congress for all the agencies under the DOI made the following testimony:

Big Cypress Hearings before the Subcommittee on Parks and Recreation of the Committee on Interior and Insular Affairs United States of America, 93rd Congress, second session page 83:

Senator Johnston. It is about the optimum use now, then, is that it?

Mr. Reed (Assistant Secretary). In the philosophy of use, this is what we would expect. I am sure it would increase in numbers as the State grows. There is no question about that. The usage will grow, but we want to keep the usage, the type of usage, to what it is now

Senator Johnston. You don't want to build a trailer park?

Mr. Reed (Assistant Secretary). No, sir, I don't want to build very much of anything. I don't want the Federal Government going in and building visitors centers or roads or anything else. This is not that kind of place

Senator Johnston. Are vehicles allowed in there?

Mr. Reed (Assistant Secretary). Yes, sir

Senator McClure. Just two questions. One is the fact that you are asking questions which I think are very pertinent to the very fact that this is a unique designation, there is none other like it, so far as I know.

Mr. Reed (Assistant Secretary). Correct, Sir.

Senator McClure. If it is absolutely unique, what is the management philosophy? It is not a park, not a recreation area, not a national seashore. It is completely new breed of cat?

Mr. Reed (Assistant Secretary). It is a new breed of cat, sir.

Senator McClure. The question comes to the management philosophy. There is also involved in this bill the standard provision for wilderness review?

Mr. Reed (Assistant Secretary). That is true. That is probably in all of our legislation. This area is not like a park in which a great deal will remain in wilderness or wilderness type of use. This not going to be that type of use at all. This is going to be used and used hard, I think

Senator McClure. If a wilderness designation should be added, it, in all likelihood, would preclude the use of any motorized vehicles, either land or water?

Mr. Reed (Assistant Secretary). Yes, sir

Senator McClure. Which bears upon the question that Senator Johnston asked about vehicles being involved?

Mr. Reed (Assistant Secretary). I would be less than honest if I did not say we have to watch carefully and monitor the use and probably may have to regulate the use of swamp buggies in the Big Cypress . . . It is almost impossible to get into without the use of a vehicle. So we do want to regulate the use of that

Senator McClure. It is regulated use rather than exclusion?

Mr. Reed (Assistant Secretary). Yes, sir

Page 82: Senator Johnston. When I say park I mean recreation area. Does that part really add anything to it?7

Mr. Reed (Assistant Secretary). Yes, sir, I think it does. With the tremendous population increase on the east coast and now the Naples area, the Big Cypress is marvelous recreation experience. The majority of the people who are here in this room, who are property owners who have used the area on weekend camps, which are numerous, have a tremendous recreation experience getting away from the urban areas of both the east and west coast

∞

In the 1970s I contracted with the National Audubon Society to guide them throughout the Preserve as they did their base line study on the resources and uses on the Big Cypress National Preserve. I contributed to their document on the topics of soil, wildlife, plants, use and ORVs. I was particularly concerned that they had not included the right amount of ORV trails in their document, see page XXX. I surmised, even then, that one day someone would look at this document and then what was really on the ground and say look what has happened since the NPS was given the land to manage. Sure enough, this happened when the Florida Biodiversity, five people, filed their litigation against the NPS, USFWS and ACoE for failure to manage ORVs, not requiring an Clean Water Act 404 permit under the Tullock Rule, and failure to properly implement the Endangered Species Act.

Camp Red Bug in 1974.

STATE OF FLORIDA

OFFICE OF GOVERNOR BOB GRAHAM

October 27, 1986

Mr. Jack Moller
610 Northwest 93 Avenue
Pembroke Pines, Florida 33024

Dear Jack:

On August 9, 1983, I initiated the Save Our Everglades Program, and over the past three years we have made significant progress in returning the Everglades to more like it was in 1900. A 12-mile segment of the Kissimmee River is now flowing through the original oxbows; work is well under way to reflood the Holey Land and Rotenberger tracts; construction has begun on converting Alligator Alley to Interstate 75; wading bird populations have increased in Everglades National Park; and over 100,000 acres of land have been purchased in the Everglades area.

In preparing to leave office as Governor, I want to give special recognition to certain individuals who played a significant role in Florida's efforts to Save Our Everglades. While thousands of people throughout Florida have contributed to our success story, a few such as you have been outstanding.

Please accept the enclosed certificate as gratitude from all those who love and care for Florida's Everglades and our State's overall well being. Your contributions have helped build a legacy as a State that truly cares for its environment.

I urge that you keep up your outstanding work toward accomplishment of the goal of the Save Our Everglades Program. In the months and years ahead, restoration and protection of our natural resources will become even more critical and difficult to achieve.

I wish you only the very best.

Sincerely,

Governor

BG/rcs

Enclosure

January 14, 1972

Mr. Edward A. Mueller, Secretary
State of Florida
Department of Transportation
Tallahassee, Florida 32304

<u>Re: Proposed I-75</u>

Dear Mr. Mueller:

I am writing as attorney for the National Wildlife Federation
and the Florida Wildlife Federation with respect to a document titled
"ENVIRONMENTAL IMPACT/SECTION 4(f) STATEMENT ADMINISTRATIVE ACTION FOR
INTERSTATE ROUTE 75 VICINITY OF FT. MEYERS IN LEE COUNTY TO MIAMI IN
DADE COUNTY." We have not yet had an opportunity to review this
document in sufficient detail to comment on its substance, but we shall
prepare and submit substantive comments within the next 60 to 90 days.
I am writing at this early stage in our review to advise you that the
document is not, and may not lawfully be considered, a draft environ-
mental statement under section 102(2)(C) of the National Environmental
Policy Act ("NEPA") and Guidelines of the Council on Environmental
Quality ("CEQ") implementing NEPA because it was prepared by the
Florida Department of Transportation rather than the Federal Highway
Administration ("FHWA").

As you know, the federal program of making grants-in-aid
to the states to reimburse a portion of the cost of building federal-
aid highways is administered by the FHWA. Except in extraordinary
circumstances, FHWA's approval of route location for a proposed highway
section in the Interstate Highway System is deemed a "major Federal
action significantly affecting the quality of the human environment"
within the meaning of section 102(2)(C) of NEPA. With respect to each
such action, section 102(2)(C) of NEPA requires "all agencies of the
Federal Government" (including FHWA) to prepare an environmental statement and file it with the CEQ.   Section 102 (2)(C) also requires
"the responsible Federal official," prior to making any environmental
statement, to consult with and obtain the comments of certain federal
agencies.

Mr. Edward A. Mueller
January 14, 1972
Page Two

Both the language of NEPA and its legislative history
indicate quite clearly that the responsibility to conduct the
environmental analysis and to prepare the statement required by
section 102(2)(C) rests with the federal officials who are to take
the action subject to NEPA, and not with any other agency or person.
As Senator Jackson said in the Senate debates on NEPA, preparing
environmental statements is "action-forcing" in the sense that the
required evaluation of environmental impacts is intended to insure
infusion of "the policies and goals defined in this act . . . into
the ongoing programs and actions of the Federal Government . . . ."
Congress intended the preparation of environmental statements to
become much more than routine paperwork for federal officials. It
was to become the method by which federal officials gained understanding about the effects of proposed actions before taking them.
It was to become the process by which federal agencies would "to
the fullest extent possible" interpret and administer "the policies,
regulations, and public laws of the United States . . . in accordance
with the policies set forth" in NEPA (Section 102(1)). The
delegation to others of responsibility for preparing environmental
statements frustrates and undermines this principal purpose of NEPA.

Moreover, the delegation of responsibility for preparing
environmental statements to agencies or persons who have an interest
in the federal action to be taken makes it impossible for the
evaluation required by NEPA to be conducted objectively. In the
federal-aid highway program, the state highway agencies are applicants
for federal grants-in-aid. They may not be expected to evaluate fully
the desirability of not taking the federal actions they propose. In
this instance, the State of Florida proposes to build Interstate
Route 75 from Ft. Meyers to Miami and to obtain reimbursement from
the Federal Government for up to 90% of its costs. The alternative
of building no highway, which the Environmental Study Panel
recommended, would undoubtedly have received closer and more impartial
scrutiny by FHWA personnel than it apparently was given by the Florida
Department of Transportation.

The procedures followed in preparing the document purporting
to be a draft environmental/section 4(f) statement for proposed I-75
may have reflected the procedures set forth in FHWA's PPM 90-1
(Aug. 23, 1971). That, however, is no excuse for failure to comply
with NEPA. To the extent that PPM 90-1 is inconsistent with NEPA's
requirement that environmental statements be prepared by "the
responsible Federal official," its provisions are invalid.

Mr. Edward A. Mueller
January 14, 1972
Page Three

        For the foregoing reasons, we urge you to advise FHWA that the Florida Department of Transportation cannot lawfully prepare an environmental statement under section 102(2)(C) of NEPA, to request that FHWA carry out the responsibilities imposed on it by NEPA, and to take no further action in connection with the document purporting to be a draft environmental/section 4(f) statement for proposed I-75.

                           Very truly yours,

                           Robert M. Kennan, Jr.
                           Counsel

                           Attorney for:
                           National Wildlife Federation
                           Florida Wildlife Federation

RMK/s

cc   The Honorable Russell E. Train
      The Honorable Herbert F. DiSimone
      Mr. Francis C. Turner
      Mr. Harry E. Stark
      Mr. P. E. Carpenter
      Jay Landers, Esq.

126 c

117

COPY

Cabinet.
Resolution to
support purchase
March 7, 1973

RESOLUTIONS

FLORIDA AUDUBON SOCIETY
BOARD OF DIRECTORS
May 17, 1973

No. 1

Interstate 75

WHEREAS previous resolutions of the Florida Audubon Society have registered opposition to the construction of Interstate 75 along the "Alligator Alley" Route, and have authorized the staff to pursue all necessary administrative and legal action necessary to prevent its construction or secure its construction along a more acceptable northern route; and

WHEREAS the primary objective of this opposition has been to protect the environment of the Big Cypress Watershed and South-west Florida from encroachment and damage related to highway construction and the undesirable patterns of urban growth and development that such highway construction would accelerate or cause; and

WHEREAS negotiations with the Governor's office and the Florida Department of Transportation arising out of this opposition have produced meaningful modifications to the original highway plan which will serve to significantly reduce and effectively control environmental damage and undesirable encroachment upon natural systems which would otherwise occur; and

WHEREAS additional commitments on the part of the State of Florida as represented by the Governor provide that the state will appropriate or authorize the expenditure of 40 million dollars to assist the federal government in acquisition of the Big Cypress Watershed for protection and management as a "National Fresh Water Reserve"; and

WHEREAS, upon examination and evaluation of the foregoing modifications and commitments it is the opinion of the Executive Director and the staff that any further legal action would be inadvisable at this time, provided that all proposed modifications to the highway plan are actually put into effect, and provided that all commitments as represented to the Society by the Governor and the Florida Department of Transportation are diligently pursued and fulfilled:

NOW THEREFORE BE IT RESOLVED By the Florida Audubon Society that the Society withhold further legal action against the construction of Interstate 75 at this time provided that:

**Florida Audubon Society threat to sue if ten items
were not agreed to, May 17, 1973, page 1**

1. The State of Florida appropriates or authorizes the expenditure of 40 million dollars to assist the federal government in acquisition of the Big Cypress Watershed.

2. The Big Cypress Watershed is actually acquired by the state and federal government.

3. The construction of Interstate 75 will not encroach on the "Six Mile Cypress Strand" in Lee County, and diligent effort is made to avoid encroachment on either unique natural features along the right of way of Interstate 75 on a north-south access through Collier and Lee Counties.

**Florida Audubon Society threat to sue if ten items
were not agreed to, May 17, 1973, page 2**

Page 2

4. No interchanges are constructed on the east-west access of Interstate 75 in the area extending from Andytown to Naples with the exception of one controlled access interchange at the Seminole Indian Reservation to provide northward access to the reservation exclusively. Appropriate barriers shall be constructed throughout the entire east-west access of the highway to prevent unauthorized access.

5. The state will purchase in conjunction with construction at least four sections of the land continuous to grade separation at the intersection of Interstate 75 and State Road 29 to provide a buffer limiting development which might otherwise create pressure to open an interchange at that location in the future.

6. The state will investigate the need and feasibility of requiring the establishment of a purchased buffer to prevent development and encroachment and possibly future pressure for an interchange at the intersection of Interstate 75 and State Road 840 in Collier County.

7. In areas not actually included by the Big Cypress acquisition along the east-west access of Interstate 75 the state shall take steps to limit development pressure which might otherwise generate demands for interchanges in the future. Mechanisms for this purpose which shall be considered by the state will include acquisition of buffer strips along the highway in fee simple title, acquisition of all access rights, designation of appropriate "areas of critical state concern" with the application of state development controls, and combinations thereof.

8. Action shall be taken...

**The Florida Board of Trustees argees to the ten items in the Florida
Audubon Society threat to litigate, April 14, 1973, page 3**

8. Action shall be taken during the construction of Interstate 75 to correct hydrolic deficiencies in the structural design of Alligator Alley. Disturbance of adjacent areas and siltation shall be controlled during construction. All hydrologic and biotic effects will concurrently be monitored by the state to assure minimum damage and prevent modification which will tend to accelerate drainage beneficial to land use changes and development. Design considerations shall also include appropriate measures to allow unhampered animal crossings at various points along the east-west access of the highway route.

9. Controlled access to public lands for recreational purposes will be provided in the Big Cypress and in Conservation Area #3. An effort will be made to generally enhance the recreational characteristics of the highway right-of-way and immediately adjacent areas to the degree compatible with environmental protection and highway design.

10. Highway design will include measures to limit positive drainage runoff into roadside canals. All such canals shall be constructed to maximize shallow literal areas which are beneficial to fish and wildlife.

BE IT FURTHER RESOLVED that this resolution shall in no way be construed to constitute an endorsement or approval of an Alligator Alley routing for Interstate 75 by the Florida Audubon Society. The Society takes the foregoing position only to further measures which will tend to minimize the adverse environmental impact of a project which otherwise would surely inflict a totally unacceptable pattern of ecological destruction upon the vital resources of the Everglades, the Big Cypress Watershed and Southwest Florida.

**Florida Audubon Society threat to sue if ten items
were not agreed to, May 17, 1973, page 4**

*The author had to present this Florida Audubon
document in the preceding manner because the
original document was on legal size paper.*

Respon to the 10 items in the Florida Audubon Society
April 14, 1973 resolution about I-75, prepared
jointly by Florida DOT and FHWA

April 14, 1973

The resolution from the Florida Audubon Society Board of Directors
dated April 14, 1973, was received by the Florida Department of
Transportation and the Federal Highway Administration after completion
of the preparation of the combination final environmental impact/
Section 1653(f) statement. The following are the Florida Department
of Transportation's and Federal Highway Administration's comments on
the items in the Florida Audubon Society's resolutions.

1. **Comment** The State of Florida appropriates or
authorizes the expenditure of $40 million to assist
the Federal Government in acquisition of the Big
Cypress Watershed.

Response The Florida Land Conservation Act provides
for a $240 million bond issue for acquisition of
Environmentally Endangered Lands and Outdoor
Recreation Lands. Governor Askew has committed
expenditure of $40 million of this amount for
acquisition of the Big Cypress Watershed. The State
expenditure of $40 million is planned to be carried
out in conjunction with Federal expenditures through
a coordinated effort by the Governor, State of
Florida, Federal Government agencies, and other
groups.

Acquisition of right-of-way for I-75, including
access rights, will be done in conjunction with
the Big Cypress acquisition.

2. **Comment** The Big Cypress Watershed is actually
acquired by the State and Federal Government.

Response Legislation to establish the Big Cypress
Watershed is currently under consideration by
Congress. The Florida Legislature passed, and
Governor Askew approved, the Big Cypress Conservation
Act of 1973. This act directs the Governor to begin
immediately an acquisition program within the Big
Cypress area on behalf of the State, pending action
by the Congress on its Big Cypress acquisition
proposal. The $40 million is included for this
State acquisition. The Florida Department of
Transportation and the Federal Highway Administration
recognize the importance of the Big Cypress Watershed
as evidenced by the steps taken to preserve and protect
this area in the planning of I-75.

3. **Comment** The construction of Interstate 75 will not
encroach on the "Six Mile Cypress Strand" in Lee
County, and diligent effort is being made to avoid
encroachment on either unique natural features along

The Florida Board of Trustees argees to the ten items in the Florida
Audubon Society threat to litigate, April 14, 1973, page 1

J2

the right-of-way of Interstate 75 on a north-south
access through Collier and Lee Counties.

Response   Meetings have been held concerning the
Six Mile Cypress Strand and the questions have been
resolved. This is documented in the Florida Audubon
Society letter of May 9, 1973 to Governor Reubin O'D.
Askew, a copy of which is attached.

4.   Comment   No interchanges are constructed on the
east-west access of Interstate 75 in the area
extending from Andytown to Naples with the exception
of one controlled access interchange at the Seminole
Indian Reservation to provide northward access to
the Reservation exclusively. Appropriate barriers
shall be constructed throughout the entire east-west
access of the highway to prevent unauthorized access.

Response   The Florida Department of Transportation
has agreed to these proposals. The Florida Department
of Transportation and the Federal Highway Administration
will proceed with further project development in
accordance with the proposal to eliminate the interchange at State Route 29 and to provide northward
access to the reservation exclusively.

These features will be presented as discussed above
at a design public hearing. Pursuant to requirements
of PPM 20-8, the approval of designs eliminating the
SR 29 interchange and providing access control features
will not be given until after the design public hearing
and an appropriate recommendation by the Florida
Department of Transportation.

There will be continuous physical barriers throughout
the project as an interstate is a limited access
facility and specifications require fencing to prohibit
unauthorized access. An attractively landscaped chain
link and cable fence will be placed approximately 60 feet
from the edge of the roadway throughout the project
which will serve as a highway safety barrier to prevent
out-of-control vehicles from entering the water distri-
bution system. It will also control unauthorized access
to the highway. In addition, the parallel water distri-
bution system will effectively control access between
the roadway and adjacent lands.

5.   Comment   The State will purchase in conjunction with
construction at least four sections of the land
continuous to grade separation at the intersection
of Interstate 75 and State Road 29 to provide a buffer

The Florida Board of Trustees argees to the ten items in the Florida
Audubon Society threat to litigate, April 14, 1973, page 2

limiting development which might otherwise create
pressure to open an interchange at that location
in the future.

Response   The State of Florida has indicated that
it will provide a buffer to limit development in the
vicinity of the intersection of Interstate 75 and
State Road 29. This will involve purchase of four
sections of land contiguous to the intersection or
any lesser amount which will effectively serve to
control development as determined by further design
and right-of-way studies by the Florida Department
of Transportation in conjunction with other appropriate
State agencies. The area around SR 29 is under consideration now for designation as an "Area of Critical
State Concern" under Florida's Land and Water Management Act.

6.   Comment   The State will investigate the need and
feasibility of requiring the establishment of a
purchased buffer to prevent development and encroachment and possibly future pressure for an interchange
at the intersection of Interstate 75 and State Road 840
in Collier County.

Response   State Road 840A will cul de sac at the north
and south right-of-way lines of Interstate 75 and no
access will be permitted at this location. A minimum
type structure to permit access across the interstate
will be considered at this and other appropriate
locations, if requested by the National Park Service
for management purposes. This road is within the area
of the Big Cypress Watershed acquisition which will
eliminate the possibility of future development and
encroachment.

7.   Comment   In areas not actually included by the Big
Cypress acquisition along the east-west access of
Interstate 75, the State shall take steps to limit
development pressure which might otherwise generate
demands for interchanges in the future. Mechanisms
for this purpose which shall be considered by the
State will include acquisition of all access rights,
designation of appropriate "areas of critical State
concern" with the application of State development
controls and combinations thereof.

Response   This concern is effectively accomplished
from Andytown to State Route 29 since for most of this
length the adjacent lands are or will be under public
control; i.e., Conservation Area #3, the Seminole
Indian Reservation, and the Big Cypress Watershed.
The section from SR 29 west to Naples is the most

The Florida Board of Turestee argees to the ten items in the Florida
Audubon Society threat to litigate, April 14, 1973, page 3

eptible area to development : the subject
section of I-75. The access rights from adjacent
lands will be acquired in accordance with Interstate
highway geometric design standards. The State of
Florida will give priority to investigations of this
area for application of its authority under the
Florida Environmental Land and Water Management Act
and work with local governments in establishing
appropriate land use controls.

In the acquisition of right-of-way for a highway,
some parcels are land locked and others are damaged
to such an extent that the value remaining after
the taking plus the damages to the remainder is
small. To the extent permitted by Federal legislation these parcels will be acquired in fee.
In other cases the Florida DOT will consult with
local and State agencies in an effort to see if
another agency is interested and has the capability
to jointly acquire the parcel in fee. Such areas
will form a partial buffer and add to the highway
aesthetics. In addition to the above steps, the
Florida Department of Transportation will:

(handwritten margin note: Creating land locked property to decrease its value for condemnation purposes.)

a. Cooperate with other interested agencies
   to the extent permissible under State law
   to acquire buffer strips along the highway
   to limit development. The size and limits
   of the areas to be obtained will be determined as design and right-of-way studies
   are developed.

(handwritten margin note: taking of private land)

b. Cooperate with other State agencies in
   establishing "Areas of Critical State
   Concern" under the provisions of the
   Florida Environmental Land and Water
   Management Act to control development
   and encroachment adjacent to the Interstate facility through the environmentally
   sensitive areas between Naples and Andytown.
   This Act permits the State to control use
   and development by means of regulations,
   permitting, zoning, and platting.

   It is the plan of the Florida Department of
   Transportation and the Federal Highway
   Administration to utilize a drainage design
   which will retain the existing drainage
   patterns of the adjacent areas. This will
   serve as deterrant to further development
   in the area.

8. Comment Action shall be taken during the construction
   of Interstate 75 to correct hydrolic deficiencies in the

**The Florida Board of Turestee argees to the ten items in the Florida
Audubon Society threat to litigate, April 14, 1973, page 4**

structural design of Alligator Alley. Disturbance of adjacent areas and siltation shall be controlled during construction. All hydrologic and biotic effects will concurrently be monitored by the State to assure minimum damage and prevent modification which will tend to accelerate drainage beneficial to land use changes and development. Design considerations shall also include appropriate measures to allow unhampered animal crossings at various points along the east-west access of the highway route.

Response   The Florida DOT and FHWA agree to correct any drainage deficiencies found to exist on the present roadway. Disturbance of adjacent areas and siltation during construction will be controlled as recommended in the Environmental Impact Statement. The drainage design of the Interstate facility as discussed in the environmental impact statement provides retention and enhancement of existing drainage patterns and sheet type flow, of the area. Animal crossings at appropriate points along the highway will be established. The Florida DOT in cooperation with agencies qualified in wildlife behavior patterns will establish the number and location of such crossings during the design development.

The need for livestock passes at the Seminole Reservation has been determined in coordination with Reservation officials and agreement has been made to provide the needed facilities. Consideration will be given to the need for other crossings during the design study.

9.   Comment   Controlled access to public lands for recreational purposes will be provided in the Big Cypress and in Conservation Area #3. An effort will be made to generally enhance the recreational characteristics of the highway right-of-way and immediately adjacent to degrees compatible with environmental protection and highway design.

Response   The Florida DOT and FHWA have agreed to provide rest area facilities. The major recreational facility will be located at the Miami Canal (Conservation Area #3) which will include provisions for boat and pedestrian access to the waterway. The location of other facilities will be determined at the design phase.

The facilities will provide for boat and pedestrian access to adjacent areas. Turnarounds to permit east or west travel will be provided at these facilities.

10.   Comment   Highway design will include measures to limit positive drainage run-off into roadside canals.

The Florida Board of Turestee argees to the ten items in the Florida Audubon Society threat to litigate, April 14, 1973, page 5

II 6

All such canals shall be constructed to maximize shallow literal areas which are beneficial to fish and wildlife.

Response   The Florida Department of Transportation and the Federal Highway Administration concur in this item as documented in the Environmental Impact Statement.

The Florida Board of Turestee argees to the ten items in the Florida Audubon Society threat to litigate, April 14, 1973, page 6

Obtained from W. Fowler 7/31/78

Region Four
P. O. Box 1079
Tallahassee, Florida 32302

November 19, 1973

Mr. Ray G. L'Amoreaux, Director
Division of Planning and Programming
Florida Department of Transportation
Tallahassee, Florida 32304

Attention: Mr. W. N. Lofroos

Dear Mr. L'Amoreaux:

Subject: Florida – Project I-75-4(1)210, Lee, Collier and
Broward Counties
I-75 from SR 82 at Ft. Myers to Andytown

Reference is made to your letter dated August 14, 1972, transmitting the Final Environmental Impact/4(f) Statement, Location Study Report and public hearing transcript and requesting approval of the FEIS and location.

The information has been reviewed, and we have been advised that the Washington Office has approved the FEI/4(f) Statement subject to conditions noted in Addenda 1 and 2 attached. As you will note in Addendum No. 2, the action taken to protect the Fakahatchee Strand through either acquisition or adoption of land development regulations under the State's Environmental Land and Water Conservation Act must have taken place and been submitted to this office prior to the request for design approval for the project involving the Fakahatchee Strand. This will prevent having any further environmental processing.

With the understanding that Addenda 1 and 2 provisions will be incorporated into the project, the location is approved in

—more—

Mr. Ray G. L'Amoreaux   2.
November 19, 1973

accord with your request, and the project may be advanced
in a normal manner subject to the above conditions. This
approval will also allow you to proceed with the work
previously authorized between Ft. Myers and SR 846 south
of Ft. Myers.

One copy of the signed PEI/4(f) Statement has been previously
furnished your office on August 28, 1973.

                              Very truly yours,

                              Sgd. P. E. Carpenter

                              P. E. Carpenter
                              Division Engineer

Addendum #2
Final Environmental Impact Statement
Florida - I-75

The Fakahatchee Strand is an important wetland area located adjacent
to the proposed Big Cypress reserve. Protection of the Strand from
development which might accompany construction of I-75 is an important
environmental objective. To some extent this will be achieved by the
proposed elimination of an interchange of State Road 29. Further
protection can be provided either through acquisition of the area
(in whole or in part) or by adoption of land development regulations
under the State's Environmental Land and Water Conservation Act.
Such regulations covering the entire Big Cypress "Area of critical
State concern," which includes the Fakahatchee Strand, have been
proposed by the State of Florida. They are currently undergoing a
process of public review and comment prior to formal action.

The State of Florida will proceed with appropriate actions to protect
the Fakahatchee Strand. Adoption of appropriate regulations under
the State's Environmental Land and Water Conservation Act, following
completion of the public meeting and review processes now underway in
the State, can provide effective control of development in the
Fakahatchee Strand; or, the State may acquire a significant portion
of the Strand. If the State notifies FHWA that either of these
actions has taken place, no further environmental processing will be
necessary. However, if neither of these actions has been completed
at the time that the State DOT requests design approval for the project,
a study will be undertaken at that time to consider what actions will
be appropriate under the circumstances then existing to minimize
adverse environmental impacts of I-75 on the Fakahatchee Strand.

United States Department of the Interior

OFFICE OF THE SECRETARY
WASHINGTON, D.C. 20240

MAR - 2 1972

Gentlemen:

There seems to be a question over the management of the Big Cypress if it becomes an authorized National Park Service area. I recognize your concern for the continuation of hunting by your members and the many others who have enjoyed Big Cypress as a recreation area.

Rumors have been deliberately started by special interests who claim setting aside the Big Cypress as a National Fresh Water Reserve by Congress would foreclose hunting, especially if it is administered by the National Park Service. Presuming Congress does not direct otherwise, let me emphatically state that these rumors are false. First, it is not intended that the reserve be managed as a national park. The National Park Service administers at least 20 different types of areas of which parks are only one. In fact, as you can see in the enclosed copy of the House bill (the Senate bill is identical), "The Secretary shall permit hunting, fishing, and trapping, etc." Second, there are many National Park Service areas in which hunting is permitted. Check the enclosed list of such areas and then also check with your national headquarters or with local Federation officers near these areas. I think you will find that the hunters are well satisfied with the National Park Service management and that hunting in these areas is in accordance with state laws.

There are rumors to the effect that all vehicles will be barred from the reserve, but again, this rumor is without foundation. A provision in the bill speaks of controlling motorized access, but this does not refer to vehicles, but the construction of highways and roads to subdivisions. We could all agree that Big Cypress requires the use of special vehicles such as air boats and swamp buggies as restriction to conventional vehicles would limit the potential uses of the reserve. In some areas though, thoughtless operators may be damaging the soil surface so that in time, compaction and erosion leads to diverting the natural flow of water. This problem of deep ruts needs to be carefully monitored to determine the best way that off-the-road vehicles can continue to operate without causing permanent damage. Some particularly sensitive areas may have to be placed out of bounds or rotated in use. If Big Cypress is to continue to give pleasure to hunters, then you will agree that good management is an absolute necessity; otherwise there would be no particular reason to protect it from the bulldozers.

The Big Cypress proposal came about following many months of study of which the Leopold report was the first of several. That report made it clear that if Big Cypress is drained, Big Cypress and the lower Everglades, as we know them today, wi'' be irreparably damaged. My flight two weeks ago over the private developments in west Collier and Lee Counties c' _lu-sively proved the point that the developers have the m ,ey to engineer and divide up Big Cypress and sell it off - . "waterfront building sites."

I am also aware that the bag of lies being used to separate us includes the assertions that this is to be a federal land grab, that property owners will be thrown off their land, forced to take a fraction of the land's value and that years will pass before any payment is made. In my opinion, that is nonsense! First, there is no way for it to be a land grab. We must pay the fair market value; and, by law, the owner participates in its determination.

Second, no one gets thrown off his land. We cannot buy anything until Congress authorizes the reserve, and appropriates the money. We are asking Congress for funding over a 10-year period, because we physically could not buy it all in less time. But most important, [the] bill provides for life estates and unless Congress directs us to do otherwise, we expect to defer purchasing lands which are being used compatibly with the objectives of the authorizing legislation. I can state without qualification that we will exploit every means legally available to us to allow compatibly used lands to remain unacquired or unpossessed by the United States for at least the lifetime of the present owners and as long as the use remains compatible. Hunting, fishing, trapping and recreation are compatible uses.

I believe that sound management of Big Cypress National Fresh Water Reserve will not only encourage and preserve quality hunting, but also will allow present access methods to continue under some

2

reasonable controls. Here we have the case: we can have our cake and eat it too; we can save this vast area from being corrupted by draglines and bulldozers, and provide south Florida with a first-class recreational area. To be sure that we will indeed have sound management and reasonable controls, we will need your help. It is usual that following enactment of a law establishing a National Park Service area, an advisory board is appointed. The board assists in the preparation of a master plan, a management plan and otherwise offers guidance to the area. I hope that you or someone from the Federation will be available to serve. In that way, we can both be sure that your concerns will be resolved.

This is not the time for friends of Big Cypress to fall apart and play into the hands of the developers. Now is the time to join together to save this area for our children's children so that they may have a taste of wilderness which we are enjoying.

Sincerely yours,

Nathaniel P. Reed
Assistant Secretary

Mr. John Jones
Florida Wildlife Federation
Tallahassee, Florida

Mr. Calvin Stone
18145 S. W. 95th Court
Miami, Florida 33157

Enclosures

LAWTON CHILES
    FLORIDA

𝔘𝔫𝔦𝔱𝔢𝔡 𝔖𝔱𝔞𝔱𝔢𝔰 𝔖𝔢𝔫𝔞𝔱𝔢

COMMITTEES:
APPROPRIATIONS
BUDGET
GOVERNMENTAL AFFAIRS
SPECIAL COMMITTEE ON AGING
DEMOCRATIC STEERING COMMITTEE

April 2, 1979

Mr. John Good, Superintendent
Everglades National Park
P.O. Box 279
Homestead, Florida 33030

Dear Mr. Good:

Since the matter of issuing final regulations to limit
and control certain activities within the Big Cypress
National Preserve is presently before you, we want to
emphasize our strong interest in the effective management of the Preserve and to comment specifically on
proposed regulations limiting the use of motor vehicles
in Big Cypress.

Big Cypress has long been recognized and acclaimed as
a unique natural resource essential to the livelihood
of Everglades National Park, an important water source
for Florida southwest coastal cities, and a valuable
area rich in recreational opportunities. When pressures
of increasing population and potential economic development seriously threatened the natural flow of water
thoughout Big Cypress, Congress was challenged to find
a way to prevent further development and, at the same
time, protect the multiple uses traditionally associated
with the area.

While we recognized the pressing need to protect the
watershed area essential to the survival of portions of
Everglades National Park, those of us who were primary
sponsors of the Big Cypress legislation were unquestion-
ably determined not to provide this protection by creating
another National Park. Instead, we structured a system of
management which would both assure the traditional pattern
of water flow to the Everglades as well as accommodate
hunting, fishing, and a variety of other recreational
activities that are not compatible with the more stringent
biological preserve management standards of Everglades
National Park. The legislative history surrounding the
establishment of the Big Cypress National Preserve in 1974

Mr. John Good
April 2
Page Two

clearly points to Congressional concern that the variety
of public uses traditionally associated with Big Cypress
be allowed to continue, and it is important that we review
the proposed regulations for the Preserve in the context
of our commitment to multiple-use management objectives for
Big Cypress.

As you are aware, public access into the Preserve is generally
by the use of motorized vehicles. Obviously, any restrictions
imposed on vehicular access affect the extent to which the
general public can use and enjoy certain areas of the Preserve.
Among those who have worked hard to protect Big Cypress are
many local residents, sportsmen, and conservation groups who
are now understandably concerned about the impact motor vehicle
use restrictions will have on traditional activities which are,
in many cases, accompanied by motor vehicles. We all realize
in some cases environmental concerns as well as competing
public demands necessitate restricting the use of motor
vehicles, but our primary concern is that any action by the
National Park Service to control or limit the use of motorized
vehicles be reasonable, equitable, and justified in terms of
public enjoyment and important resource protection.

Section 7.86(a) of the proposed regulations for Big Cypress
National Preserve ensures public participation in future
decisions affecting permanent closures or restrictions of
areas from motor vehicle use. The public comment period
affords an opportunity to assess reaction to proposed restrictions and ensures essential coordination with appropriate
Federal, State, and local agencies. Although it would be
impracticable to require a public comment period when the
Superintendent finds it necessary to temporarily close or
restrict areas from motor vehicle use, it is important,
nonetheless, that any action taken affecting vehicular
access be coordinated with appropriate agencies. For this
reason we suggest that the regulations require the Superintendent to consult with the Executive Director of the Florida
Game and Fresh Water Fish Commission before imposing any
closures or restrictions of an area from motor vehicle use.
Prior consultation will, in our view, ensure better coordination of the Commission's fish and wildlife management activities
with the administrative actions of the National Park Service.

Mr. John Good
April 2
Page Three

We appreciate having the opportunity to participate in
the review of proposed special regulations for the Big
Cypress National Preserve and look forward to hearing
from you in response to our comments and suggestions.
We stand ready to support you in your continued efforts
to preserve the natural values and protect the public uses
associated with the Big Cypress National Preserve.

Most sincerely,

LAWTON CHILES

RICHARD (DICK) STONE

DANTE FASCELL

DON FUQUA

L. A. (SKIP) BAFALIS

ANDY IRELAND

LC/glt

CC: Mr. Robert L. Herbst
     Assistant Secretary for Fish, Wildlife and Parks
     U.S. Department of Interior

United States Environmental Protection Agency

United States Department of the Army

AUG   4 1995

MEMORANDUM FOR THE FIELD

SUBJECT: Applicability of Clean Water Act Section 404 to Vehicle Use in Waters of
the U.S.

On August 25, 1993, the Army Corps of Engineers (Corps) and the U.S.
Environmental Protection Agency (EPA) issued a final rule (the Tulloch rule) that
revised the definition of "discharge of dredged material" within the meaning of the Clean
Water Act Section 404 regulatory program. The definition was revised to clarify that the
term "discharge of dredged material" includes discharges associated with mechanized
landclearing, ditching, channelization, and other excavation activities that destroy or
degrade wetlands or other waters of the United States. In light of questions that have
arisen regarding the application of the Tulloch rule to vehicular traffic, this joint
memorandum is being issued to clarify that, as a general matter and as explained below,
the Corps and EPA do not interpret the Tulloch rule as applying to normal, routine use
of a vehicle or vehicles through wetlands.

<u>Discussion</u>

In making this clarification, the agencies are guided by the underlying purpose of
the Tulloch rule, which was to close regulatory loopholes that, in the past, had enabled
some projects to be designed specifically so that they did not require Section 404 review,
even though virtually identical activities with the same environmental impacts were
subject to regulation. The rule was proposed pursuant to a settlement agreement in
<u>North Carolina Wildlife Federation v. Tulloch</u>, a lawsuit that charged EPA and the
Corps with failing to regulate ditching and other excavation activities that destroyed
several hundred acres of pocosin wetlands in North Carolina. The extensive destruction
of wetlands and other waters associated with the residential development and golf course
which led to the lawsuit are illustrative of the types of projects that did not undergo
Section 404 review due to the regulatory loopholes in existence prior to the final rule.
These loopholes allowed the developers in <u>Tulloch</u> to avoid regulation by using
sophisticated and expensive excavation methods, such as drag-lines and backhoes with
sealed buckets and sealed containers resting on truck beds, to ensure that only
"incidental" discharges of dredged material were redeposited in the wetlands. The
environmental impacts resulting from these methods, however, were no different than

those resulting from projects using less sophisticated methods involving the same or similar types of equipment, but with larger discharges of dredged material, which required Section 404 authorization.

In order to close these regulatory loopholes, the Tulloch rule subjects to regulation under Section 404 "any addition, including any redeposit, of dredged material, including excavated material, into waters of the United States which is incidental to any activity, including mechanized landclearing, ditching, channelization, or other excavation." 40 CFR Section 232.2 and 33 CFR Section 323.2(d)(1)(iii) (definition of discharge of dredged material) (emphasis added). While the identification of activities involving discharges provided in this definition is not exhaustive, it is reflective of the agencies' intent to subject to regulation the enumerated activities, as well as other activities involving discharges that are not specifically enumerated but are similar in character to those identified. As discussed in the preamble to the Tulloch rule, the specifically identified activities were, prior to adoption of this regulation, subject to disparate treatment under Section 404 depending upon the amount of soil movement associated with the activity. The underlying purpose of the Tulloch rule was to remove this disparity and ensure that mechanized landclearing, ditching, channelization, excavation, and similar activities were subject to regulation in a consistent and rational manner. In contrast to these activities, normal use of vehicles has not been subject to disparate treatment under the Section 404 program (indeed, such activities were not regulated at all prior to the Tulloch rule). In this important respect, therefore, such normal vehicular traffic is not fundamentally similar to the activities specifically identified in the regulation.

In light of this background, the Corps and EPA wish to clarify that, as a general matter, the driving of a vehicle or vehicles through wetlands does not require authorization pursuant to Section 404 under the Tulloch rule. Specifically, driving a vehicle such as a car, off-road-vehicle (ORV), or farm tractor through a wetland in a manner in which such a vehicle is designed to be used is not subject to regulation under Section 404, except as discussed below. The agencies emphasize that their determination that, as a general matter, vehicle use in wetlands is not regulated by Section 404 is based upon operation of the vehicle in a manner consistent with its designed use. For example, questions have been raised to the agencies as to whether use of Florida's Big Cypress Preserve by large ORVs is covered by Section 404. Based on the agencies' understanding that such ORVs will be driven in the manner in which the vehicles are normally used, the Corps and EPA wish to clarify that such vehicle use is not the type of activity that the Tulloch rule was intended to regulate.

However, as the agencies stated in the preamble to the Tulloch rule, vehicular traffic may be subject to regulation under "extraordinary" circumstances. As an example, the agencies believe that such circumstances may exist if vehicles were to be used in a manner inconsistent with their normal use. This would occur if the vehicles are used in such a way that the activity may reasonably be considered as fulfilling a function comparable to the activities specifically identified in the Tulloch rule (e.g., lining up of one or more vehicles in a wetland and repeatedly spinning the vehicle wheels in order to create ditches to alter the wetland). In the agencies' view, use of vehicles in this manner would be analogous to use of a boat propeller for prop-dredging, which the Corps and EPA indicated in the Tulloch rule preamble would be subject to Section 404 regulation, see 58 FR 45023 (Aug. 25, 1993).

While vehicular traffic is not, as a general matter, subject to regulation under Section 404, the Corps and EPA will continue to work with Federal and State agencies seeking to address any environmental effects that result from vehicle use in wetlands under their regulatory authorities. For example, with regard to Florida's Big Cypress Preserve noted above, use of the Preserve by ORVs requires authorization from the National Park Service (NPS), and the Corps and EPA will continue to provide assistance to the NPS as it seeks to ensure that ORV use is undertaken in a manner that is consistent with the purposes and functions of the Preserve.

If you have any questions regarding this memorandum, please contact Hazel Groman of EPA's Wetlands Division at (202) 260-8798 or Sam Collinson of the Corps' Regulatory Branch at (202) 272-0199.

Robert H. Wayland III, Director
Office of Wetlands, Oceans and Watersheds
U.S. Environmental Protection Agency

Michael Davis, Chief
Regulatory Branch
U.S. Army Corps of Engineers

3

RESOLUTION NO. 88-29

A RESOLUTION OF THE CITY OF FORT LAUDERDALE,
FLORIDA, ENDORSING REST AND RECREATIONAL ACCESS
SITES TO PUBLIC LANDS IN COLLIER COUNTY, FLORIDA,
FROM INTERSTATE 75 FOR USE BY OFF-ROAD VEHICLES,
BOATING AND HIKING INTERESTS.

WHEREAS, the proposed construction of Interstate 75 may greatly diminish access to public properties in Collier County, including the Big Cypress National Preserve; and

WHEREAS, such properties have been historically utilized for such recreational purposes as off-road vehicles, boating and hiking by members of the general public, including residents of the City of Fort Lauderdale; and

WHEREAS, the Department of Interior, National Park Service, is currently developing a General Management Plan (GMP) for the Big Cypress National Preserve concerning rest and recreational access sites which would ensure the continued use of such public areas by off-road vehicles, boating and hiking interests; and

WHEREAS, the interests of the citizens of Fort Lauderdale and the entire State of Florida will best be served by preservation of recreational access by off-road vehicles, boating and hiking interests from Interstate 75 to public lands within Collier County, including the Big Cypress National Preserve;

NOW, THEREFORE, BE IT RESOLVED BY THE CITY COMMISSION OF THE CITY OF FORT LAUDERDALE, FLORIDA:

SECTION 1.   The City Commission of the City of Fort Lauderdale, Florida, endorses development of rest and recreational access sites within the National Park Service's General Management Plan (GMP) for the Big Cypress National Preserve within Collier County, Florida for off-road vehicles, boating and hiking uses.

SECTION 2.   That the City Clerk is hereby directed to furnish a certified copy of this Resolution to the Secretary of the United States Department of Interior via the Director of the National Park Service.

ADOPTED this the 2nd day of February, 1988.

Mayor
ROBERT O. COX

ATTEST:

GUV OFF. OF EN~ ~~~ TEL+:~04-922-6~00~~~ ~NOV 09~95 ~:12 NO.004 P.02

STATE OF FLORIDA

Office of the Governor

THE CAPITOL.
TALLAHASSEE, FLORIDA 32399-0001

LAWTON CHILES
GOVERNOR

November 6, 1995

Honorable Janet Reno
Attorney General
Department of Justice
Tenth Street and Constitution Avenue, N.W.
Washington, D.C. 20530

Dear Janet:

This letter is to request your assistance in resolving an issue regarding recreational access and use of the Big Cypress National Preserve. The case known as "Florida Biodiversity Project vs. Roger Kennedy" (Civ. No. 95-50-CIV-FTM-24D) is currently being litigated in the U.S. District Court, Middle District of Florida, Ft. Myers Division, by the Department of Justice representing the Departments of Interior and the Army, and the EPA. A proposed settlement agreement between the Plaintiff and Defendants has been filed and is being considered by the Judge. My understanding is that a decision by the Judge on the Agreement is imminent.

Flori~ . ~~rests in the case are being represented by the Florida Game and Fresh Water Fish Co: .~:~ :~ as Friend of the Court. The Florida Wildlife Federation and individual representatives of Florida sportsmen are intervenors. The Department of Justice and plaintiffs developed the proposed settlement agreement without the benefit of participation by the Game and Fresh Water Fish Commission and the intervenors. It does not consider the legitimate historic and recreational uses of the Big Cypress National Preserve by Florida citizens, or acknowledge the intent of Congress to provide for traditional recreational activities as stated in the Big Cypress National Preserve Act.

The Department of Justice could help rectify this situation by agreeing to, or in the alternative not opposing, modifications to the settlement agreement which would:

1) provide that future changes to the agreement should require the approval of all parties, including intervenors, or approval of the Court;

2) preserve the National Park Service's ability to regulate Off-Road-Vehicle activities pursuant to its General Management Plan for the Big Cypress National Preserve (paragraph 7, settlement agreement);

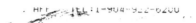

Honorable Janet Reno
November 6, 1995
Page Two

3) strike paragraphs eight and nine from the agreement since these issues were never raised by plaintiffs in the Lawsuit and therefore should not be part of the settlement; and,

4) provide language in the Agreement that recognizes the intent of Congress in establishing the Big Cypress National Preserve to ensure "the preservation, conservation, and protection of the natural scenic, hydrologic, floral and faunal, and recreational values of the Big Cypress..."

For many years Florida and the federal government, with the support of environmental and recreational organizations, have worked cooperatively to protect and preserve the Everglades and Big Cypress systems. Since 1983, some 170,500 acres have been acquired in the Big Cypress Swamp. Two new national wildlife refuges have been created--the Florida Panther and Ten Thousand Islands National Wildlife Refuges. Significant improvements in the flow of freshwater to the Everglades have been accomplished through the conversion of Alligator Alley to I-75. Wildlife crossings have been installed along I-75/Alligator Alley and State Road 29. Congressional approval of the Big Cypress National Preserve Addition and Everglades National Park Expansion Acts will add more than a quarter of a million acres to federal holdings in Big Cypress and Everglades.

I have long advocated protection and public use of the Big Cypress and sponsored the legislation that created both the National Preserve and its Addition. While our protective efforts have been very successful, we also need to continue our commitment to reasonable public access and use. The recommended amendments to the settlement agreement would greatly benefit this long-standing commitment.

Your consideration of this request would be deeply appreciated.

With kind regards, I am

Sincerely,

LAWTON CHILES

LC/mrs

United States Department of the Interior

NATIONAL PARK SERVICE

EVERGLADES NATIONAL PARK
AND
FORT JEFFERSON NATIONAL MONUMENT
P. O. BOX 279
HOMESTEAD, FLORIDA 33030

IN REPLY REFER TO:
W24
BICY

MAR 1 2 1979

Mr. L. Jack Moller
610 N.W. 93rd Avenue
Pembroke Pines, Florida 33024

Dear Mr. Moller:

We have received your request that the proposed special regulations for
Big Cypress National Preserve be withdrawn.

In order to comply with the Congressional directive in Public Law 93-440,
the enabling act establishing Big Cypress National Preserve, special regulations must be developed for activities such as motorized vehicles, hunting,
fishing, trapping, etc. Without the regulations, these uses, nontraditional
in many units of the National Park Service, would be prohibited in Big
Cypress National Preserve.

It would be helpful to us if you could specify the statements which you
consider difficult to understand. Written comments will be accepted until
March 30, 1979.

Sincerely,

Claude L. McClain

ACTING Superintendent

Attorney General Reno
October 24, 1995
Page 1

Reno10.95.2

October 24, 1995

L. Jack Moller
610 NW 93 Ave
Pembroke Pines, FL
33024

Attorney General J. Reno
Attorney General's Office
Washington, D.C.

Honorable Janet Reno:

For many years you worked with my students in Dade County and taught them and I many important principals about America. One of those principales concerns discrimination. It is this that I have found most surprising and disturbing because I have found myself on the side of being discriminated against by, of all agencies, the one you are responsible for.

In recent litigation, Florida Biodiversity vs National Park Service, et el., the court accepted me and three others as intervenors. Yet we, our lawyers, were denied access to the judicial process involving negotiations. Your staff lawyer felt so strongly about not allowing us to be involved that they did not even review the documents we produced which supported our interest, and the publics, in this case.

Once the plaintiff and Justice Department reached a negotiated settlement our attorney(s) received a copy with a telephone conversation that was summarized as, "this is it, we (the Justice Department) are not interested in your clients position or any changes to this settlement." Our attorney was able to get a few minor alterations but not enough to make a significant difference in the settlement. Had our material been reviewed and even better had we been able to attend the negotiation table the final out come would have been much different.

ɔ

Further, our lawyer reported to us that your staff said, "you should not be surprised that you were not at the negotiation table because that is the way Justice Department works." This, in my opinion, is wrong. Not only is wrong because we, or any intervenor should be involved in the negotiations but I know of one case were interested parties in a Justice Department case were involved heavily in the negotiation settlement.

When the Federal Government, through the Justice Department, filed suite against the State of Florida, South Florida Water Management District, for polluting Federal properties in Florida, namely Loxihatchee Wildlife Refuge and Everglades National Park, others were involved in the negotiated settlement. I was a part of that litigation on the side, again as in the last case, of the Federal Government. My involvement was providing funds and leadership to help the Florida Wildlife to be considered a "friend of the court."

Our representative was able to sit at the table of negotiations and be a full participant in the activity. Additionally those corporate interest in the Everglades Agriculture Area (EAA), they were not an intervenor on the side of the state, were allowed to participate by the Justice Department. The handling of this case and the more recent case in which I was denied access to the process clearly indicates to me that your Department is extremely selective in how they do business. Another term for selective is discrimination.

The EAA people were merely stake holders without court standing just has I was a stake holder in the Florida Biodiversity vs National Park Service, et.el. case. But, I had court standing as an intervenor and still denied access. In the earlier case filed by Dexter Lehtinin the stake holders were allowed by the Justice Department to attend and fully participate in the negotiation process. Their denial in this more recent has stopped me from effectively participating in this litigation resulting in my interest being damaged.

It is my opinion had I been one of the wealthy EAA corporations I would have been allowed to attend and participate in the recent court case. But not being a wealthy person I was denied even though I had qualified as an intervenor and had proper legal counsel.

The reason a person files for intervenor status and is accepted by the court is because they have a very high degree of investment in the issue, intervenors are serious stake holders. As such their interest are not going to be adequately or be properly

ﮮ

Attorney General Reno
October 24, 1995
Page 3

represented by the defendant's lawyer. Thus I was considered by the court to qualify as an intervenor. However your staff prevented me from obtaining access to the process and circumvented the court's consideration of my position.

To me this is a discriminatory act based on ones financial status.

I look forward to hearing from you on this issue and seeing you in Miami again. And, once again I am shocked that you would allow this type of discriminatory action to occur under your leadership.

Sincerely,

L. Jack Moller

cc: President Clinton
       Governor Chiles
       Senator Graham
       Senator Mack
       Representative C. Shaw
       Representative P. Goss
       Bill Horn, Wild Legislative Fund of America
       Sue Lamson, National Rifle Association
       Manly Fuller, Florida Wildlife Federation
       Lee Chamberlain, Everglades Co-ordinating Council
       Bob Apgar, Esq.
       David O. Charland, Co-intervenor
       Barbara Powell, Co-intervenor
       Wayne Jenkins, Co-intervenor

United States Department of the Interior

NATIONAL PARK SERVICE

BIG CYPRESS NATIONAL PRESERVE
S. R. BOX 110
OCHOPEE, FLORIDA 33943

IN REPLY REFER TO:

D3415(BICY)
Tract # 731-99

MAR 7 1984

L. Jack Moller
610 NW 93 Avenue
Pembroke Pines, Florida 33024

Dear Jack,

I am sorry that you were disappointed with my response on the ORV data but unfortunately, at this time the data cannot be provided without expending a great deal of manpower and funds which are just not available.

In regards to the information on buggies alone, this information is interspersed with the 6000+ other permits. Since we have begun this process over 1,025 buggies have been permitted. If funds and manpower become available, one of my high propities is to have this type of information computerized and I would be more than happy to provide this information for you at that time.

In regard to vehicular access to your property, I provide the following. I consider the access road to your exempt property to be similar to a private drive. It would not fall under the category of a deeded maintained and named road similar to Turner River Road. Nevertheless, vehicles traversing this road directly to and from your property would not require our ORV permit so long as they operate on the "maintained" portion of this road.

As for maintenance on your road: As this road is and has been privately maintained this would be allowed so long as it remains substantially as it is. Any significant change would require all applicable permits prior to any work being done. Smoothing the road and filling small pot-holes would be considered appropriate in order to maintain the road at its present condition.

I hope this clarifies the situation for you. If I can be of further assistance, feel free to contact me.

Fred J. Fagergren
Superintendent

United States Departmentof the Interior

National Park Service
SOUTHEAST REGIONAL OFFICE
75 Spring Street, S. W.
Atlanta, Georgia, 30303

IN REPLY REFER TO:

N21(SER-PC)

JUN 1 2 1990

Mr. L. Jack Moller
610 NW 93rd Avenue
Pembroke, Florida 33056

Dear Jack:

Superintendent Fagergren conveyed to me your concerns about the language in the draft I-75 Recreational Access Plan/Environmental Assessment which states "public hunting will not be permitted in the Addition until protection of the panther is assured." I can clearly understand your concern that this section is too open-ended and could mean the National Park Service would not open this area to hunting for many years.

I have informed the authors of the document that this is not our intention and that this point must be clarified in the final document. Our intention is to ensure that we comply with the Endangered Species Act and consult with the U.S. Fish and Wildlife Service under section 7 prior to opening areas to hunting. Please note that the draft plan indicates on page 9 that, in order to develop hunting management proposals, further data must be collected on: white-tailed deer and other game; past levels of hunting in the Addition; the status and protection needs of the Florida panther; and other critical resources.

We would hope that this formal letter alleviates your concerns. It is our intention to collect the data necessary to make hunting management determinations within 3 years of acquiring title and access to property in the Addition.

Thank you for bringing this item to our attention.

Sincerely,

Robert M. Baker
Regional Director
Southeast Region

United States Department of the Interior

NATIONAL PARK SERVICE
BIG CYPRESS NATIONAL PRESERVE
S. R. BOX 110
OCHOPEE, FLORIDA 33943

IN REPLY REFER TO:

L7617 (BICY)

February 20, 1991

We are pleased to enclose the Finding of No Significant Impact (FONSI) and Statement of Findings (SOF) for the I-75 Recreational Access Plan/Environmental Assessment. In early 1990, we provided you with a draft of this Plan. The enclosed documents constitute the approval of the Plan. The Plan has been transmitted to the Florida Department of Transportation so that these conceptual plans can be incorporated into the construction plans for I-75.

Questions should be directed to this office at (813) 695-2000.

Fred J. Fagergren
Superintendent

United States Senate
WASHINGTON, D.C. 20510

February 25, 1988

Sonny Nomes
17101 SW 200th Street, E-34
Miami, Florida 33187

Dear Sonny:

Thank you for contacting me to share your thoughts. I appreciate
hearing from you and having the benefit of your views.

I am pleased to report that legislation I introduced to expand the Big
Cypress National Preserve has passed the Senate. This is a unique proposal in that it calls for using highway funds, which must be expended
for completion of I-75, to accomplish equally important goals of environmental restoration and wildlife protection. Alligator Alley, the
cross-state highway going from Andytown in Broward County to Naples,
has disrupted the natural water flow in the Big Cypress Preserve area.
The road functions as a dam in some areas, causing unnatural pooling
of water while at the same time interrupting the important sheet flow
so essential to Everglades National Park. The construction of I-75
along Alligator Alley provides an important opportunity to correct
these hydrological problems.

We also have an opportunity to protect the endangered Florida panther
and many other animals that are killed crossing the Alley. The proposed fencing and canal system along the interstate will serve as a
barrier for animals as they approach the road, and strategically located bridge underpasses will allow panthers and other animals to pass
under the highway safely.

Finally, I have included language in this bill which affirms the recreational uses of the Preserve. I am a strong believer in making public
lands as accessible as possible to taxpayers for their education and
enjoyment.

The House has already passed a similar measure. I will be working to
secure resolution of the difference in these two bills and appreciate
knowing of your interest.

With kind regards, I am

                              Most sincerely,

                              LAWTON CHILES

LC/ahs
Enclosure

LAWTON CHILES
FLORIDA

COMMITTEES:
APPROPRIATIONS
BUDGET
GOVERNMENTAL AFFAIRS
SPECIAL COMMITTEE ON AGING
DEMOCRATIC STEERING COMMITTEE

United States Senate

September 14, 1988

Mr. L. Jack Moller
610 N.W. 93rd Avenue
Pembroke Pines, FL 33024

Dear Mr. Moller:

I wanted to get back in touch with you to share a copy of my
statement on the Senate Floor regarding passage of the Big
Cypress Addition. I hope that this information will address your
concerns.

Your letter pointed out that some recreational opportunities
currently enjoyed in the Big Cypress Preserve are not
"traditionally" part of the National Park Service's philosophy on
park management. Let me point out that our amendment to S. 90
specifically covers those recreational uses currently enjoyed in
the Preserve and does not address National Park Service policy in
general. I have made my hope clear that any changes in the
number of hunting days or types of allowable activities should be
the result of thorough study and analysis, public comment, and
proper documentation of degradation of resources.

Again, thank you for contacting me.

With kind regards, I am

Most sincerely,

LAWTON CHILES

LC/vmp

Enclosure

United States Department of the Interior

NATIONAL PARK SERVICE
BIG CYPRESS NATIONAL PRESERVE
S. R. BOX 110
OCHOPEE, FLORIDA 33943

IN REPLY REFER TO:

A3821 (BICY)

September 22, 1989

L. Jack Moller
610 NW 93rd Avenue
Pembroke Pines, Florida 33027

Dear Jack,

In response to your recent telephonic inquiry I would acknowledge my awareness
of a proposal by the National Parks and Conservation Association (NPCA) that the
area of Big Cypress National Preserve south of U.S. Highway 41 be added to
Everglades National Park. I understand this was one of a number of boundary
changes NPCA recommended occur for units of the National Park System.

I would note this proposal did not originate at Big Cypress National Preserve.
Big Cypress has made no proposal for any portion of Preserve lands to be added
to Everglades National Park.

Sincerely,

Fred J. Fagergren
Superintendent

PETER DEUTSCH
20TH DISTRICT, FLORIDA

COMMITTEE ON FOREIGN AFFAIRS
SUBCOMMITTEE ON EUROPE AND
THE MIDDLE EAST
SUBCOMMITTEE ON WESTERN HEMISPHERE AFFAIRS

COMMITTEE ON BANKING, FINANCE
AND URBAN AFFAIRS
SUBCOMMITTEE ON FINANCIAL INSTITUTIONS
SUPERVISION, REGULATION AND DEPOSIT INSURANCE
SUBCOMMITTEE ON HOUSING
AND COMMUNITY DEVELOPMENT
SUBCOMMITTEE ON CONSUMER CREDIT
AND INSURANCE

COMMITTEE ON MERCHANT MARINE
AND FISHERIES

Congress of the United States
House of Representatives
Washington, DC 20515-0920

MAILING ADDRESS
425 CANNON HOUSE OFFICE BLDG.
WASHINGTON, DC 20515
(202) 225-7931
(202) 225-8456 (FAX)

MAIN DISTRICT OFFICE

10100 PINES BLVD.
PEMBROKE PINES, FL 33025
(305) 437-3936
(305) 437-4776 (FAX)

DADE (305) 371-8721
KEY LARGO (305) 852-0159
BIG PINE (305) 872-3916
KEY WEST (305) 294-5815

July 5, 1994

Mr. L. Jack Moller
610 NW 93rd Ave
Pembroke Pines, FL 33024-6368

Dear Mr. Moller:

Thank you for your recent letter regarding hunting and ORV management in the Big Cypress National Preserve. You mentioned your concerns about a recent staff briefing that was held in my office. I would like to correct your understanding of the circumstances and content of this meeting.

Legislative staff commonly attend informational briefings on a variety of topics. The meeting you referred to in your letter was called specifically and solely to discuss genetic restoration for the endangered Florida Panther with representatives from the National Parks & Conservation Association and the National Zoo. This was not a formal briefing for Members of the Florida Congressional delegation, but rather an informational meeting for interested staff. Although I did not personally attend this meeting, my staff has advised me that hunting and ORV use were not discussed.

Again, thank you for your letter regarding hunting and ORV use in the Big Cypress National Preserve. I do not plan to support proposals that would limit recreational activities in Big Cypress. If you have any specific concerns regarding genetic restoration for the Florida Panther, I would be pleased to hear about them.

Sincerely,

Peter Deutsch
Member of Congress

PD\mb

Florida Department of Transportation

JEB BUSH
GOVERNOR

THOMAS F. BARRY, JR.
SECRETARY

August 20, 2001

Mr. L. Jack Moller
610 NW 93 Avenue
Pembroke Pines, FL 33024

RE: Public Records Request No. 01-08273

Dear Mr. Moller:

This is to respond to your inquiry regarding severance of access and land purchase costs along I-75 (Big Cypress National Perserve) in Collier County.

This office has researched the files for that portion of I-75 (Big Cypress National Perserve) from State Road 29 to the L-29 Canal. The total cost for acquiring the right of way in this area was approximately $45,368,102.00 Due to the age of this project, it was not possible to separate the cost for severance of access and land purchase. Therefore, the amount provided includes both.

If you have any further questions, please feel free to contact my office at 1-800-292-3368, extension 2579.

Sincerely,

James S. Crackel
Programs, Budget &
Management Systems Administrator

JSC:rh

Cc: Cheri Kelley, T. E. Small, W. M. Owings, B. F. Wolcott, V. J. Luster,
      Project Correspondence File

To: Jack Mollen
From: Rick Smith

STATE OF FLORIDA

Office of the Governor

THE CAPITOL
TALLAHASSEE, FLORIDA 32399-0001

LAWTON CHILES
GOVERNOR

May 29, 1991

Mr. Robert M. Baker, Regional Director
Southeastern Regional Office
National Park Service
U.S. Department of the Interior
75 Spring Street, Southwest
Atlanta, Georgia 30303

RE: Plan Approval and Finding of No Significant Impact I-75
    Recreational Access Plan/Environmental Assessment, Big
    Cypress National Preserve, Florida. SAI: FL9005241544CR

Dear Bob:

I want to thank you and your staff for developing the Interstate
Highway 75 (I-75) Recreational Access Plan. Uncountable hours
have gone into this effort by your staff, State agency personnel,
conservation organizations and individuals.

We are not completely satisfied with the National Park Service
Plan because of its strict limitation on public access,
particularly at the Mile Marker 31 access point to the Big
Cypress National Preserve. Justification for these proposed use
reductions is lacking. We are also concerned with the procedures
for determining how and when access is to be provided into the
Addition lands.

Notwithstanding these concerns, it is very important that we
forge ahead with the construction of recreational access
facilities without lengthy delay. We therefore ask that
implementation of the proposed plan be expedited.

Since we are not convinced that the public interest or
Congressional intent have been satisfied, it is the State's
intent to pursue further issues pertaining to additional public
access and recreation, and the timing of baseline studies.

Mr. Robert M. Baker
Page Two

The Big Cypress National Preserve and Addition, an
environmentally sensitive highway, and accommodation of public
use and enjoyment of our public land is of vital importance to
Florida. These are some of the reasons why the Save Our
Everglades Program is my highest environmental priority.
Implementation of a recreational access plan for I-75 is a key
part of achieving these objectives. Therefore, the National Park
Service, the Federal Highway Administration and the State of
Florida would best serve Florida's environment and its people by
expediting the implementation of the current recreational access
plan.

Any apparent conflicts in the positions of State agencies as
expressed in the attached letters were reconciled in an
interagency meeting convened by my office May 21, 1991.

We appreciate the opportunity to review this plan. I would
appreciate meeting with you in the near future to begin
addressing the unresolved issues.

With kind regards, I am

                              Sincerely,

                              LAWTON CHILES

LC/rms

cc: Colonel Robert M. Brantly, Game and Fresh Water Fish
        Commission
     Carol Browner, Department of Environmental Regulation
     Ben Watts, Department of Transportation
     Fred Fagergren, Big Cypress National Park

NATHANIEL P. REED

POST OFFICE BOX 1213
HOBE SOUND, FLORIDA 33475

PHONE (772)546-2666
FAX (772)546-5019

October 13, 2003

L. Jack Moller
610 NW 93 Ave.
Pembroke Pines, FL 33024

Dear Jack,

I received a vast amount of material from Eric and you and devoured it during this past week.

I made a number of calls to those people who I trust for a different view over the current state of the on going disputes that wrack the management of the Big Cypress Preserve. I spoke to eminent ecologists, members of the NPS, fishing guides, and members of the south Florida environmental community.

Here is my decision: I am 70 years of age. Although in reasonable physical condition, I am suffering through a series of attacks of arrhythmia. I will need medical attention for several months to insure that I am not a victim of stroke.

I am still actively in business. Although busy, I find time to work on a series of everglades restoration issues that fascinate me. I have three grandsons who live seven miles west of our home who on returning from school and finishing their homework fish with me in the Indian River every afternoon.

I serve on the boards of the National Geographic Society, the Natural Resources Defense Council, Hope Rural School and advise a number of other state and national environmental groups. I have a limited amount of time. I select projects where I have the opportunity to make a difference. For instance, I will be Co Chair of an Urban Land Institute effort to examine why regional planning has failed in Florida. I am serving on the board of a group that wishes to pass a constitutional amendment forcing review of the $8.7 billion of exemptions from Florida's sales taxes.

I have examined a potential role in trying to arrive at consensus on management issues within the Big Cypress. Although the current situation is terrible, marked by mistrust and past and present grievances clouding every decision, I do not see any way that the parties can reach consensus. Both sides are totally resistant to change. The ORV users and hunters want the Big Cypress managed for them and in their view as the least damaging alternative. The environmental interests are determined to halt what they consider to be practices that undermine the overall mission of the Service to "guard and protect" the ecosystem. The guides think that all sides have gone too far and that it is impossible to reach an agreement. Experts on the Florida panther talk about the lack of faith and judgment of the Wildlife Commission including the fact that one year

L. Jack Moller
October 13, 2003
Page Two

old deer are now legal prey despite the need to provide deer for the cat population. Members of the NPS are determined in their belief that the "users" are totally committed to "their" way and couldn't care less about the state of the environment or the other potential users of the Preserve.

I could spend ten years trying to arbitrate between user groups and not make an impression.

I have written Fran Maninella and urged her to appoint an "extraordinary" superintendent who will listen to all sides, bring a sense of order to the staff and make decisions, tough decisions and live by them unless overturned in court.

Jack, I will always have a soft spot in my heart for the hunters and fishers-outdoorsmen- who joined forces to urge the creation of the Big Cypress Preserve. I have always acknowledged that their support was determinant in the Preserve's creation. However, from the start I knew that many practices of the day would have to change. I knew that preservation of the ecosystem came first and would remain the greatest priority of the Service. I knew that the Service would have a very difficult time managing use and managing people who were used to doing their own thing when and where they chose to go.

I have made the firm decision that I am not going to attempt to mediate the on going dispute. The depth of disagreement, the remembrances of wounds real or perceived are simply too great for me to spend time on without the prospect of success.

The best I can hope for is the appointment of an extraordinary superintendent. Frankly, it may take another generation who are not battle scared to work out a management plan that is 80% acceptable to all.

With best wishes,

Nathaniel Reed

cc: Fran Maninella
       Eric Kimmel
       Terry Rice
       Johnny Jones
       Joe Browder

United States Department of the Interior

NATIONAL PARK SERVICE
Southeast Regional Office
Atlanta Federal Center
1924 Building
100 Alabama St., S.W.
Atlanta, Georgia 30303

IN REPLY REFER TO: A3821 (SERO)

May 11, 2001

Mr. L. Jack Moller
610 NW 93 Avenue
Pembroke Pines, Florida 33024

Dear Mr. Moller:

Your letter dated April 8, to Secretary of the Interior, Gale A. Norton, has been
forwarded to this office for reply.

As of March 2, 2001, the National Park Service has acquired 535,747.51 acres within the
original preserve. Based on current GIS technology, there are actually 581,767.89 acres
within the authorized boundaries of the original preserve. Since the National Park
Service only owns 535,747.51 acres, they can still acquire 34,252.49 acres and remain
within the legislative mandate. Your claim that the National Park Service can no longer
acquire land within the original preserve because they have exceeded the 570,000 acre
legislative ceiling is incorrect.

As you are aware, the final Recreational Off-Road Vehicle (ORV) Management Plan was
signed in September 2000. This was part of the settlement agreement in a lawsuit
brought about by the Florida Bio-Diversity Project in 1995 that alleged past management
practices resulted in the impairment of Preserve resources. The plan addresses an ORV
permit program, vehicle specifications, a system of designated access points and trails,
rules governing the operation of vehicles and enforcement of those rules, strategies for
restoring areas impacted by ORVs, education needs, research needs, and other
management strategies, such as number limits for access points and trail miles, as well as
the need for restoration of previous damage.

The Final ORV Plan does not significantly change the off-road vehicle specifications or
require anyone to scrap or junk their current off-road vehicle for a new design. Vehicles
are inspected to ensure that they meet the minimum vehicle specifications and to gather
data for future research.

As stated previously, the property owned by you in Big Cypress National Preserve meets
the criteria under the enabling legislation as an exempt property. The term Acquisition
Deferred is the administrative term used by the National Park Service Lands Office in

Naples, Florida. This term does not represent any change in status of lands or in land acquisition policy.

Your question regarding commercial vehicle access in the preserve is presently under review of the Solicitor's Office, Department of the Interior. The Ranger who asked you the question about your running a commercial venture from your property within the preserve was acting on his own initiative. He had observed you on a number of occasions with different people in the preserve. You are not under investigation and it is certainly your right to show people around the preserve. The Ranger was not wrong in asking you a simple question. Illegal commercial ventures do occur in the preserve and it is the Rangers responsibility to inquire about such activities. We will notify you of the Solicitor's decision when it arrives.

The question of what constitutes a taking is far from a "..simple question..", but there has been no denial by the National Park Service (NPS) of reasonable access to your property. You sold your private access right of way (ROW) in 1987 to the Florida Department of Transportation for $31,000.00. When the National Park Service acquired the private parcels within the Pines and Palms Ranch project, all rights of private access ("deeded ROW's") the former land owner might have owned were terminated. None of the NPS acquired lands were subject to public access because Collier County never accepted the developer's dedication ("dedicated ROW"). The developer's deeded dedication was in fact recorded in the county seat; however, the recording is meaningless because it was never accepted by the county. You, as well as others who own property within the Preserve, may continue to cross closed Federal Lands to reach your property via designated access points and trails.

The National Park Service is not taking landowners "rights of access" by enforcing the off-road vehicle plan nor are they using this plan to constitute a condemnation or taking of an owner's property.

We have addressed your concerns and issues on these subjects several times now and hope we have fully satisfied all of your questions.

Thank you for your continued interest in Big Cypress National Preserve.

Sincerely,

Jerry Belson
Regional Director
Southeast Region

cc:
Tract #731-99

FLORIDA FISH AND WILDLIFE CONSERVATION COMMISSION

DAVID K. MEEHAN	H.A. "HERKY" HUFFMAN	JOHN D. ROOD	QUINTON L. HEDGEPETH, DDS
St. Petersburg	Deltona	Jacksonville	Miami
	EDWIN P. ROBERTS, DC	RODNEY BARRETO	SANDRA T. KAUPE
	Pensacola	Miami	Palm Beach

ALLAN L. EGBERT, Ph.D., Executive Director
VICTOR J. HELLER, Assistant Executive Director

OFFICE OF THE EXECUTIVE DIRECTOR
(850)487-3796   TDD (850)488-9542

February 25, 2002

Ms. Fran Mainella, Director
National Park Service
U. S. Department of the Interior
1849 "C" Street NW
Washington, DC 20240

RE: Big Cypress National Preserve

Dear Ms. Mainella:

Thank you for taking time out of your busy schedule to talk with us and with representatives of the Florida Wildlife Federation recently. I would like to expand on some of the themes we discussed and give you my perspective on Big Cypress National Preserve (Preserve) issues.

Right up front, I believe the working relationship between the Fish and Wildlife Conservation Commission (FWC) and the National Park Service (NPS) continues to deteriorate. Regretfully, this has been going on for many years, in part a result of conflicting philosophical approaches to land management, different agency priorities, jurisdictional disputes, and even personality conflicts. My perspective is that neither side is listening to the other very well anymore, and we need to rebuild that working relationship. While I am speaking primarily about the Preserve, the course of events there affects other areas of our federal/state relationship (Biscayne Bay National Park's Fishery Management Plan comes to mind).

I believe it is fair to say that the creation of the Preserve was viewed at the time as a partnership between the federal government and the State of Florida. The Bear Island area was purchased by Florida and became the initial contribution to the Preserve (eventually totaling over $40 million dollars in land acquisition). Hunters, conservationists, hikers, and outdoor

620 South Meridian Street • Tallahassee • FL • 32399-1600
www.floridaconservation.org

enthusiasts were united endorsing the creation of the Preserve. The former Game and Fresh Water Fish Commission quickly established the Preserve as a state wildlife management area in order to develop a cooperative hunting program. Over time, our staff and our hunting and fishing constituents viewed the joint roles of the NPS/FWC as one of co-management. We know now that this perception has led to a painful misunderstanding. The NPS never considered that it shared management responsibility with any agency and consistently endeavored to counter that perception by rulemaking, unilateral policy decisions, and assertion of jurisdictional authority. That has been evident in the many years of debate and eventual FWC acquiescence in passing rules at the request of NPS staff, even though we rarely agreed that those rules were necessary or biologically justified.

There are many hurdles to accomplishing a more effective partnership, not the least of which are the attitudes and biases of FWC administration and staff. It is not my intent to suggest that the problem lies entirely with one side or the other. But I want to bring to your attention some of the issues that have caused us the greatest concern. As I mentioned earlier, a big problem has been that where we perceived a partnership, NPS acknowledges only a "delegation" of authority to FWC to manage public hunts. This may satisfy the NPS need to demonstrate what it perceives to be its exclusive management authority, but over the long haul it has squelched cooperation on fish and wildlife issues of mutual concern. I do not believe that the NPS must necessarily "abandon" its responsibilities for wildlife and land management or violate federal law by trusting a state agency to apply its expertise in support of fish and wildlife management. I have not seen any credible evidence that FWC rules and policies for the last 25 years have resulted in diminished fish and wildlife populations or health. Yet, year after year, some of our most basic game management rules and practices are called into question, data collection techniques and results are challenged, and efforts are made to limit our role in endangered and threatened species work.

Our differing approaches to partnership and co-management (terms your staff have rebuffed in correspondence) have led to similar disconnects with regard to the concept of "consultation and cooperation". I can summarize the distance between our agencies by referring to Mr. Jerry Belson's February 2001 letter to our former FWC chair, Ms. Julie Morris. He states: "The NPS has a responsibility to consult and cooperate with the State of Florida, which we take very seriously and plan to continue. Consultation is not synonymous with consensus. Our authorities do not allow co-management or management by consensus for Federal lands. We must work within the parameters of the laws and policies of the NPS."

Ms. Fran Mainella
February 25, 2002
Page 3 of 5

We agree that the laws creating and adding to the Preserve dictate consultation and cooperation. And while we do not expect consensus on all matters, we have felt on occasion that NPS consultation amounted to little more than notification. This problem was highlighted over the last three years when NPS implemented "emergency closures" in response to high and low water conditions. In some cases, possible impacts to wildlife populations or habitat were cited as reasons for the closures. Our staff felt these concerns were exaggerated and that the closures would result in significant and unnecessary disruption of established hunting seasons and recreational activities. There was either little opportunity to discuss these views with NPS, or our comments were disregarded. In fairness, FWC staff have occasionally failed to adequately consult your agency from time to time on matters of mutual concern, and we need to do better.

A number of our employees (and many of our hunting and fishing constituents) have been involved in Preserve issues for over 20 years. They remember the unique conditions leading to the establishment of the Preserve, and its recognition of traditional uses like hunting and ORV access. Much of the distrust and skepticism about NPS policies and intentions is a result of what we see as an inexorable, deliberate transformation of the Preserve into a national park with ever-increasing restrictions on access and allowable uses. NPS staff have always maintained that the Preserve shall be managed as a unit of the national park system (i.e., like a national park) and express little appreciation for the Preserve's unique history and uses. South Florida's sportsmen and women observe the trend and conclude that the ultimate objective of the NPS is to eliminate all but a token amount of hunting, sufficient only to comply with federal law.

This fear of NPS intentions is only heightened by NPS handling of the Addition Lands. You heard some of the concerns expressed by Manley, Jack and Franklin during our phone conversation. We echo those concerns. Again with state involvement, the common presumption was that the Addition Lands would be just that; additions to the existing Preserve, managed in accordance with existing Preserve rules and guiding policies. Years later, the Addition Lands are closed to all but limited pedestrian access. Planning efforts recently initiated by the superintendent now seem to be focusing on setting aside large areas as Wilderness. Taken together with the recently enacted ORV plan, over half of the Preserve has or apparently soon will be closed to traditional vehicular access for hunters, froggers, fishermen, and backcountry travelers. We recognize and support the need for reasonable ORV regulations and controls. However we remain concerned that the actions of the NPS have unfairly restricted ORV's while basing such restrictions on biological assumptions that are not supported by fact.

Ms. Fran Mainella
February 25, 2002
Page 4 of 5

A final example of the level to which our relationship has deteriorated is our "cooperative" research program for the Florida panther. FWC staff with a long history of expertise handling and studying this animal are constantly questioned and second-guessed by the NPS staff working on panthers, to the extent neither agency has much desire to work with the other. Yet, work together we must, given our overlapping interests and the narrow range of this species. FWC attempted to accommodate NPS's interests last year by issuing Big Cypress Preserve staff a permit to conduct independent panther capture activities. A necessary condition of that permit was that NPS staff coordinate daily with FWC staff involved in capture work, to ensure the two capture teams didn't inadvertently interfere with one another. We were surprised to learn, when NPS submitted its final report under that permit, that not a single one of the NPS's independent capture efforts were coordinated with FWS staff. We are lucky no animals were harmed as a result! Rather than work to resolve this problem, we have learned NPS staff have applied for a federal permit to conduct future panther capture activities, and have expressed an intent not to seek renewal of their state permit. We believe this is counter to Department of the Interior policy, and certainly counter to a spirit of mutual cooperation.

I offer this litany of issues recognizing that few solutions have been offered. Your effort to initiate meaningful dialogue between the agencies is perhaps the best first step that could be taken. I sense that you share my disappointment that both of our respective agencies have failed our constituents by refusing to acknowledge the authority, responsibility, and expertise of the other, and that needs to be addressed in a new memorandum of understanding between us. The agreement needs to forge a clear and more specific working relationship that allows us to share our resources and expertise more effectively and without constant rancor. It also needs to clearly articulate those areas of responsibility that each agency is willing to defer to the other. I accept that this will not be easy, but I believe it must be done.

Sincerely,

Allan L. Egbert, Ph.D.
Executive Director

ALE/crb

Cc: Commission Members

Ms. Fran Mainella
February 25, 2002
Page 5 of 5

Bcc: Mr. Max Peterson, IAFWA
      Mr. Manley Fuller
      Mr. Jack Moller
      Mr. Franklin Adams
      Mr. Victor J. Heller
      Mr. Frank Montalbano
      Mr. Mark Robson

United States Department of the Interior

NATIONAL PARK SERVICE
Big Cypress National Preserve
HCR 61, Box 110
Ochopee, Florida 34141-9710

IN REPLY REFER TO:

L48 (BICY-S)

March 19, 2004

Mr. L. Jack Moller
2723 Round Hill Court
Katy, Texas 77494

Dear Mr. Moller:

This is in response to your letter dated March 14, 2004, in which you requested information concerning wilderness at Big Cypress National Preserve (preserve).

You asked for a definition of "previous wilderness status" and when to expect a return of the preserve to this status. We are not familiar with this term nor do we recall ever making a commitment to such a status. Perhaps you are referring to the term "wilderness character." The Legislative History of the preserve, Senate Report 93-1128 dated August 22, 1974, states:

> "Since the area included in the preserve is largely undeveloped at the present time and because it will be managed in a manner which will assure its return to the true wilderness character which once prevailed, it will offer many outdoor recreation opportunities to the visiting public. During significant portions of the year, primitive camping, hiking, and sightseeing will be popular activities. Naturalist and wildlife observers will come to see the flora and fauna in their natural setting and hunters and fishermen will continue to find the area popular. While the use of all terrain vehicles must be carefully regulated by the Secretary [of the Interior] to protect the natural, wildlife and wilderness values of the preserve, the bill does not prohibit their use along designated roads and trails."

Congress clearly intended that the wilderness character of the preserve be protected. To this end, the National Park Service will continue to keep development within the preserve consistent with this intent and to the extent necessary to protect the resource and recreational values, while providing opportunities for all visitors to experience the preserve's unique resources. We will also continue to restore areas through the removal of exotic plants and abandoned fill sites.

The "massive boardwalks" and "huge new visitor center" you cite are primarily on existing roadside filled sites and thus do not compromise wilderness values. The welcome center that is being developed at the preserve is intended to be a multi–agency operation, providing information on all the agencies in the area. The boardwalks will provide resource protection while also providing safe access for the visiting public.

These amenities will foster a greater appreciation by the visiting public for the fragile resources of the preserve and other natural and cultural areas by providing interpretive opportunities and safe access to viewing areas, in keeping with Senate Report 93-1128:

> "Construction of physical facilities of any kind would be minimized and would be limited to those developments which are essential to the preservation and management of the area and the safety of the public. To the extent such facilities are deemed necessary and appropriate they would be constructed in a manner which would minimize their impact on the environment and their intrusion on the natural setting."

We hope this information is helpful. Thank you for your interest in this unit of the National Park Service.

Sincerely,

Carol A. Clark
Acting Superintendent

cc:
Gale Norton, Secretary of the Interior
Fran Mainella, Director, National Park Service
Patricia Hooks, Southeast Regional Director, National Park Service

United States Department of the Interior

NATIONAL PARK SERVICE
Big Cypress National Preserve
HCR 61, Box 110
Ochopee, Florida 34141-9710

IN REPLY REFER TO:

L48 (BICY-S)

March 31, 2004

Mr. L. Jack Moller
2723 Round Hill Court
Katy, Texas 77494

Dear Mr. Moller:

This is in response to your letter dated March 22, 2004, in which you requested information concerning wilderness and other issues at Big Cypress National Preserve.

In our March 19, 2004, letter to you we cited a paragraph from the Legislative History of the Preserve that stated, "...it [the Preserve] will be managed in a manner which will assure its return to the true wilderness character which once prevailed..." The rest of that paragraph listed recreational activities, such as camping, birdwatching, hunting, and use of all-terrain vehicles, that Congress envisioned to be compatible with this type of management. Our management of the Preserve is consistent with the intent of Congress. Page 76 of the Preserve's General Management Plan (GMP) states:

> "The intent of development is to provide structures for quality visitor recreation and interpretation and for NPS operations while limiting any further modification of natural and cultural resources. To obtain this objective, most development would take place at existing disturbed sites."

At the time the Preserve was established, large areas already exhibited wilderness character in that they were mostly undeveloped. In the years since, we have sought to protect these areas by making every effort to restrict development to previously disturbed sites, as stated in the GMP. We have facilitated the return to wilderness character of disturbed areas of the Preserve in several ways, including 1) restoring disturbed sites through removal of fill material and allowing native plants to revegetate or through exotic plant removal, and 2) implementing the 2000 Recreational Off-Road Vehicle (ORV) Management Plan, which will result in a sustainable trail system providing for the needs of hunters and ORV users while allowing many areas impacted from past ORV use to recover.

Section 2(c) of the Wilderness Act of 1964, P.L. 88-577, provides a detailed definition of wilderness, although it is not clear that Congress had this definition in mind when referring to the "wilderness character" of the Preserve. It is probably safe to assume that the intent was to return most of the Preserve to the state that existed prior to human disturbance. Some areas will never return to this condition, as they necessarily must remain developed for administrative and visitor-related services. For this reason, and because restoration is an ongoing process, it is not feasible to plan for a point at which wilderness character for the Preserve has been obtained. Exotic species will always have to be controlled, prescribed fire must always be utilized, and so on, in order to achieve and maintain desired conditions.

As for your question concerning ORV trail access points, these are currently planned for Phase III of the six-phase ORV trail project which we hope to be constructed during the fiscal year 2008-2009 timeframe. Prior to then, we will follow procedures under the National Environmental Policy Act (NEPA) and secure appropriate permits from state and federal regulatory agencies. During the EA and permitting processes, we will seek public and agency input on the location and extent of these sites. Until then, we will look at each access point for completed trails to see if temporary improvements not involving wetlands or environmental impacts can be made.

If you have further questions, please contact me at 239-695-1103. Thank you for your interest in Big Cypress National Preserve.

Sincerely,

Carol A. Clark
Acting Superintendent

cc:
Gale Norton, Secretary of the Interior
Fran Mainella, Director, National Park Service
Patricia Hooks, Southeast Regional Director, National Park Service

2001 05/08 TUE 07:57 FAX   ᴪ004

FLORIDA FISH AND WILDLIFE CONSERVATION COMMISSION

JAMES L. "JAMIE" ADAMS, JR.	BARBARA C. BARSH	QUINTON L. HEDGEPETH, DDS	H.A. "HERKY" HUFFMAN
Bushnell	Jacksonville	Miami	Deltona
DAVID K. MEEHAN	JULIE K. MORRIS	TONY MOSS	EDWIN P. ROBERTS, DC	JOHN D. ROOD
St. Petersburg	Sarasota	Miami	Pensacola	Jacksonville

LLAN L. EGBERT, Ph.D., Executive Director
ICTOR J. HELLER, Assistant Executive Director

OFFICE OF THE EXECUTIVE DIRECTOR
(850) 487-3796 TDD (850) 488-5☐

October 25, 2000

Mr. Jerry Belson
Southeast Regional Director
U. S. Department of Interior
National Park Service
100 Alabama Street, 1924 Building
Atlanta, Georgia 30303

Dear Mr. Belson:

We are writing pursuant to a discussion and resulting motion passed by the Florida Fish and Wildlife Conservation Commission (FWC) at our September 2000 meeting in DeLand, Florida. That discussion was spawned by concern among Commissioners regarding what we believe to be an already strained and perhaps further eroding relationship between our agency and the National Park Service (NPS) relating to our respective roles in the management of the Big Cypress National Preserve (Preserve). This letter is written with the sincere hope that we might stimulate a more mutually constructive relationship between our agencies more consistent with that we believe the U. S. Congress contemplated in establishing the Preserve with the passage of Public Law (PL) 93-440 in 1974.

Many of our concerns stem from NPS interpretation and actions pursuant to the provisions of PL 93-440 which address consultation with the appropriate state agency relating to restrictions relating to hunting, fishing and trapping. Please understand that this is not intended as a challenge to the NPS' exercise of authority or legal compliance with the provisions of PL 93-440. We, nevertheless, recognize and believe that provisions for consultation were included in the legislation to provide reassurance, albeit perhaps legally hollow reassurance, to those who, for various reasons, were opposed to creation of the Preserve and more specifically opposed to the dedication of state-owned lands for the Preserve's purposes. In fact, we

Mr. Jerry Belson
October 25, 2000
Page 2

believe that Congress intended that "consultation" be synonymous with a
reciprocity of opinion, rather than being synonymous with notification.
Irrespective of Congress' intent, we recognize that Congress' action may
have been specific enough to create the illusion of protection for these
interests, without actually providing that protection.

The upshot is that many Floridians feel betrayed by the empty
assurances that the legislation proffered. We are not so naive as to believe
that the NPS will retreat from the posture of unilateral authority it has
assumed. We do, however, believe that the NPS could very well move
toward making the "consultation" exercise more meaningful than the simple
notification process which it has become. Please consider the greater good
that might be accomplished by expanding the exercise of "consultation"
toward the mutual exchange of views and reciprocity of opinion that the
term literally embodies.

We would welcome the opportunity to discuss this matter further with
the NPS at your convenience. Thank you for your consideration of our
proposal.

Sincerely,

Julie K. Morris
Chairman

JM/fm/pm
\\Wildnet\dow\NPSchairman.wpd
WLD 8-5-2 (Big Cypress)

cc: Commission Members
      Mr. John Donahue
      Dr. Allan L. Egbert

United States Department of the Interior

NATIONAL PARK SERVICE
Big Cypress National Preserve
HCR 61, Box 110
Ochopee, Florida 34141-9710

IN REPLY REFER TO:

A3821 (BICY-S)

March 5, 2004

William H. Losner, Chairman and President
c/o 1st National Bank of South Florida
1550 North Krome Avenue
P.O. Box 128-33090-0128
Homestead, Florida 33030

Dear Mr. Losner:

We have received your second letter dated, February 20, 2004 regarding the designated trails in the Stairsteps area of Big Cypress National Preserve.

I have flown over the area many times and our position remains that allowing airboat use over the entire area causes more ecosystem damage than concentrating use on designated trails. We understand your preference to the contrary. The intent of Congress, as articulated in the Senate and House reports that comprise part of the preserve's legislative history both contained identical language discussing the management of the Preserve that directs that the area "will be managed in a manner which will assure its return to the true wilderness character which once prevailed", and "[w]hile the use of all-terrain vehicles must be carefully regulated by the secretary [of the interior] to protect the natural wildlife and wilderness values of the preserve, the bill does not prohibit their use along designated roads and trails."

While the impacts occurring to the trails as a result of concentrated use may not be as pleasing to you as dispersing over undamaged wetlands, limiting ORVs, including airboats, to designated trails results in a major reduction in the spatial extent of the preserve affected by ORVs. If you care to discuss this further you may call Mr. Ed Clark at (239) 695-1108. Thank you for your correspondence.

Sincerely,

Carol A. Clark
Acting Superintendent

cc:
Carol A. Clark, BICY
Ron Clark, BICY
Ed Clark, BICY
Central Files

United States Department of the Interior

NATIONAL PARK SERVICE
Big Cypress National Preserve
HCR 61, Box 110
Ochopee, Florida 34141-9710

A3821 (BICY-SUPT)

May 21, 2001

Mr. Michael Warren
18133 NW 19th Street
Pembroke Pines, Florida 33029

Dear Mr. Warren:

This letter is in response to your correspondence dated May 9, 2001, in which you seek
information on companies and/or individuals that operate a business within Big Cypress
National Preserve.

Our records indicate that there are two (2) companies that operate businesses within the
Preserve. Both of these companies provide a service to the general public. You may
contact these companies for the information you seek concerning the number of
employees, customers, types of activities provided, etc. The companies are listed below:

North Carolina
Outward Bound School
Everglades Programs
P.O. Box 454
Everglades City, Florida 33929
(813) 695-2200
Don Obert, Everglades Program Director

North American Canoe Tours
65 Black Point Road
Niantic, CT 06357
(941) 695-4666
David Harraden, President

Thank you for your interest and concern in the commercial business available within the
Preserve.

Sincerely,

John J. Donahue
Superintendent

2001 05/08 TUE 07:56 FAX ☒002

United States Department of the Interior

FWC-OED

FEB −7 2001

NATIONAL PARK SERVICE
Southeast Regional Office
Atlanta Federal Center
1924 Building
100 Alabama St., S.W.
Atlanta, Georgia 30303

RECEIVED

IN REPLY REFER TO:
(SER-D)

FEB 5 2001

Ms. Julie K. Morris
Chairman, Florida Fish and Wildlife
 Conservation Commission
620 Meridian Street
Tallahassee, Florida 32399-1600

Dear Ms. Morris:

I was pleased to receive your recent correspondence relating to consultation between the Florida Fish and Wildlife Conservation Commission (FFWCC) and the Big Cypress National Preserve (BICY), a unit of the National Park System in the Southeast Region. I assure you that the National Park Service (NPS) also is very interested in having meaningful consultation between our agencies.

As you have described in your letter to me, there appears to be a misunderstanding about management authority and expectations at BICY that has existed for many years. The NPS, through the superintendent, is the manager of these Federal lands and the wildlife therein. No other entity is authorized to manage or make management decisions for BICY.

The NPS has a responsibility to consult and cooperate with the State of Florida, which we take very seriously and plan to continue. Consultation is not synonymous with consensus. Our authorities do not allow co-management or management by consensus for Federal lands. We must work within the parameters of the laws and policies of the NPS.

The National Park Service has delegated the management of the hunt to your agency for the past twenty-five years, but that delegation does not cede NPS management authority to FFWCC; and we cannot abandon our responsibilities for wildlife and land management in BICY. A mutual recognition of our respective roles in this situation is the basis for a successful relationship.

I would suggest as a first step that we attempt to reach an understanding on what the law directs and what is an appropriate role for FFWCC at BICY. I would also be interested in finding ways to enhance consultation and cooperation. Therefore, I suggest that you have Dr. Egbert contact Superintendent Donahue and set up a meeting for them to discuss their respective responsibilities and begin a mutually satisfying relationship.

Sincerely,

FOR *Patricia A Hooks*

Jerry Belson
Regional Director
Southeast Region

South Florida Ecosystem Restoration Land Acquisition Strategy
Federal Projects and Joint Federal/State Projects

Prepared by the Florida Natural Areas Inventory, November 2003, with funding provided by the Florida Department of Environmental Protection

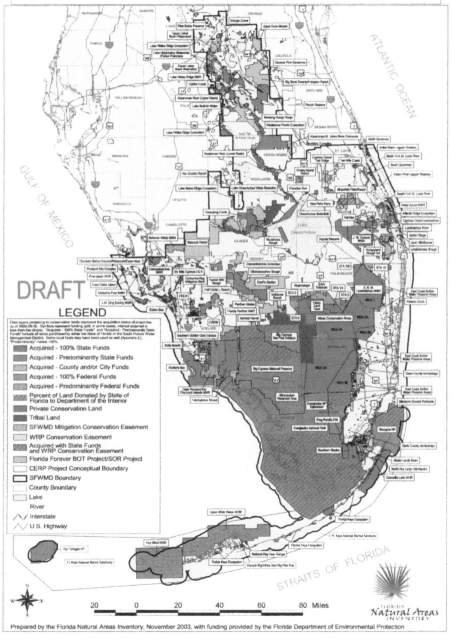

South Florida Ecosystem Restoration
Land Acquisition Update

Panther Habitat

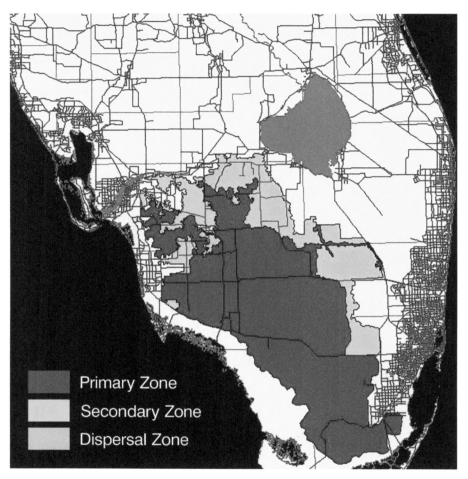

Created by Daryl Lands, FWC, panther expert, 2005

Panther Road Kills as of 2005

Caloosahatchee Ecoscape

Panther roadkills

12 Mile Slough WEA

Ok Slough State Forest

Devils Garden, ALICO

Dinner Island WEA

Panther Glades

Barfield Ranch

Big Cypress National Preserve

Created by Daryl Lands, FWC, Panther Expert

Our least cost pathway analyses identifies habitat areas critical to maintaining connectivity.

Habitat loss or fragmenting existing panther habitat may jeopardize ability to maintain current panther population.

Land on the Florida Forever list

Public owned land

Male and Female Panther Home Range 2003-04

Created by Daryl Lands, FWC, 2005

Average male panther home range size is 102,875 acres

Average female panther home range size is 38,557 acres

Professional Report
Wilderness Recovery: Thinking Big in
Restoration Ecology

Reed F. Noss

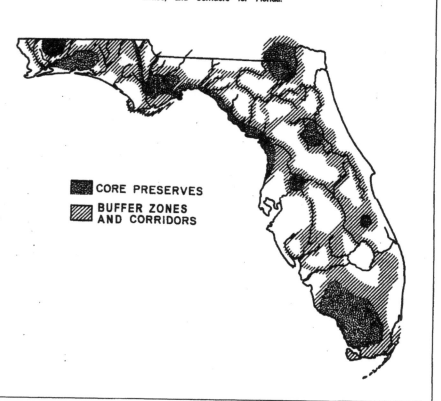

Figure 2. A Proposed Wilderness Recovery Network of Preserves, Buffer Zones, and Corridors for Florida.

CORE PRESERVES

BUFFER ZONES AND CORRIDORS

Adapted from Noss (1985a and 1987).

Department of
Environmental Protection

Marjory Stoneman Douglas Building
3900 Commonwealth Boulevard
Tallahassee, Florida 32399-3000

Jeb Bush
Governor

Colleen M. Castille
Secretary

April 21, 2005

MEMORANDUM

TO: The Acquisition and Restoration Council

FROM: Eva Armstrong, Director
           Division of State Lands

SUBJECT: Summary of Babcock Ranch Negotiations

The purpose of this memorandum is to inform you of the sequence of events during the Babcock Ranch negotiations. The information provided outlines third party companies that wee potential participants in the acquisition.

Should you have any questions regarding this memorandum, please call Eva Armstrong, Director, Division of State Lands at 245-2555.

EA/jw
Attachments

Babcock Negotiations Summary
April 15, 2005

7/2/04   DSL approved first appraisal $460,000,000
8/11/04   DSL approved second appraisal $450,000,000
9/04-11/04   Ongoing meetings with representatives of Babcock and DSL staff to
                discuss various purchase options for Babcock Corporation including real
                estate assets.

Companies interviewed by DSL staff for possible participation in purchase
of Babcock were as follows:

- Land South Holdings, Inc. with Evergreen Investments
  Purchase Plan - Corporate Stock Purchase

- Pomcor Realty Inc.
  Purchase Plan - 1033 Land Exchange under the IRS tax code

- Midcoast
  Purchase Plan – Asset recovery-re-engineers corporations
  including C Corp.

  Eliminated/rejected by family attorneys-did not think investment
  Plan was applicable.

- WCI
  Purchase Plan – not planned yet

  Explored possibilities with state on 3/4/05. Unable to move fast in
  the public arena. Willing to discuss again if deal fails with other
  partners.

- Pulte Home Corp.
  Purchase Plan – not planned yet

  Explored possibilities with state on 3/3/05. Did not materialize.

- Plum Creek
  Purchase Plan – not planned yet

  Explored possibilities with state. Did not materialize.

- TNC
  Would have tax liability issue.

2

- The Conservation Fund
  Would have tax liability issue.

- National Fish and Wildlife
  Unable to handle transaction with such high dollar amount
  recommended TNC or Conservation Fund.

12/15/04   State offers Babcock $400 million (87% of approved value). Family
              declines indicating withdrawal from negotiations.

1/5/05   Babcock family pursues possibility of sale to Lee County at asking price
              of $480 million.

2/05   Lee County declines to pursue eminent domain for Babcock acquisition.
              Family again states asking price of $480 million.

2/16/05   DSL met with Babcock representatives to restart negotiations. Both
              parties agree that state cannot purchase stock and a third party will be
              needed.

2/16-4/12/05 Pomcor indicates eminent domain needed for their company to facilitate
              1033 land exchange under the IRS tax code.

              State determines not to pursue eminent domain and continues to discuss
              possible purchase of real estate assets from Evergreen Investment Partners
              and LSH provided Evergreen is successful in purchasing Babcock
              Corporation.

Summary of contract terms: Evergreen Investment Partners and LSH (Evergreen) based
              on offer price to Babcock Corporation for $455,000,000.

              1. Purchase price for the real estate acquisition by the state locked in for
                 5 years.
              2. State to purchase parcels in five separate transactions over 5 year
                 period at locked in values.
              3. The state's carrying costs covered by the investment purchaser.
              4. The state would receive immediate management control over the
                 property through a negotiated management agreement with Evergreen.
              5. The current Babcock employees would continue to manage the
                 property through a corporate leasing contract with Evergreen until the
                 State is ready to take over and/or make changes.

                 - See Exhibit A for details and flow chart of Evergreen transaction.

3

4/05   DSL sends letter outlining 2 offers to Babcock representatives.

                First offer is cash purchase by the State in the amount of $455,000,000.
                the Babcock family would have to pay taxes.

                Second offer is for $455,000,000 with state and third party which would
                purchase Babcock Corporation and sell real estate assets to the state. Third
                party would assume tax liability.

4/12/05   Letter from Babcock representatives received by DSL declining both
                offers from State.

ACQUIRING BABCOCK RANCH
Questions and Answers
April 2005

What is the State of Florida doing?
As part of its continuing efforts to preserve the Babcock Ranch, the Department of Environmental Protection extended two offers to the owners of the Babcock Corporation to purchase the environmentally-sensitive land in Lee and Charlotte counties.

What did the offers involve?
The Department is proposing two options for a fiscally-sound acquisition of Babcock Ranch that would keep the State from assuming the tax liability of the corporation:
* Acquire the real estate assets of the Babcock Corporation, which includes the 91,000-acre Babcock Ranch, for $455 million through the *Florida Forever* program, in partnership with Lee and Charlotte counties. Acquisition would be subject to approval by the Governor and Florida Cabinet (the Board of Trustees).
* Facilitate an agreement between the Babcock Corporation and a third party that would purchase the Corporation and the real estate assets. The third party would then sell to the State close to 80,000 acres of environmentally-sensitive land, including a near 16,500-acre conservation easement, allowing Florida to conserve the most pristine landscapes of Babcock Ranch.

Have owners of the Babcock Corporation expressed any interest in the offers?
The Department has maintained an open dialogue with the corporation's representatives. Shareholders have indicated a firm term of the transaction as a 100% stock acquisition in the Babcock Florida Company rather than selling the real estate alone to the State.

Can the State buy and keep the stock of the Babcock Corporation?
No. The Florida Constitution prohibits state agencies, counties and municipalities from becoming a joint owner or stockholder of any corporation, association or partnership. Under the Constitution, the State cannot acquire the company and continue its management and operation. If the State were to acquire the company and then immediately dissolve it, Florida's taxpayers would be assuming the corporation's tax liability.

In addition to the Constitutional restrictions, the State can only use *Florida Forever* funds to acquire real estate, not to purchase stock. The 10-year, $3 billion *Florida Forever* fund was established for acquiring environmentally-sensitive land, restoring water resources and preserving historical and cultural sites.

What does that mean to Florida's taxpayers?
If the State acquired the corporation stock without third party involvement, dissolved the company and sold the land to the Board of Trustees, Florida's taxpayers would be responsible for paying the associated corporate income taxes, estimated at 39.5 percent of the sale. A local government would also face the same financial considerations.

How much would the taxes cost the State?
Because Florida law limits the expenditure of *Florida Forever* funds to real property, the State would need to fund its share of the purchase of the Babcock Corporation from General Revenue. Assuming the final price is at or near the appraised value of $450-$460 million, the State would need another $181.7million for corporate income taxes.

Has a State agency ever purchased a for-profit corporation?
No. In 1998, the St. Johns River Water Management District considered acquiring farm corporations along Lake Apopka. The district sought to purchase all the stock of a corporation where the only asset was the real estate. The Attorney General stated that the State could only acquire corporate stock under limited, strictly controlled, circumstances. Where the purpose was to acquire an asset held by the company and immediately dissolve the company, the state could acquire the stock without violating the spirit of the constitutional prohibition. The Attorney General also stated, however, that the district was prohibited from assuming any liability of the corporation including taxes.

Since both the State and local governments are generally prohibited from purchasing the stock, can a non-governmental organization purchase the Babcock Corporation?
The State has actively evaluated the option of a non-profit organization such as the Conservation Fund, The Nature Conservancy and the National Wildlife Federation purchasing the stock and real estate and then selling the land to the State of Florida. The organizations were unable to participate because of the large size of the acquisition or because of facing the same tax consequences as the State in acquiring the company's stock.

Can the state file eminent domain to acquire the corporation or property?
According to the Attorney General's Office, eminent domain is to be used solely for acquiring real property if it serves a public purpose, but not to acquire stock. If the State condemned the property, the current corporation owners would assume the liabilities of the corporation, including any federal taxes due when conveying the property to the State. The internal revenue code gives the owner of condemned property three years to exchange like kind properties to minimize tax consequences for an unwilling seller.

What happens next?
Owners of the Babcock Corporation are considering the Department's offers. A response is expected on Tuesday, April 12, 2005.

2

April 6, 2005

Eva:

We are always willing to help The State of Florida to protect important
conservation lands. In the case of Babcock Ranch, we have had several
meetings with representatives of the owners, and discussed the project with
you informally from time to time. With respect to the financial issues in this
instance, in our view, sale of the corporation to a non-profit entity would not
extinguish any taxes due from the sale of appreciated stock. We would also
be working from the same list of appraisers which the state uses, if transfer
to the state would be the ultimate goal..

TNC has historically worked with corporate entities who own lands needed
for conservation purposes, and on other occasions has obtained loans from
TNC's Board of Governors to hold land which the government wants, for
which government funds would be available subsequently. However, in this
case, I cannot see how either of these abilities would be helpful, given the
tax issues and an outright sale.

Vicki

Victoria Tschinkel   **The Nature Conservancy**
Florida State Director   Tallahassee Office
                                625 North Adams Street
vtschinkel@tnc.org   Tallahassee, FL 32301
(850) 222-0199 (Phone)
(850) 222-0973 (Fax)

nature.org

ARTICLE VII

FINANCE AND TAXATION

SECTION 10. Pledging credit.--Neither the state nor any county, school district, municipality, special district, or agency of any of them, shall become a joint owner with, or stockholder of, or give, lend or use its taxing power or credit to aid any corporation, association, partnership or person; but this shall not prohibit laws authorizing:

(a) the investment of public trust funds;

(b) the investment of other public funds in obligations of, or insured by, the United States or any of its instrumentalities;

(c) the issuance and sale by any county, municipality, special district or other local governmental body of (1) revenue bonds to finance or refinance the cost of capital projects for airports or port facilities, or (2) revenue bonds to finance or refinance the cost of capital projects for industrial or manufacturing plants to the extent that the interest thereon is exempt from income taxes under the then existing laws of the United States, when, in either case, the revenue bonds are payable solely from revenue derived from the sale, operation or leasing of the projects. If any project so financed, or any part thereof, is occupied or operated by any private corporation, association, partnership or person pursuant to contract or lease with the issuing body, the property interest created by such contract or lease shall be subject to taxation to the same extent as other privately owned property.

(d) a municipality, county, special district, or agency of any of them, being a joint owner of, giving, or lending or using its taxing power or credit for the joint ownership, construction and operation of electrical energy generating or transmission facilities with any corporation, association, partnership or person.

History.--Am. H.J.R. 1424, 1973; adopted 1974.

ARTICLE VII

FINANCE AND TAXATION

SECTION 11. State bonds; revenue bonds.--

(a) State bonds pledging the full faith and credit of the state may be issued only to finance or refinance the cost of state fixed capital outlay projects authorized by law, and purposes incidental thereto, upon approval by a vote of the electors; provided state bonds issued pursuant to this subsection may be refunded without a vote of the electors at a lower net average interest cost rate. The total outstanding principal of state bonds issued pursuant to this subsection shall never exceed fifty percent of the total tax revenues of the state for the two preceding fiscal years, excluding any tax revenues held in trust under the provisions of this constitution.

(b) Moneys sufficient to pay debt service on state bonds as the same becomes due shall be appropriated by law.

(c) Any state bonds pledging the full faith and credit of the state issued under this section or any other section of this constitution may be combined for the purposes of sale.

(d) Revenue bonds may be issued by the state or its agencies without a vote of the electors to finance or refinance the cost of state fixed capital outlay projects authorized by law, and purposes incidental thereto, and shall be payable solely from funds derived directly from sources other than state tax revenues.

(e) Bonds pledging all or part of a dedicated state tax revenue may be issued by the state in the manner provided by general law to finance or refinance the acquisition and improvement of land, water areas, and related property interests and resources for the purposes of conservation, outdoor recreation, water resource development, restoration of natural systems, and historic preservation.

(f) Each project, building, or facility to be financed or refinanced with revenue bonds issued under this section shall first be approved by the Legislature by an act relating to appropriations or by general law.

History.--Am. C.S. for C.S. for S.J.R. 612, 1984; adopted 1984; Am. proposed by Constitution Revision Commission, Revision No. 5, 1998, filed with the Secretary of State May 5, 1998; adopted 1998.

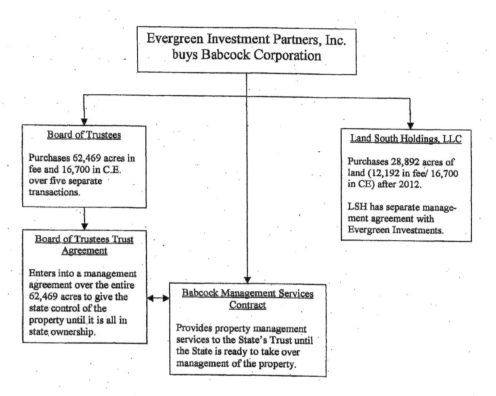

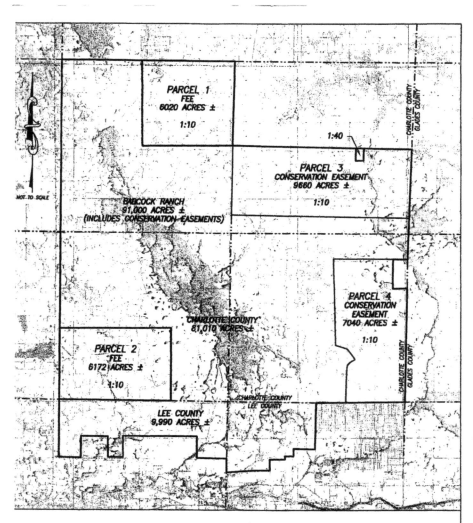

BABCOCK RANCH
CHARLOTTE COUNTY, FLORIDA
MARCH 14, 2005

West Bay Area Vision Map

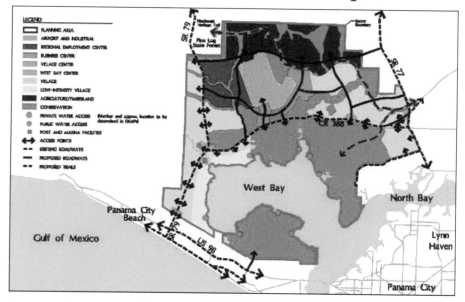

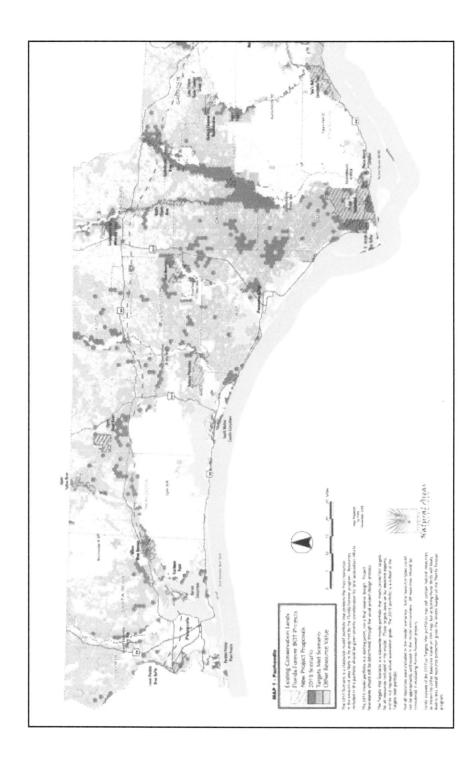

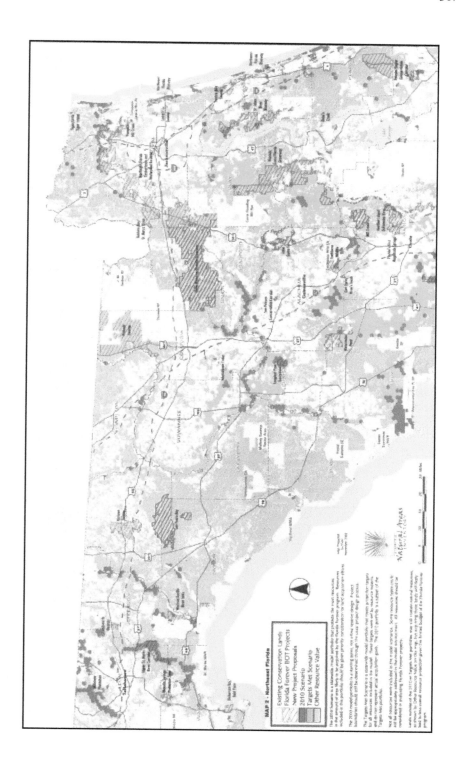

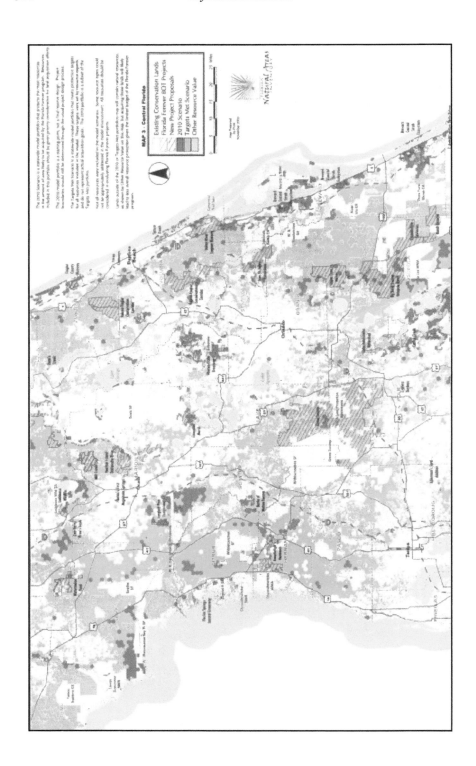

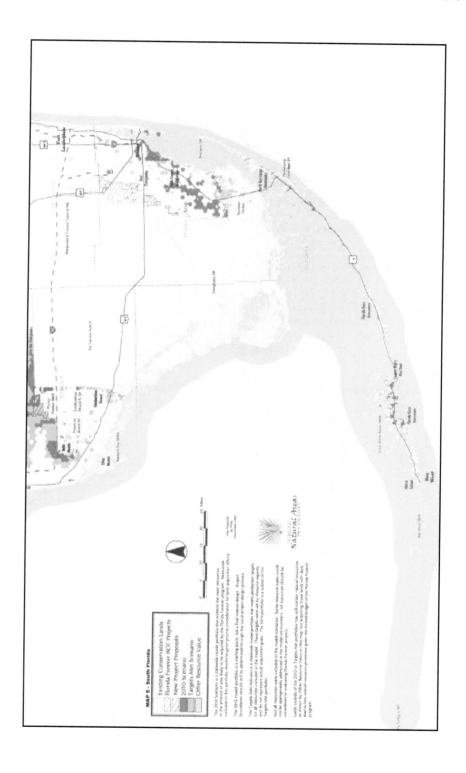

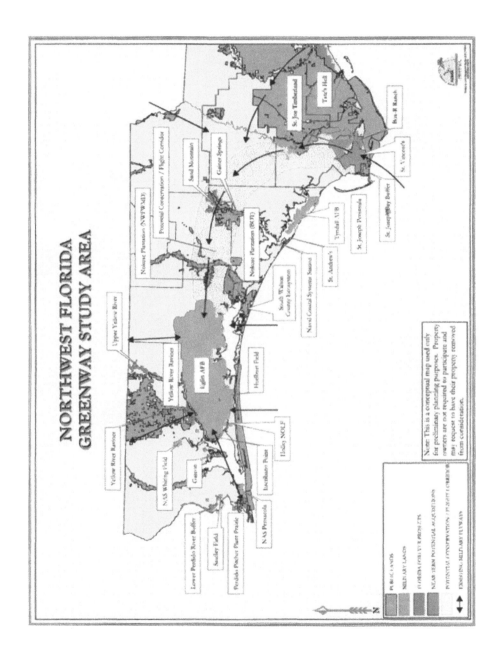

Email from Mr. Tim Towls, Florida Fish, Wildlife and Conservation Commission, after more than ten years of telling the DOI/ACoE that they want to put too much water in the Everglades, he is still having to tell them this. The Federal folks want to drown the Florida Everglades.

****
Forwarded Message:
Subj: RE: Information for Consideration in Development of Alternative 4.
Date: 4/8/2005 1:07:55 PM Central Standard Time
From: tim.towles@MyFWC.com
To: plinton@sfwmd.gov, Bruce_Boler@nps.gov
CC: amayes@consensusbuildersinc.com, Amy.L.Swiecichowski@saj02.
usace.army.mil, Barbara.B.Cintron@saj02.usace.army.mil, Barry_Rosen@fws.
gov, bmills@sfwmd.gov, cal@sfwmd.gov, ca.alvarez@earthlink.net, christine_
chan@nps.gov, cotara@miamidade.gov, Dan.Vogler@saj02.usace.army.mil,
Dan_Nehler@fws.gov, ddrum@sfwmd.gov, Debbie.R.Peterson@saj02.usace.
army.mil, inger.hansen@dep.state.fl.us, Jacob.R.Davis@saj02.usace.army.
mil, James.M.Riley@saj02.usace.army.mil, Jerrell.T.Pennington@saj02.usace.
army.mil, jl3353@aol.com, joe.walsh@MyFWC.com, joffre_castro@nps.gov,
Jon.Moulding@saj02.usace.army.mil, joseph_terry@nps.gov, Jose.Lizarribar@
saj02.usace.army.mil, kelliott@sfrestore.org, kevin_kotun@nps.gov, Kevin_
Palmer@fws.gov, Kimberley.A.Taplin@saj02.usace.army.mil, Larry.E.Taylor@
saj02.usace.army.mil, lawrence@sfrestore.org, levinm@miamidade.gov,
lmccart@sfwmd.gov, lphillip@sfwmd.gov, Luis.A.Alejandro@saj02.usace.army.
mil, martiv@miamidade.gov, mbansee@sfrestore.org, Richard.E.Punnett@
saj02.usace.army.mil, Robert.A.Evans@saj02.usace.army.mil, Ryan.S.Bishop@
saj02.usace.army.mil, Sara_O'Connell@nps.gov, Sherry_Mitchell@nps.
gov, ssculley@sfwmd.gov, Steve_Traxler@fws.gov, Susan.B.Sylvester@saj02.
usace.army.mil, Terry.l.rice@worldnet.att.net, tom@mfl.org, Trent.L.Ferguson@
saj02.usace.army.mil, villas@miamidade.gov, William.J.Gallagher@saj02.
usace.army.mil
Sent from the Internet

Paul and PDT,

I believe that Paul did an excellent job of providing a summary of the flow transect information for the alternatives that have been run up to this date. From this analysis, it is clear that the flows delivered to Shark River Slough as a whole, and to the eastern portion of SRR (T are more than sufficient in all of the alternatives modeled so far, since they all exceed the average annual flows predicted by what has been authorized in CERP (D-13R). It should also be noted that Alt. 3 (72,000 acre-feet) out-performed the West bookend (62,000 acre-feet) in moving greater quantities of flows through WCA-3B and into Northeast Shark River Slough without greatly increasing high water impacts to tree islands in WCA-3B.

I agree that we should strive to move as much flows through WCA-3B as possible, but without creating impounding effects against the L-30 levee that will lead to the loss of tree island habitat similar to what has already been witnessed in southern WCA-3A. Neither should we move so much water through WCA-3B that water quality there would be compromised, and natural Everglades plant communities converted to cattail marsh (a defacto STA). Some increase in cattail coverage was observed following the Pilot Test in 1994, and in areas where sawgrass ridge die-off occurred due to higher than normal water levels in WCA-3B in the spring of 1998. Hence, the introduction of excessive quantities of water of extreme depths as predicted under the West Bookend would likely result in impacts to marsh plant communities as well as tree islands. The type of hydrological conditions predicted by the West bookend or similar iterations such as the current alternative (A4W7OU) being proposed by ENP would most likely not be conducive to the maintenance of the ridge and slough landscape.

It is clear from Paul's High Water summary, using the 2.5 and 3.0 ft depth criteria, that at this point, only the East bookend run simulates extreme high water depths in WCA-3B that are less than those predicted to occur with implementation of CERP. From our agency's standpoint, CSOP should be implemented as an intermediate step towards the CERP. This step-wise process will allow the vegetative communities that are now in place in WCA-3B and northeast SRS to adapt to the new hydrologic regimes by effecting a shift upslope on the elevational gradient. Alternative 3 (7.5% Period of Record) predicts extreme (>2.5 ft) depths in WCA-3B that are already greater than those predicted by CERP (6% POR). However, it should also be noted that the 2.5 ft depth criteria being used by Paul to measure potential impacts to tree islands is more permissive than the criteria that we have established based on field data from the WCAs (including WCA-3B) that is incorporated into the Hydrologic Suitability for Elevated Everglades Tree Islands performance measure. This performance measure uses a 2.0 foot criteria and NSM for assessing high water impacts. Using this criterion, Alternative 3 predicts water levels greater than 2.0 ft for 26% POR which exceeds the NSM 4.6.2 level (23% POR). We also believe that the NSM bar of high water exceedence is most likely set too high in WCA-3B and northeast Shark River Slough. Consequently, I believe that continuing to development future alternatives that further exceed NSM and CERP predictions for high water conditions in WCA-3B would be considered as unacceptable by the FWC. I strongly believe that the PDT should build upon the beneficial aspects of Alternative 3 rather that use our valuable time in modeling a "west bookend-like" alternative such as the one that is currently being proposed because I don't think that such an alternative would be considered as a viable one by the PDT.

The recommendations put forth by Paul Linton have been well thought out, and I hope that the COE will agree to build the next alternative based on his recommendations. Although I have some concern about not having the ability to close Weir 1 when stages in WCA-3B become excessively high, I would be willing to look at the model results. Perhaps a sensitivity run could be done with the weir closing to evaluate the difference.

Also, if plugs are modeled in the L-67A canal, we would like to have them placed at an elevation of 4.0 ft. NGVD as was done in the Pilot Study for moving waters across the L-67s into WCA-3B. This level facilitated reasonable boat passage during most water levels conditions.

——Original Message——
From: Linton, Paul [mailto:plinton@sfwmd.gov]
Sent: Friday, April 08, 2005 11:12 AM
To: Bruce_Boler@nps.gov
Cc: Analee Mayes (E-mail); Swiecichowski, Amy L SAJ Contractor; Barbara
Cintron (E-mail); Barry Rosen (E-mail); Mills, Brenda; Neidrauer, Calvin;
Carlos Alvarez (E-mail); Christine Chan (E-mail); Antonio Cotarelo (E-mail);
Dan Vogler (E-mail); Daniel Nehler (E-mail); Drum, Deborah; Debbie Peterson
(E-mail); Inger Hansen (E-mail); Jacob Davis (E-mail); James Riley (E-mail);
Jerrell Pennington (E-mail); Joette Lorion (E-mail); Walsh, Joe; Joffre Castro
(E-mail); Jon Moulding (E-mail); Joseph Terry (E-mail); Jose SAJ Lizarribar
(E-mail); Kate Elliot (E-mail); Kevin Kotun (E-mail); Kevin Palmer (E-mail);
Kim Taplin (E-mail); Larry Taylor (E-mail); Joan Lawrence (E-mail); Marcia
Levinson (E-mail); McCarthy, Linda; Phillips, Luna; Luis Alejandro (E-mail);
Victor Martin (E-mail); Marsha Bansee (E-mail); Richard Punnett (E-mail); Bob
Evans (E-mail); Ryan Bishop (E-mail); Sara O'Connell (E-mail); Sherry Mitchell
(E-mail); Sculley, Shawn; Steve Traxler (E-mail); Susan Sylvester (E-mail);
Terry Rice (E-mail); Towles, Tim; Tom MacVicar (E-mail); Trent Ferguson
(E-mail); Sonia Villamil (E-mail); Bill Gallagher (E-mail)
Subject: RE: Information for Consideration in Development of Alternative 4.

Bruce and PDT

I am providing the following brief responses to your comments:

1. Flow through WCA-3B

Bruce As described in my e-mail I used the flow transect to provide estimates of the flow to northwestern (Transect 17) and northeastern (Transect 18) Shark River Slough (SRS) for all the runs discussed. The flow transect number include both routes (through the eight passive weirs along L-67A and S-333). In the CERP D13R V3.5 an average annual flow 434,000 and 487,000 across Transects 17 and 18 respectively. My discussion never referenced (subtracted the flow through S-333) when discussing the portion of flow through WCA-3B. If I incorporated the S-333 route (subtracted the S-333 flow from transect's 18 flows) the ratio's provided would be higher.

From a policy perspective I am concerned that you or your agency or both did not like what congress authorized in the Comprehensive Everglades Restoration Plan (CERP) and now are trying to substantively change the CERP through this precursor project (the Combined Structural and Operational Plan [CSOP] for the Modified Water Deliveries to Everglades National Park [MWD ENP] and the C-111 Canal projects).

2. Performance Measures and Indicators for WCA-3B

There is a fundamental disagreement between our agencies (SFWMD and ENP) on the Tree Island Performance Measures. Certainly, there is more information on Tree Island Harm (including mortality) in WCA-3A because WCA-3A has taken the brunt of the high water; WCA-3B is basically rainfall driven and there are no levee in Everglades National Park (ENP) to pond water to depths and duration comparable to WCA-3B.

It does not make sense to meaningfully exceed the CERP depth and duration in WCA-3B and most likely cause Tree Island Harm in the interim period between CSOP and CERP.

If your argument it is ok to exceed CERP levels in WCA-3B because we do not have the level of science to predict the harm precisely I would other the counter opinion that the lack of certainty warrantee caution.

If your are also arguing that it is ok to harm WCA-3B because it's not a primary objective of CSOP this s not convincing and makes it sound like the development of objectives and selection of performance measures have resulted in diminished concern (value) of WCA-3B.

It should be noted the SFWMD never approved the reference "Purpose and Objective" paper and withdrew support for its development when after approximately three month of pressure to have SFWMD Governing Board approve this paper and allegation of stalling by the SFWMD (due to request by the SFWMD staff for clarifying language on Planning Conditions and the term "target minimum" which the SFWMD staff indicated should say only "minimum") it was revealed that it was ENP's refusal to clarify the vague Flood Damage Reduction language which referred to a "target minimum" was base on retaining the ability to reduce Flood Damage Reduction below the identified minimum should it be necessary to achieve the environmental restoration goal of ENP.

Regardless of the fact that the Purpose and Objective Paper was never approved by the SFWMD Governing Board, Item Number 5 states that preservation of fish and wildlife resources of which I believe Tree Islands are a resource.

Lastly the CSOP team does not determine we provide recommendations to the USACE which evaluates them and produces a document which goes through a public approval process (e.g. EIS and ROD).

Paul

Mr. Paul Linton, P.E. Lead Engineer
South Florida Water Management District
3301 Gun Club Road
West Palm Beach, Florida, 33408
Office 561-682-2871
Mobile 561-718-2830
Facsimile 561-682-0100

-----Original Message-----
From: Bruce_Boler@nps.gov [mailto:Bruce_Boler@nps.gov]
Sent: Friday, April 08, 2005 8:59 AM
To: Linton, Paul
Cc: Analee Mayes (E-mail); Swiecichowski, Amy L SAJ Contractor; Barbara
Cintron (E-mail); Barry Rosen (E-mail); Mills, Brenda; Neidrauer,
Calvin; Carlos Alvarez (E-mail); Christine Chan (E-mail); Antonio
Cotarelo (E-mail); Dan Vogler (E-mail); Daniel Nehler (E-mail); Drum,
Deborah; Debbie Peterson (E-mail); Inger Hansen (E-mail); Jacob Davis
(E-mail); James Riley (E-mail); Jerrell Pennington (E-mail); Joette
Lorion (E-mail); Joe Walsh (E-mail); Joffre Castro (E-mail); Jon
Moulding (E-mail); Joseph Terry (E-mail); Jose SAJ Lizarribar (E-mail);
Kate Elliot (E-mail); Kevin Kotun (E-mail); Kevin Palmer (E-mail); Kim
Taplin (E-mail); Larry Taylor (E-mail); Joan Lawrence (E-mail); Marcia
Levinson (E-mail); McCarthy, Linda; Phillips, Luna; Luis Alejandro
(E-mail); Victor Martin (E-mail); Marsha Bansee (E-mail); Linton, Paul;
Richard Punnett (E-mail); Bob Evans (E-mail); Ryan Bishop (E-mail); Sara
O'Connell (E-mail); Sherry Mitchell (E-mail); Sculley, Shawn; Steve
Traxler (E-mail); Susan Sylvester (E-mail); Terry Rice (E-mail); Tim
Towles (E-mail); Tom MacVicar (E-mail); Trent Ferguson (E-mail); Sonia
Villamil (E-mail); Bill Gallagher (E-mail)
Subject: RE: Information for Consideration in Development of Alternative 4.

Paul et al.,

I would have responded to your proposal sooner, but I have been working on the TT Report. ENP is concerned with several aspects of the SFWMD proposal, including:

1) Your analysis of flows through 3B during CERP runs fails to account for overland flow, as the CERP runs provide only flows through structures. In CERP modeling there are several miles of canal and levee removed in L-67A that is apparently unaccounted for in the CERP runs. In essence, this is several miles of weir-like flows at ground level that are apparently omitted from the calculation. Once this omission is corrected, your evaluations of comparative flows would be more meaningful.

2) We are especially concerned with your position that a performance indicator (HSI Ridge and Slough Suitability Index) should be elevated to a planning constraint for purposes of evaluating alternatives. We assume it is this HSI that you are using in conjunction with the 2X2 model to predict 2.5 ft. hydroperiods for 3B. It was our understanding that the SFWMD in collaboration with other agencies as part of CSOP development of PMs, determined that the HSI PMs were unsuitable to be used as PMs due to many inherent weaknesses (i.e., lack of calibration, weakness of model outputs, etc.). The CSOP team determined that they would be more appropriate as performance indicators, since they were not reliable enough (according to RECOVER, as well) to be used as PMs. A performance indicator woud have less weight than a PM, since they do not have as strong scientific support.

According to definitions provided by the Corps, a Constraint means a "limit imposed on the CSOP from applicable statutory and regulatory requirements." The only planning constraints for CSOP were the following, according to the purposes and objectives document.

3.3 Planning Constraints

1. Restoration of the ENP will be accomplished in a manner consistent with the ENP's enabling legislation and the mission of the National Park Service. (Source: 48 Stat. 816: May 30, 1934 and U.S.C., Chapter 1, Subchapter 1, Section 1:1916).

2. Minimize adverse effects to federally listed species under the Endangered Species Act. (Source: USACE 1992 GDM, Chapter E: Objectives and Constraints, Section 4: Problems and Constraints, page 26)

3. Minimize adverse effects to state listed endangered or threatened species or species of special concern consistent with Florida Statutes and regulations. (Source: Chapter 372, Florida Statutes (2001); Chapter 68, Florida Administrative Code)

4. Meet applicable water quality standards.

5. Maintain the original purposes of the C&SF project of flood damage reduction, regional water supply for agricultural and urban areas, prevention of saltwater intrusion, preservation of ENP, water supply to the ENP, preservation of fish and wildlife resources, recreation, navigation and ecosystem restoration.

6. Ensure no significant impact to existing habitat of endangered or threatened Species (Source: USACE 2000 GRR and Final SEIS 8.5 SMA, Section 4.0 Evaluation criteria, 4.2 Project Requirements, page 38).

7. Ensure consistency with other applicable federal and State laws and regulations.

It is difficult for ENP to understand how the SFWMD could elevate a performance indicator to a constraint that not only trumps all of the PMs our team developed, but also trumps all of the other planning constraints. Is it the position of SFWMD that the authorized planning constraints for CSOP should be modified to include an HSI? What is the justification for this?

—Bruce

Map taken from SFWMD 2005 Annual Report

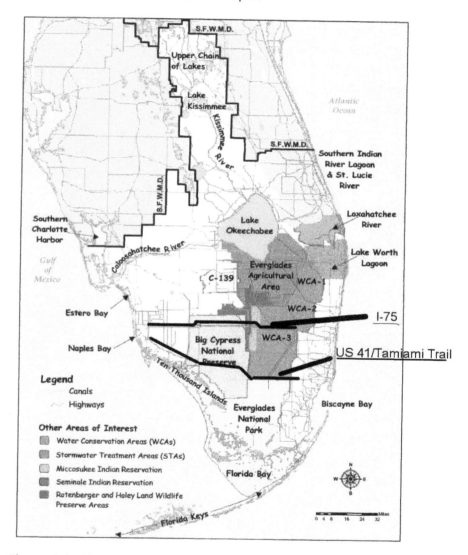

Figure 1-1. Major features of the South Florida environment within the boundaries of the South Florida Water Management District. [Note: See also **Figure 5-50** of this volume for major hydrological features in South Florida.]

Governor's Sustainable Commission of South Florida

CHAIRMAN

Richard A. Pettigrew
1550 Madruga Ave., Suite 412
Coral Gables, FL 33146
(305) 669-6973
(305) 669-6974/FAX
E-Mail: NONE

LEGISLATURE

Sen. Howard C. Forman
32nd District
Quality Communities Committee
Senate Office Bldg.
Tallahassee, FL 32399-1100
10400 Griffin Rd., Suite 104, Cooper
City, FL 33328
(850) 487-5103
S/C 277-5103
(954) 680-5632
S/C 430-4175
(954) 680-4176/FAX
E-Mail: forman.howard.web@leg.state.
fl.us

Rep. John Rayson
90th District
Natural Resources Committee
320 The Capitol
Tallahassee, FL 32399-1300
950 N. Federal Highway, Suite 109
Pompano Beach, FL 33062
(850) 448-0260
S/C 278-0260
(850) 292-4506/FAX
(954) 467-4268
(954) 467-4305/FAX
E-Mail: rayson.john@leg.state.fl.us

STATE

Charles Aller, Director
Natural Resources Committee
Office of Agricultural Water Policy
The Capitol, LL-29
Tallahassee, FL 32399
(850) 488-3022
(850) 488-7585/FAX
E-Mail: allerc@doacs.state.fl.us

John Anderson, President & CEO
Quality Communities Committee
Enterprise Florida, Inc.
390 N. Orange Ave., Suite 1300
Orlando, FL 32801
(407) 316-4600
(407) 425-1921/FAX
E-Mail: coverstreet@enterprise.state.
fl.us

Quinton Hedgepeth
Natural Resources Committee
Florida Game and Fresh Water Fish
Commission
2375 SW 27th Ave.
Miami, FL 33145
(305) 856-2300
(305) 856-0921/FAX
E-Mail: NONE

Steven Seibert, Secretary
Quality Communities Committee
Florida Dept. of Community Affairs
2555 Shumard Oak Blvd.
Tallahassee, FL 32399-2100
(850) 488-8466
S/C 278-8466
(850) 921-0781/FAX
E-Mail: steven.seibert@dca.state.fl.us

Thomas F. Barry, Jr., Secretary
Quality Communities Committee
Florida Dept. of Transportation
605 Suwannee St., MS 59
Tallahassee, FL 32399-0450
(850) 414-5205
(850) 488-3111/FAX
E-Mail: tom.barry@dot.state.fl.us

David Struhs, Secretary/Vice Chair
Natural Resources Committee
Florida Dept. of Environmental
Protection
3900 Commonwealth Blvd.
Tallahassee, FL 32399-3000
(850) 488-1554
S/C 278-1554
(850) 488-7093/FAX
E-Mail: struhs_d@epic9.dep.state.fl.us

REGIONAL

Mitchell Berger
SFWMD Governing Bd. Member
Natural Resources Committee
100 NE Third Avenue, Suite 400
Ft. Lauderdale, FL 33301
(954) 525-9900
(954) 523-2872/FAX
E-Mail: mberger@bdslaw.com

Robert Duane, Planning Director
Quality Communities Committee
Southwest FL Regional Planning
Council
c/o Hole, Montes & Assoc.
4880 6th Ave. SW
Naples, FL 33999
(941) 262-4617
(941) 262-3074/FAX
E-Mail: bob.duane@holemontes.com

John F. Flanigan Esq.
Board Member
Natural Resources Committee
Treasure Coast Regional Planning
Council
c/o Moyle, Flanigan, Katz, Kolins,
Raymond & Sheehan, P.A.
625 N. Flagler Dr., 9th Floor
West Palm Beach, FL 33401
(561) 659-7500
(561) 659-1789/FAX
E-Mail: jflanigan@moylelaw.com

Debra S. Harrison
South FL Regional Planning Council
Natural Resources Committee
8075 Overseas Highway
Marathon, FL
(305) 289-1010
(305) 289-0113/FAX
E-Mail: forpanda@bellsouth.net

LOCAL GOVERNMENT

Burt Aaronson, Commissioner
Quality Communities Committee
Palm Beach County Commission
PO Box 1989
West Palm Beach, FL 33402
(561) 355-2205
(561) 355-3990/FAX
E-Mail: baaronson@palm-beach.fl.us

Miguel Diaz de la Portilla
Quality Communities Committee
Miami-Dade County Commission
111 NW 1ˢᵗ St., Suite 230
Miami, FL 33128
(305) 375-4834
(305) 375-4838/FAX
E-Mail: NONE

Suellen H. Fardelmann, Mayor, *Quality Communities Committee*
City of Cooper City Hall
9090 SW 50ᵗʰ Place
Cooper City, FL 33328
(954) 434-4300
(954) 434-5099/FAX
E-Mail: cooperch@bellsouth.com

Pamela S. Mac'Kie, Commissioner
Quality Communities Committee
Collier County Commission
Administration Bldg.
3301 Tamiami Trail East
Naples, FL 34112
(941) 774-8097
(941) 774-3602/FAX
E-Mail: pmackie367@aol.com

Lori Nance Parrish, Commissioner
Natural Resources Committee
Broward County Commission
115 S. Andrews Ave., Rm. 401
Ft. Lauderdale, FL 33301
(954) 357-7005
(954) 357-7044/FAX
E-mail: Lparrish@co.broward.fl.us

Steve Shiver, Mayor
City of Homestead
Natural Resources Committee
790 N. Homestead Blvd.
Homestead, FL 33030
(305) 247-8898
(305) 248-7429/FAX
E-Mail: sshiver@shiver.com

Clara K. Williams, Mayor
Quality Communities Committee
City of Riviera Beach
600 West Blue Heron Blvd.
Riviera Beach, FL 33301
(561) 845-4092
(561) 840-3438/FAX
E-Mail: NONE

BUSINESS

Luis Ajamil
Executive Vice President
Quality Communities Committee
Bermello, Ajamil & Partners, Inc.
2601 S. Bayshore Dr., 10th Floor
Miami, FL 33133
(305) 859-2050
(305) 859-9638/FAX
E-Mail: luis_ajamil@bamiami.com

Ernie Caldwell, Vice President
Natural Resources Committee
Governmental and Environmental
Affairs
Berry Holding Company
PO Box 5609
Winter Haven, FL 33880
(941) 324-4988 ext. 226
(941) 324-9492/FAX
E-Mail: NONE

Michael Collins, Captain
Natural Resources Committee
Florida Keys Guide Association
PO Box 803
Islamorada, FL 33036
(305) 852-5837
(305) 852-0240/FAX
E-Mail: NONE

W. Arthur Darling,Executive Director
Natural Resources Committee
Sunshine State Milk Producers
PO Box 547666
Orlando, FL 32854
(407) 648-4311
(407) 648-2009/FAX
E-Mail: darlinga@msn.com

J. Noble Hendrix M.D., Owner
Natural Resources Committee
Hendrix Farms
25399 SW 157 Ave.
Homestead, FL 33031
(305) 665-5868
(305) 247-0240/FAX
E-Mail: HendrixFms@aol.com

Margaret F. Megee
Quality Communities Committee
8106 Presidential Court
Cape Canaveral, FL 32920
(407) 784-1607
E-Mail: NONE

William J. Payne, Attorney
Natural Resources Committee
11211 Prosperity Farms Road
Building B, Suite 106
Palm Beach Gardens, FL 33410
(561) 625-6480
(561) 625-5979/FAX
E-Mail: bpayne@csra.com

Roy Rogers, Senior Vice President
Quality Communities Committee
Gov't. Relations and Planning
Arvida
1205 Arvida Parkway
Weston, FL 33327
(954) 384-8000
(954) 384-3026/FAX
E-Mail: rrogers@arvida.com

Macolm S. Wade Jr.. Senior Vice
President
Natural Resources Committee
U.S. Sugar Corp.
PO Drawer 1207
Clewiston, FL 33440
(941) 983-8121
(941) 983-4804/FAX
E-Mail: mccorvey@ussugar.com

Charles J. Zwick, Retired Chairman
Natural Resources Committee
Southeast Banking Corporation
1 Alhambra Plaza, Suite 1115
Coral Gables, FL 33134
(305) 448-8828
(305) 448-4572/FAX
E-mail: C17JZ@prodigy.net

PUBLIC INTEREST

John M. DeGrove, Director
Quality Communities Committee
FAU/FIU Joint Center for
Environmental and Urban Problems
University Tower
220 SE 2nd Ave., Suite 709
Ft. Lauderdale, FL 33301
(954) 762-5255
S/C 238-5255
(954) 760-5666/FAX
E-Mail: jdegrove@fau.edu

Loly Espino
Natural Resources Committee
Economatrix, Inc.
501 Brickell Key Dr., Suite 502
Miami, FL 33131
(305) 371-2710
(305) 371-4959/FAX
E-Mail: mdespino@aol.com

Maggy Hurchalla
Natural Resources Committee
5775 SE Nassau Terrace
Stuart, FL 34997
(561) 287-0478
E-Mail: mhurchalla@hotmail.com

Dexter Lehtinen, Attorney
Miccosukee Tribe of Indians
Natural Resources Committee
Lehtinen, O'Donnell, Vargas & Reiner
7700 N. Kendall Drive
Miami, FL 33156
(305) 279-1166
(305) 279-1365/FAX
E-Mail: lyonese@aol.com

L. Jack Moller, Delegate
Florida Wildlife Federation
Quality Communities Committee
610 NW 93rd Ave.
Pembroke Pines, FL 33024
(954) 432-1361
FAX: NONE
E-Mail: ljmoller@aol.com

Terry L. Rice, Ph.D.
Research Scientist
Natural Resources Committee
Southeast Environmental Research
Program
University Park Campus
Miami, FL 33199
(305) 348-3095
(305) 971-4832/FAX
E-Mail: tlrice@adelphia.net

Carol B. Rist, Past President
Quality Communities Committee
Miami-Dade & Broward League of
Women Voters
18014 SW 83rd Ct.
Miami, FL 33157
(305) 255-5275
(305) 255-5275/FAX
E-mail: ristck@aol.com

Herbert Robinson
Dean of Student Services
Miami-Dade Community College
11011 SW 104 St., Room 3204
Miami, FL 33176
(305) 237-2304
(305) 237-0980/FAX
E-Mail: hrobinso@mdcc.edu

Stuart Strahl, Ph.D.
Executive Director
Natural Resources Committee
National Audubon Society
Everglades Restoration Campaign
444 Brickell Ave., Suite 850
Miami, FL 33131
(305) 371-6399
(305) 371-6398/FAX
E-Mail: sstrahl@audubon.org

Michele Thomas
Seminole Tribe of Florida
Natural Resources Committee
Brighton Reservation
Route 6, Box 666
Okeechobee, FL 34974
(941) 763-4128
(941) 763-5077/FAX
E-Mail: NONE

Bernard J. Yokel
Natural Resources Committee
313 Pond Road
Mt. Dora, FL 32757
(352) 383-0501
E-Mail: bjy313@iag.net

NON-VOTING MEMBERS

Billy Causey, Superintendent
Natural Resources Committee
U.S. DOC National Oceanic and
Atmospheric Administration
Florida Keys National Marine
Sanctuary
PO Box 500368
Marathon, FL 33050
(305) 743-2437
(305) 743-2357/FAX
E-Mail: bcausey@ocean.nos.noaa.gov

John H. Hankinson Jr.
Regional Administrator
Natural Resources Committee
U.S. Environmental Protection Agency
Atlanta Federal Center
61 Forsyth Street, SW
Atlanta, GA 30303-8909
(404) 562-8357
(404) 562-9961/FAX
E-Mail: hankinson.john@epamail.
epa.gov

Col. Joe R. Miller, District Engineer
Natural Resources Committee
USACOE, Jacksonville District
OESAJ-DE
PO Box 4970400
W. Bay Street
Jacksonville, FL 32232-0019
(904) 232-2241
(904) 232-1213/FAX
E-Mail: joe.r.miller@saj02.usace.
army.mil

Richard G. Ring, Superintendent
Natural Resources Committee
U.S. Dept. of Interior
Everglades National Park
40001 State Rd. 9336
Homestead, FL 33034
(305) 242-7710
(305) 247-6211
(305) 242-7711/FAX
E-Mail: dick_ring@nps.gov

Terrence (Rock) Salt
Executive Director
Quality Communities Committee
South Florida Ecosystem Restoration
Task Force
Florida International University
OE Bldg. Room 148
Miami, FL 33199
(305) 348-1665
(305) 348-1667/FAX
E-Mail: rsalt@sfrestore.org

Special Guest
Present at Our Meetings

J. Allison DeFoor II
Everglades Policy Coordinator
Executive Office of the Governor
The Capitol, Room 1501
Tallahassee, FL 32399-0001
(850) 488-5551
S/C 278-5551
(850) 922-6200/FAX
E-Mail: allison.defoor@laspbs.state.fl.us

Big Cypress fox squirrel.

Printed in the USA
CPSIA information can be obtained
at www.ICGtesting.com
LVHW070741091123
763323LV00024B/53